INTRODUCTION TO
OBJECT-ORIENTED
PROGRAMMING AND

C++

INTRODUCTION TO OBJECT-ORIENTED PROGRAMMING AND

C++

By

Yashavant P. Kanetkar

BPB PUBLICATIONS
B-14, CONNAUGHT PLACE, NEW DELHI-1

FIRST EDITION 2004 REPRINTED 2005

Distributors:

MICRO BOOK CENTRE
2, City Centre, CG Road,
Near Swastic Char Rasta,
AHMEDABAD-380009 Phone: 26421611

COMPUTER BOOK CENTRE
12, Shrungar Shopping Centre, M.G. Road,
BANGALORE-560001 Phone: 5587923, 5584641

MICRO BOOKS
Shanti Niketan Building, 8, Camac Street,
KOLKATTA-700017 Phone: 2826518, 2826519

BUSINESS PROMOTION BUREAU
8/1, Ritchie Street, Mount Road,
CHENNAI-600002 Phone: 28534796, 28550491

DECCAN AGENCIES
4-3-329, Bank Street,
HYDERABAD-500195 Phone: 24756400, 24756967

MICRO MEDIA
Shop No. 5, Mahendra Chambers, 150 D.N. Road,
Next to Capital Cinema V.T. (C.S.T.) Station,
MUMBAI-400001 Ph.: 22078296, 22078297, 22002732

BPB PUBLICATIONS
B-14, Connaught Place, **NEW DELHI-110001**
Phone: 23325760, 23723393, 23737742

INFO TECH
G-2, Sidhartha Building, 96 Nehru Place,
NEW DELHI-110019
Phone: 26438245, 26415092, 26234208

INFO TECH
Shop No. 2, F-38, South Extension Part-1
NEW DELHI-110049
Phone: 24691288, 24641941

BPB BOOK CENTRE
376, Old Lajpat Rai Market,
DELHI-110006 PHONE: 23861747

Price : Rs. 150/-

ISBN 81-7656-863-5

Published by Manish Jain for BPB Publications, B-14, Connaught Place, New Delhi-110 001 and Printed by him at Pressworks, Delhi.

Dedicated to
Prabhakar Kanetkar

About the Author

Yashavant Kanetkar is an author of more than a dozen books on C/C++/VC++/COM/DirectX/.Net programming. His books are amongst the highest-selling titles in Asia. He has several technology articles to his credit and is a regular columnist for Express Computers and Developer 2.0 published in association with the venerable Dr Dobb's Journal. In recognition of his efforts Microsoft awarded him the "Best .NET Technical Contributor" award from Microsoft for the year 2003.

Yashavant obtained his B.E. from VJTI Bombay and his M. Tech. from IIT Kanpur. A Mechanical Engineer by education, he switched to computers a decade ago and hasn't looked back since. His current affiliations include being a Director of KICIT, a training company and DCube Software Technologies.

Acknowledgments

Any book is a team effort. While the author may be the most visible player the contributions of author's colleagues and teammates make the book possible. It is such a pleasure to acknowledge those contributions. Here is my little list of people who made this book happen…

Nandita Shastri should top this list. She did an incredible job in diligently poring over every single page of this book to get it into the form that you see before you.

Soumitra, Vishal, Reshma and Indira helped iron out the appendices and the programs contained in it.

Thanks also to the rest of the team who kept their sense of humour alive when mind got strained at times.

The merit that the readers find in these chapters is largely due these individuals, any errors and inconsistencies are, alas, mine.

Contents

Introduction

Most C++ programmers are former C programmers. I too migrated to C++ from C. While learning the initial concepts of C++ one is so busy comparing them with C that one often ends up doing C programming in C++. That is one pitfall that this book has diligently tried to avoid.

C++ is simple, however, the jargon associated with it is not. It takes time and several hours of programming before one understands that the underlying concept behind features like Encapsulation, Inheritance, Polymorphism, Overloading, Templates, Exceptions are very simple. I have made a concentrated effort to keep out the jargon as much as is reasonably possible and explain the underlying concepts. I have also tried to support this understanding with examples and programs. Most programming examples in this book are fully workable programs rather than mere fragments of code. In my experience a program that can actually compile and run explains a great deal more than mere fragments of code.

Not only should one know the syntax and working of the C++ language but also the Object oriented concepts that they help implement. I have made a sincere effort to make these complicated concepts digestible for readers who may have little real-life programming experience.

Programming is all about confidence, and to help you boost yours you would find Exercises at the end of each chapter. I would advise that you attempt them before moving on to the next chapter. You would rarely regret it.

Lastly, this book is an attempt to make you think in Object-oriented manner rather than in procedural manner. I am hopeful that you would find these efforts worthwhile.

1
Principles of Object Oriented Programming

1.1 Introducing OOP

It is important for us to understand what is OOP, why do we need it, what does it do that traditional languages like C, Pascal and Basic don't and what are the principles behind OOP. This chapter addresses these issues and provides an overview of the features to be discussed in the rest of the book.

While designing software a guideline that should be followed is 'The expression of an algorithm should model the application domain that it supports'. Or in other words the solution to a problem should resemble the problem that it solves. That is, the observer should be able to recognize the purpose of the solution without necessarily knowing the problem in advance. For example, when you see a properly designed inventory control system, you recognize that its purpose is to maintain a record of stock quantities and locations. You recognize these things because the solutions resemble and therefore remind you of the problems that they solve. In a similar sense the purpose of a programming language is to express with algorithms the solution to a data processing problem. The techniques used in that expression determine how successfully the solution models its problem domain. Earlier, procedural programming was used for expression of an algorithm. Of late it is being replaced by object-oriented programming.

The earliest computers were programmed in binary. Mechanical switches were used to load programs. With the advent of mass storage devices and larger and cheaper computer memories, the first high-level computer programming languages came into existence. With their arrival, instead of thinking in terms of bits and bytes, programmers could write a series of English like instructions that a compiler could translate into the binary language of computers. These languages were simple in design and easy to use because programs at that time were primarily concerned with relatively simple tasks like calculations. As a result, programs were pretty short, limited to about a few hundred lines of source code.

As the computer's capacity and capability increased, so also did the ability to develop more complex computer programs. However, the earlier programming languages were found wanting in performing the complex programming tasks. These languages suffered from the following limitations:

(a)   There were no facilities to reuse existing program code. Wherever the same piece of code was required, it was simply duplicated.

(b)   The control was transferred via the dangerous *goto* statement. As a result, there was too much jumping around in the program, often without any clear indication of how, where and why the control is flowing.

(c)   All variables in the program were global. Tracking down spurious changes in global data in long convoluted programs was a very tedious job.

Writing, understanding and maintaining long programs became a programmer's nightmare. The programmers felt an urge to develop new languages with new features that would help to create more sophisticated applications. The breakthrough occurred in late 60's and early 70's with the introduction of procedural programming. The programming done using languages like C, COBOL and FORTRAN is called procedural programming. The long programs that the programmer found difficult to comprehend could now be broken down into smaller units of few hundred statements. Functions/subroutines/procedures were introduced in these languages to make the programs more comprehensible to their human creators. A program could now be divided into functions, with each function having a clearly defined purpose and a clearly defined interface to the other functions in the program. A typical organization of a program built using procedural programming principle is shown in Figure 1.1.

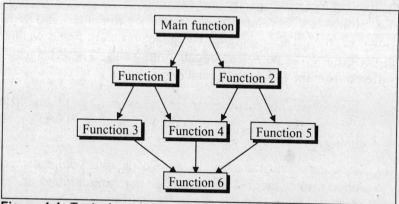

Figure 1.1. *Typical structure of a procedure-oriented program.*

A procedural program is built by breaking down the program's primary purpose into smaller pieces that then become functions within the program. Each function can have its own data and logic. Information is passed between functions using parameters and functions can have local data that cannot be accessed outside the function's scope. The entire program may have global data that can be shared by all the functions. Figure 1.2 shows the relationship between data and functions in procedural programming.

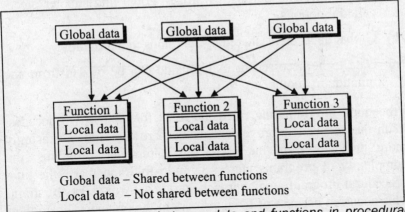

Figure 1.2. *Relationship between data and functions in procedural programming.*

By isolating processes within functions, a procedural program minimizes the chance that one procedure will affect another. This also makes it easier to isolate problems, if any. Procedural programming helps you to write cleaner code and maintain control over each function. There is less need of global variables, which are now replaced by local variables that have a smaller and more controllable scope. All this makes the development and maintenance of code fast as well as efficient.

A new concept came into existence with procedural programming—*Abstraction*. Abstraction permitted the programmer to look at an entity without being concerned with is internal details. In a procedural program it is enough to know which task is performed by function. It does not matter to the programmer how that task is performed so long as the function does it reliably. This is called functional abstraction and is the corner stone of procedural programming.

Thus following are the highlighting features of procedural programming.

(a) Program's main purpose is broken down into smaller pieces called functions.

(b) Global data can be shared by functions in a program.

(c) Data to be accessed or manipulated can be passed from one function to another.

Procedural programming ruled the roost for almost two decades. With the constant improvement in the hardware and increasingly more demands from the users for feature-rich programs, the complexity of programs increased multi-fold and that's the time procedural programming approach started showing signs of strain. This occurred because of the weakness in the procedural paradigm (organizing principle) itself. One of the key reasons for the failure of procedural languages was the role played by data.

In a procedural language, the whole emphasis is on doing things. Subdivision of a program into functions continued this emphasis. Functions do things just as single program statements do. What they do may be more complex, but the emphasis is still on doing. Data is given a second-class status in the procedural paradigm even though data is the reason for program's existence. For example, in a payroll processing application the important part isn't the function, which displays the data, or the function that checks for correct input; the important part is the payroll data itself.

Procedural programming languages like C and Pascal define data structures (arrays, structures, unions, enums, etc.) and provide functions that inspect or change the data from any place in the program. When the program grows beyond a reasonable size it becomes unmanageable since the data structures are available throughout the program and changing them in one part may have repercussions on other part of the program.

Another problem with procedural programming is that its primary components—functions and data—don't model the real world very well. For example, suppose you are writing a program to create the elements of a GUI: menus, windows, etc., there are no obvious program elements to which a menu or a window would correspond. This is because the procedural programming paradigm emphasizes on fitting a problem to the procedural approach of a language.

Thus, following are the disadvantages of the procedural programming.

(a) Poor representation of real world model.

(b) Manipulation of global data in one function may have repercussions in another.

(c) Complete emphasis on doing things (procedure) rather than on data on which things are being done.

To overcome the limitations felt in procedural programming, object-oriented programming was introduced.

1.1.1   Comparing Procedural Programming and OOP

The world and its applications are not organized into values and procedures separate from one another. Problem solvers in other crafts do not perceive the world that way. They deal with their problem domains by concentrating on the objects and letting the characteristics of those objects determine the procedures to apply to them. To build a house, grow a tomato, or repair a carburetor, first you think about the object and its purpose and behavior. Then you select your tools and procedures. The solution fits the problem.

The world is, therefore, object-oriented, and the object-oriented programming paradigm expresses computer programs in ways that model how people perceive the world. Because programmers are people, it is only natural that our approach to the work of the world reflects our view of the world itself.

The object-oriented paradigm is built on the foundation laid by the procedural programming concepts and data abstraction. Data abstraction does for data what functional abstraction does for operations. With data abstraction, data structures can be used without having to be concerned about the exact details of implementation. For example, floating-point numbers are abstracted in programming languages. You are not required to know how a floating-point number is represented in binary while assigning a value to it. Likewise, you are not bothered how binary multiplication takes place while multiplying floating-point values. Abstraction for floating-point numbers has existed in programming languages since long. However, it is only recently languages have been developed to define your own abstract data types.

The fundamental change in OOP is that a program is designed around the data being operated upon rather than upon the operations themselves. This is to be expected once we appreciate that the very purpose of the program is to manipulate data.

The basic idea behind object-oriented language is to combine into a single unit, both, the data and the functions that operate on the data. Such a unit is called an object.

An object's functions, called member functions in C++, typically provide the only way to access its data. If you want to read a data item present in an object, you call a member function in the object. It will read the item and return the value to you. You can't access the data directly. The data is hidden, so it is safe from accidental alteration. Data and its functions are *encapsulated* into a single entity.

If you want to modify the data in an object, you know exactly what functions interact with it—the member functions in the object. No other functions can access the data. This simplifies writing, debugging, and maintaining the program.

A C++ program typically consists of a number of objects, which communicate with each other by calling one another's member functions. The organization of a C++ program is shown in Figure 1.3.

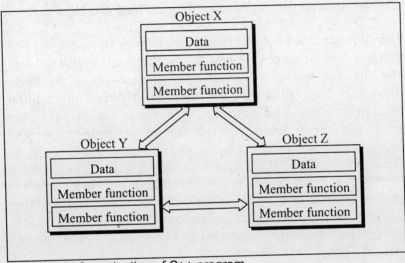

Figure 1.3. *Organization of C++ program.*

Thus, rather than trying to fit a problem to the procedural approach of language, OOP attempts to fit the language to the problem.

Object-oriented programming reduces dependencies between different parts of a program. An object contains data structures and a set of operations for inspecting and manipulating them. All operations that require the knowledge of data structures are directly associated with the structures, rather than being spread throughout the program. Combining the data and the operations that inspect and modify the data brings in huge benefits. This arrangement ensures that you do not directly manipulate the data, instead you request functions associated with the data to do this job for you. Thus, part of the program that requests action to be performed on the data structures remains separate from the part, which fulfills the request. As a result, now the parts of the program do not depend on each other through the data structures but through the functionality that the parts promise to provide. When you approach a programming problem in an object-oriented language you do not ask how the problem will be divided into functions. Instead you ask how it will be divided into objects.

When you approach a programming problem in an object-oriented language, you no longer ask how the problem will be divided into functions, but how it will be divided into objects. Thinking in terms of objects, rather than functions, has a surprisingly helpful effect on how easily programs can be designed. This results from the close match between objects in the programming sense and objects in the real world.

The match between programming objects and real world objects is the happy result of combining data and functions. The resulting objects offer a revolution in program design. No such close match between programming constructs and the items being modeled exists in a procedural language.

Thus following are the highlighting features of object-oriented programming.

(a) Emphasis is on data rather than on procedures.

(b) The programming problem is divided into objects.

(c) Data and the functions that operate upon it are tied together.

(d) Objects can communicate with one another through functions.

(e) Models the real world objects very well.

There is more to OOP programming than just binding the data and functions together. OOP, for example, facilitates creating reusable code that can eventually save a lot of work. A feature called polymorphism permits us to create multiple definitions for operators and functions. Another feature called inheritance permits us to derive new classes from old ones. As you can see, OOP introduces many new ideas and involves a different approach to programming than the procedural programming. In short, in OOP, instead of concentrating on tasks, we concentrate on representing concepts.

1.1.2   OOP Languages

Any language can implement the object-oriented features. For example procedural languages like C and Pascal can use the object-oriented features. But the programming can become clumsy and confusing when the programs become large. A language that is specially designed to support the OO features makes it easy to implement the OO features.

The language should support several features to be called as OO language. Depending upon the features they support, the languages can be categorized into two:

–   Object-based programming languages
–   Object-oriented programming languages.

Object-based programming is the style of programming that primarily supports encapsulation and object identity. Major features that are required for object-based programming are:

–   Data encapsulation
–   Data hiding and access mechanisms
–   Automatic initialization and clean up of objects
–   Operator overloading

Languages that support programming with objects are said to be object-based programming languages. They do not support inheritance and dynamic binding. Ada, Visual Basic are the object-based programming languages.

Object-oriented programming incorporates all of object-based programming features along with two additional features, namely, inheritance and dynamic binding. Languages that support these features include C++, Smalltalk, Java and C#.

Whether to use an object-based language or object oriented language depends on characteristics and requirements of an application.

1.1.3   Advantages of OOP

OOP offers benefits not only to the designer of the program but also to the end users. Given below is the list of benefits.

(a) The inheritance feature permits reuse of existing classes.

(b) OOP reduces the development cycle time since its easy to use the existing tried and tested modules rather than coding them from scratch.

(c) The data hiding facility available in classes prevents the programmers from making honest mistakes. It also secures the data from accidental misuse from other parts of the program.

(d) OOP permits us to divide the problem domain into objects and then map to those in the program.

(e) It is easy to partition the work in a project based on objects.

(f) It is easier to capture and manage the complexity of a large problem through OOPs.

(g) It is easier to upgrade an existing system when the software is built in the form of a group of recognizable objects.

(h) OOP provides programmers a convenient way to create new data types.

Note that the extent to which the above benefits would accrue depends upon the type of the problem as well as the experience of the designer of the system.

1.2 Features of OOP

Before we start with C++ as an object oriented language, it is necessary to understand few features of OOP. We would discuss them in this section.

1.2.1 Objects and Classes

In procedural programming a problem is approached by dividing it into functions. Unlike this, in object-oriented programming the problem is divided into objects. Thinking in terms of objects rather than functions makes the designing of program easier. The examples that can be treated as objects are employees in a payroll processing system, GUI elements like windows, menus, icons, etc., customers, sales persons in a sales tracking system and so on. These objects occupy memory just like other variables.

Most languages offer primitive data types like *int*, *long* and *float*. Their data representation and response to arithmetic, assignment and relational operators are defined as part of the language. However, the language does not know user-defined data types. The programmer defines its format and behaviour by defining a *class*. For example, there can be a user-defined data type to represent dates. The compiler and the computer do not know about dates. Programmers have to define the behaviour of dates by designing a date *class*. This class expresses the format of date and the operations that can be performed on it. The way we can declare many variables of the primitive type *int*, we can define many objects of the *date* class. A class serves as a blueprint or a plan or a template. It specifies what data and what functions will be included in objects of that class.

1.2.2 Encapsulation

Encapsulation is the mechanism that binds together the code and data it manipulates, and keeps both safe from outside interference and misuse. The advantage of encapsulated code is that the outside world knows how to access it and thus can use it regardless of the implementation details and without fear of unexpected side-effects. In C++ the basis of encapsulation is a *class*. The purpose of a *class* is to encapsulate complexity and C++ provides mechanisms for hiding the complexity of implementation inside the *class*.

1.2.3   Data Abstraction

In layman's language abstraction tells users everything that they may want to know about an object and nothing else. In C++ language an abstraction indicates what data can an object hold and what functions can it perform on the data. How these functions are performed is abstracted away. For example, a stack may be viewed as an abstraction. The stack can be understood and used once we come to know the features like push and pop that it provides, without bothering about how it stores the data or how the push and pop operations are performed.

1.2.4   Inheritance

Inheritance is a process of creating new classes, called *derived classes* from existing or *base classes*. The derived class inherits all the capabilities of the base class and can either refine some of its features or add totally new features of its own. For example, we can build a set of classes that describe a library of publications. There are two primary types of publications—periodicals and books. We can create a general *publication* class by defining data items for the publisher name, the number of pages and the accession number. Publications can be retrieved, stored and read. For performing these operations we can write functions in the *publication* class. Next, we can define two derived classes named *periodical* and *book*. A periodical has a volume and issue number and contains articles written by different authors. Data items for these should be included in the definition of the *periodical* class. The *periodical* class will also need a function, *subscribe*. Data items for the *book* class will include the names of its author a cover type (hard or soft) and its ISBN number. As you can see, the *book* class and the *periodical* class share the characteristics of *publication* class while having their own unique attributes. This entire scenario is depicted in Figure 1.4.

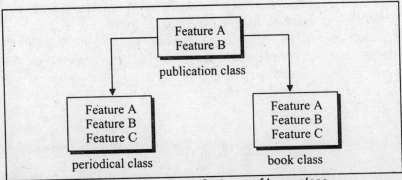

Figure 1.4. *Derived class inherits features of base class.*

Inheritance facilitates the concept of reusability. We reuse the base class to create the derived class.

1.2.5 Polymorphism

Polymorphism means the ability to assume several forms. In object-oriented programming context this refers to the ability of an entity to refer to objects of various classes at runtime.

We would understand polymorphism by extending the same example of the *publication*, *periodical* and *book*. Our base class, *publication*, defines methods for storing and retrieving data. A periodical may be stored in a binder, while a book is usually placed on a shelf. Furthermore, the way to find a specific periodical is different from finding a book. Periodicals are located through a guide to periodical literature, while books are found using a card catalogue system. Based on this we can design a 'find through periodical literature' function for a periodical and a 'find through card catalogue' function for a book. OOP provides an elegant facility called *polymorphism* to handle this situation. In our example, the retrieval method for a periodical is different from the retrieval method for a book, even though the end result is same. Polymorphism permits you to define a function for retrieving a publication that can work for both periodicals and books. When a periodical is retrieved, the retrieve function that is specific to a periodical is used, but when a book is retrieved, the retrieve function associated with a book is used. The end result is that a single function name can be used for the same operation performed on related derived classes even if the implementation of that function varies from one class to another. This is shown in Figure 1.5.

C++ has three mechanisms that help us to implement polymorphism. These are:

-   Function overloading
-   Operator overloading
-   Virtual functions

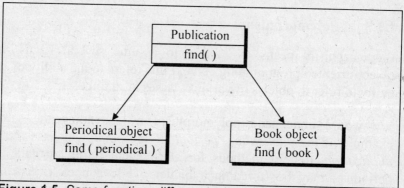

Figure 1.5. *Same function, different implementations.*

1.2.6   Dynamic Binding

The term dynamic binding refers to the binding of a function call to the code to be executed as a response to this call. Dynamic binding takes place in polymorphism where, which function is to call is decided at run-time. The function to be called is decided according to the type of the contents of the pointer using which the function is called.

1.3 Overview Of OOP Using C++

Like C, C++ began its life at Bell Labs, where Bjarne Stroustrup developed the language in the early 1980s. In his own words, "C++ was primarily designed so that programmers would not have to program in assembler, C, or various modern high-level languages. Its main purpose is to make writing good programs easier for the programmer." Stroustrup based C++ on C because of C's brevity, its suitability to system programming, and its widespread availability. C++'s OOP aspect was inspired by a computer simulation language called Simula67. Stroustrup added OOP features to C without significantly changing the C component. Thus C++ is a superset of C, meaning that any valid C Programming is a C++ program too.

1.3.1   Creating C++ Programs

A C++ program consists of a series of statements. These statements must appear in the same order in which we wish them to be executed; unless of course the logic of the problem demands a deliberate 'jump' or transfer of control to a statement, which is out of sequence. Here is the first C++ program. It calculates and prints the average marks obtained by student.

```
// The first C++ program
#include <iostream.h>
```

```
void main( )
{
    char str [ 40 ] ;
    int m1, m2, m3, avg ;

    cout << "Enter your name: " ;
    cin >> str ;

    cout << "Enter marks in three subjects: " ;

    cin >> m1 >> m2 >> m3 ;
    avg = ( m1 + m2 + m3 ) / 3 ;

    cout << "Your name is " << str ;
    cout << endl << "And your average marks are " << avg ;
}
```

Here is some sample interaction with the program.

```
Enter your name: Saurav Gupta
Enter marks in three subjects: 44  72  64
Your name is Saurav Gupta
And your average marks are 60
```

If you come from a C background you would find at least some part of the program familiar. The way of writing the program, the *main( )* function, the assignment statement are same as they used to be in C. However, there are some important differences in the Input/Output statements and the file that is included. Let us now discuss each statement in the program in detail.

1.3.2   Program Statements

As said earlier, a C++ program is a set of statements. Like C, in C++ also each statement is terminated by a semicolon (;). Given below is a discussion of the statements that we used in this program.

Comments

C++ supports two types of comments. C programmers are familiar with the /* */ style of commenting. Anything lying within the /*... */ pair is ignored by the compiler. C++ additionally supports the // notation for commenting. For example,

c = 5.0 / 9 * (f - 32) ; // conversion formula

Here, everything following // till the end of line is treated as comment. Usually /* */ style is used for commenting out a block of code, whereas, // is used for single line comments.

Input/Output Statements

Before we look at the Input/Output statements used in the program, consider the following statement:

cout << "God, Give me common sense!" ;

This statement causes the phrase in the quotation marks to be displayed on the screen. A complete description of this statement requires an understanding of objects, operator overloading, and other topics we won't discuss until later in the book, but here's a brief preview.

The identifier *cout* (pronounced "C out") is actually an object. It is predefined to correspond to the *standard output stream*. A *stream* is an abstraction that refers to a flow of data. The standard output stream normally flows to the screen display, although it can be redirected to other output devices.

The operator << is called the *insertion* or *put to* operator. It directs the contents of the variable on its right to the object on its left.

Contrary to *cout*, to receive input through the keyboard what is used is an identifier *cin*. The word *cin* (pronounced "C in") is an object, predefined in C++ to correspond to the *standard input stream*. This stream represents data coming from the keyboard (unless it has been redirected). The >> is the *extraction* or *get from* operator. It takes the value from the stream object on its left and places it in the variable on its right. For example, in the following statement receives a number from the keyboard and stores it in a variable *age*.

```
cout << "Enter your age " ;
cin >> age ;
```

Now that we have understood how to write Input/Output statements, let us turn our attention back to the program. Right at the beginning of the program we have included the file 'iostream.h'. It contains declarations that are needed by *cout & cin* identifiers and << & >> operators. Without these declarations the compiler won't recognize *cout & cin* and will think that << & >> are being used incorrectly.

The first pair of *cout* and *cin* used in the program are straightforward. *cout* outputs a message asking for the name and *cin* receives that name in the string *str[ ]*.

Note the repeated use of the extraction operator >> in the second *cin* statement. This is perfectly legal. This is known as cascading of operators. It is a better idea than having three independent *cin*s. However, using this capability eliminates the opportunity to prompt the user between inputs. As you may have guessed cascading of insertion operators is also allowed.

Look at the last *cout* statement. You would find the use of an unfamiliar word in this statement, *endl*. This is known as a *manipulator*. It causes a linefeed to be inserted in the output stream. As a result, the phrase following it appears on a fresh line. The same effect could have been obtained by sending the newline character ('\n').

Variables, Declaration and Assignment

As in C, the type of every variable used in a program must be declared before using it. In our program we have declared the variables *m1*, *m2*, *m3* and *avg* as integers. Similarly we have declared *str* as a character array capable of holding 40 characters.

The assignment statement remains same as in C. Like C, we can use different forms of assignment statements as shown below:

```
// Chained assignment
i = j = k = 25 ;  // assigns 25 to each variable

// Embedded assignment
i = ( j = 30 ) +  25 ;  // assigns 30 to j and 55 to i

// Compound assignment
i = j = k = 5 ;
i += 10 ;  // same as i = i + 10
i -= 5 ;  // same as i = i - 5
j *= 15 ;  // same as j = j * 15
k /= 2 ;  // same as k = k / 2
k %= 5 ;  // same as k = k % 5
```

1.3.3   Class Declaration

A class is a user-defined data type. Like a structure, it too can hold data and functions together. We would now see a simple example that shows how to declare a class and how to use a class variable.

```
#include <iostream.h>
class a
{
```

```
        int i ; float j ;
        public:
            void setdata ( int ii, float jj )
            {
                i = ii ;
                j = jj ;
            }
            void printdata( )
            {
                cout << i << " " << j ;
            }
};

void main( )
{
    a z1 ;
    z1.setdata ( 10, 50.34 ) ;
    z1.printdata( ) ;
}
```

We have declared a class *a* having data of type *int* and *float*. The class also holds two functions *setdata( )* and *printdata( )*. They are called member functions of class *a*. In *main( )* we have declared an object *z1* of the class *a*. The member functions are called using this object. We have passed two values to the *setdata( )* function. In this function we have assigned these values to *i* and *j*. We have displayed values of *i* and *j* in the *printdata( )* function.

At this juncture it would suffice to say that class is a datatype and an object is an instance of this data type. Classes and objects have many more features. We would discuss these features in detail in Chapter 4.

1.3.4 · Compiling a C++ Program

The process of compiling a C++ program differs according to the operating system. Under Unix we would use *cc* command to compile the program. The command

```
cc pr1.c
```

at Unix prompt would compile the program contained in the 'pr1.c' source file. The compiler would produce 'pr1.o' object file. At run-time, this file is linked with the library functions to produce an executable file.

Under DOS, we would usually use Turbo C++ or Borland C++ compilers to compile the program. They provide an IDE (Integrated Development Environment) to write, edit, save and execute the program. In Turbo C++ the program gets compiled and executed by pressing the Ctrl + F9 keys. Figure 1.6 shows the entire process of building a program.

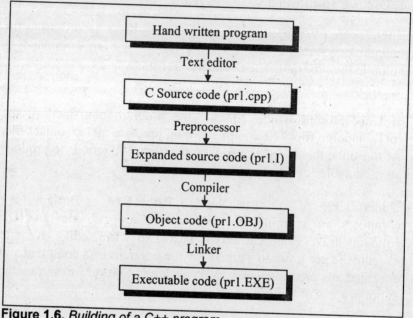

Figure 1.6. *Building of a C++ program.*

To run a C++ program under Windows we can use Microsoft Visual C++ compiler. In VC++ compiler we have to press Ctrl + F5 to compile and run the program.

Exercises

[A] State True or False:

(a) Object oriented programming languages permit reusability of the existing code.

(b) Languages earlier than procedural programming languages made use of only global variables.

(c) In Object Oriented programming languages the only way to transfer control from one place in the program to another is by using the *goto* statement.

(d) The main emphasis of OOP is on algorithms rather than on data.

(e) It is easier to write, understand and maintain programs in Object Oriented languages as compared to Procedural languages.

(f) Data is given a second-class status in Procedural programming languages.

(g) Encapsulation means combining data of different types into a single unit.

(h) Procedural programming languages do not model the real world data as well as the Object Oriented programming languages.

(i) A class permits us to build user-defined data types.

(j) Objects are to classes as variables are to data types.

(k) In procedure-oriented programming, all data are shared by all functions.

(l) Inheritance means the ability to reuse the data values of one object by other objects.

[B] Fill in the blanks:

(a) The ability of a function or operator to act in different ways on different data types is called _____.

(b) The process of building new classes from existing ones is called _____.

(c) If a class A inherits its properties from class B, then A and B are known as_____class and _____class, respectively.

(d) Pascal and C are _____ languages, whereas, C++ is_____language.

[C] Answer the following:

(a) What do you mean by Abstraction and Encapsulation?

(b) Where does dynamic binding become useful?

(c) Explain the process of compilation of a C++ program in Turbo C++ compiler.

2
Elements Of C++ Language

2.1 Using Tokens and Identifiers

Now that we are through with our first program let us look at the finer details of any C++ program. The smallest individual units in a program are called tokens. The constants, variables, keywords and operators used in any program are tokens. Let us discuss them one by one.

2.1.1   Keywords

Keywords are used to implement specific language features. They cannot be used as identifiers in a program. In addition to the keywords available in C, a number of new keywords were added in C++. A list of all keywords available in C++ is given in Table 2.1.

asm	bool	catch	class
const_cast	delete	dynamic_cast	explicit
friend	inline	mutable	namespace
new	operator	private	protected
public	reinterpret_cast	static_cast	template
this	throw	try	typeid
using	virtual		

Table 2.1. *Keywords.*

We would postpone the discussion of the new keywords introduced in C++ as well as the object-oriented features of C++ to subsequent chapters.

2.1.2   C++ Identifiers

The variable names, function names, array names, class names, etc. are collectively known as *identifiers*.

The rules for constructing identifiers in C++ are given below:

(a) A variable name is any combination of alphabets, digits or underscores.

(b) The variable name cannot start with a digit.

(c) Variable names are case sensitive, so *abc*, *ABC*, *Abc*, *aBc*, *ABc* are all distinct variable names.

(d) Keyword cannot be used as a variable name.

(e) There is no limit on length of a variable name.

2.1.3   Variables and Constants

A quantity that may vary during program execution is called a variable. Variable names are names given to different locations in memory. C++ allows us the flexibility of defining variables at the point where they are used.

Constants refer to fixed values that do not change during execution of the program. C++ supports several types of constants like integer, character, real and string. Remember that these constants do not have memory locations. Here are a few examples…

```
'Z'        // character constant
629        // integer constant
255.12     // real constant
012        // octal integer constant
0X39       // hexadecimal integer constant
"OOP"      // string constant
L'Z'       // wide character constant
L"OOP"     // wide-character string constant
```

A wide character constant may contain either one or two characters, whereas, a wide-character string constant can contain any number of characters. The wide-character is used for those character sets that need two bytes to represent each character.

2.2   Introducing Data Types

As the name suggests Data Types represent the different types of data that a language supports. C++ supports primary (basic) and secondary (derived) data types. Not only this it lets you define your own data types as well. These are shown in Figure 2.1.

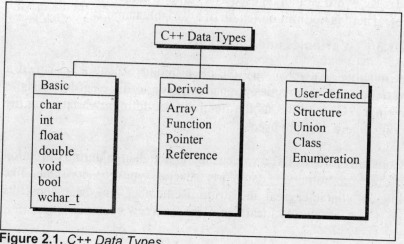

Figure 2.1. *C++ Data Types.*

2.2.1   Basic Data Types

Except for the type *void* the other primary data types may have modifiers preceding them. A modifier is used to alter the meaning of a primary data type to suite a particular situation. Given below are the common modifiers that are applied to various primary data types:

(a) *signed*, *short*, *long* and *unsigned* are applied to integer data type.

(b) *unsigned* and *signed* are applied to character data type.

(c) *long* can also be applied to *double* data type.

Given below are some sample declarations of variables using these modifiers.

```
short int a ;
short a ;
unsigned int a ;
long int a ;
unsigned long a ;
unsigned char ch ;
```

The size and range of data types are dependent upon the processor type and the compiler. For example, for 16-bit environments like DOS or Windows 3.1, an integer is 16 bits long with a range -32768 to 32767. For 32-bit environment like Windows 2000, an integer is 32 bits long with a range -2147483648 to 2147483647. Table 2.2 lists the size and range of different data types.

Operation	Bytes	Range
char	1	-128 to 127
unsigned char	1	0 to 255
signed char	1	-128 to 127
int	2	-32768 to 32767
unsigned int	2	0 To 65535
signed int	2	-32768 to 32767
short int	2	-32768 to 32767
unsigned short int	2	0 to 65535
signed short int	2	-32768 to 32767
long int	4	-2147483648 to 2147483647
signed long int	4	-2147483648 to 2147483647
unsigned long int	4	0 to 4294967295
float	4	3.4E-38 to 3.4E+38
double	8	1.7E-308 to 1.7E+308
long double	10	3.4E-4932 to 3.4E+4932

Table 2.2. *Size and range of data types.*

The *void* data type is used for three purposes. These are as follows:

(a) To specify that a function is not going to return any value.

(b) To specify that a function does not receive any argument. For example, the function *myfunc* shown below neither receives any argument, nor returns any value.

```
void myfunc ( void )
{
    cout << "E-governance is likely to weed out corruption..." ;
    cout << "Since machine neither accepts money nor gives money" ;
}
```

(c) To declare a generic pointer as in,

```
void *p ;
```

2.2.2   Derived Data Types

The derived data types are built using primary data types. The declaration and usage of derived data types like arrays and pointers is same as that in C.

Every variable occupies space in memory. That memory space has a particular address. We can access this address using pointer. We would learn pointers in detail in Chapter 8.

An array is a set of similar data types. When a program needs to hold several values of same type, it is a better idea to declare an array instead of several variables to hold the values. The following code shows how to declare an array and initialise the array elements.

```
int arr [ 100 ] ;
for ( int i = 0 ; i < 100 ; i++ )
    arr [ i ] = i ;
```

Here, *int* specifies the type of the variable, just as it does with ordinary variables and the word *arr* specifies the name of the array. The *[100]* however is new. The number *30* tells how many elements of the type *int* will be in our array. This number is often called the 'dimension' of the array. The bracket ([ ]) tells the compiler that we are dealing with an array. The individual elements in the array can be referred with subscript, the number in the brackets following the array name. This number specifies the element's position in the array. All the array elements are numbered, starting with 0. Thus, *arr[2]* is not the second element of the array, but the third. The subscript can also be a variable.

Consider the following array declaration:

int arr [8] ;

What happens in memory when we make this declaration? 16 bytes get immediately reserved in memory, 2 bytes each for the 8 integers (under Windows/Linux the array would occupy 32 bytes as each integer would occupy 4 bytes). And since the array is not being initialized, all eight values present in it would be garbage values. As shown in Figure 2.2 all the array elements would always be present in contiguous memory locations.

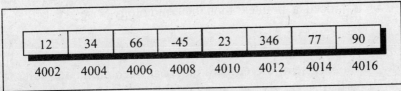

12	34	66	-45	23	346	77	90
4002	4004	4006	4008	4010	4012	4014	4016

Figure 2.2. *Arrangement of array in memory.*

Pointers are closely related with arrays. The array name *arr* represents the base address of the array. It means that the array name is actually a pointer containing the base address of the array. Base address is the address of 0th element of the array. Here, *arr* would contain *4002* i.e address of 0th element.

Functions in C++ have undergone major changes. Many of these changes are directed towards exploiting the object-oriented features of C++. These changes are so many and so powerful that we have one complete chapter dedicated to it (Chapter 3).

C++ introduced a new derived data type called reference. Look at the following code.

```
int i = 10 ;
int &j = i ;
cout << endl << "i = " << i << " j = " << j ;
```

And here is the output...

```
i = 10 j = 10
```

In this program *j* is called *reference* of *i*, whereas *i* is called a *referent*. A reference is indicated by using the & operator in the same way we use the * operator to indicate a pointer. Note the following important points:

(a) When we initialize *j* with *i*, address of *i* gets stored in *j*. Thus, *j* is indeed a pointer, though terminology-wise we call it a reference.

(b) Internally a reference is nothing but a *const* pointer. *const*, because once a reference variable has been defined to refer to a particular variable, it cannot refer to any other variable.

(c) To dereference a reference we do not have to use a * operator.

(d) Since the reference is automatically dereferenced, any time we use a reference we end up using a referent.

(e) A reference must always be initialised. Thus the following set of statements produce an error.
```
int y = 4 ;
```

```
int &z ;  // error
z = y ;
```

(f) We can also create a reference to a pointer. The declaration of such a reference would look like this:

```
char *p = "Hello" ;
char *&q = p ;
```

(g) We cannot create a pointer to a reference. This can be explained with the help of following code:

```
int  p ;
int *q  ;  // pointer to an integer
int  &r = p ;  // reference to an integer
int * &s = q ;  // reference to pointer - OK
int & *t = &r ;  // Error - attempt to create pointer to a reference
```

(h) A variable can have multiple references. Changing the value of one of them effects a change in all others.

(i) We cannot create a reference to a reference. For example, the following code would be wrong.

```
int q ;
int &p = q ;
int &&r = p ;  // Error
```

(j) We can create a reference to an array. For example:

```
int  a[ ] = { 3, 7, 6, 9, 5 } ;
int ( &p ) [ 5 ] = a  ;
```

Though an array of pointers is acceptable, an array of references is not. Let us understand why. As in C, in C++ too an array name acts as pointer to zeroth element of the array. Hence, had an array of references been allowed the array name would have become a pointer to the zeroth element, i.e. a pointer to a reference. But a pointer to a reference is not feasible, hence an array of references is also infeasible.

2.2.3   User-Defined Data Types

The concepts of structures, unions, enums that one learns in C are applicable even in C++. However, like functions these data types have also been upgraded to suit object oriented programming. Additionally, C++ permits us to define a user-defined data type called *class*. The variables built from this user-defined data type are called *objects*. Objects are the central theme around which every OO program weaves its story. We would learn about the enhancements made to structures in Chapter 4 and about classes & objects from Chapter 4 onwards till the time you have read the last page of this book.

Unions are user-defined data types the way structures are. Both structures and unions are used to group a number of different variables together. But while a structure enables us to treat a number of different variables stored at different places in memory, a union enables us to treat the same space in memory as a number of different variables. That is, a union offers a way for a section of memory to be treated as a variable of one type on one occasion, and as a different variable of a different type on another occasion.

An enumerated data type is another user-defined data type. It provides a way for associating names with numbers. Once associated we can use the names in place of numbers.

This can help in making the program listing more readable, which can be an advantage when a program gets complicated or when more than one programmer would be working on it. Using enumerated data type can also help you reduce programming errors.

A point to note. Unlike C, which defines types of *enum*s to be integers, which treats *enum* values as integers, in C++ each enumerated data type retains its own separate type. As a result, we cannot assign an *int* to an *enum* as shown below:

```
enum style { solid, dashed, dotted, dashdot } ;
style linestyle = 5 ;  // Error.
```

A special type of *union* and *enum* has been added in C++— *anonymous union* and *anonymous enum*. An anonymous union does not have a union name (tag), and its elements can be accessed directly without using a *union* variable. Following example illustrates this:

```
union
{
     int i ;
     char ch [ 2 ] ;
} ;
```

Both *i* and the array *ch[ ]* share the same memory locations and can be accessed directly simply by saying,

```
i = 10 ;
ch [ 0 ] = 'A' ;
```

Simply omitting the *union* name in the declaration does not make the *union* an anonymous *union*. For a *union* to qualify as an anonymous *union*, the declaration must not declare a variable of the *union* type.

Anonymous *unions* are subject to additional restrictions:

- When declared globally they must be *static*.
- Their elements can be *public*, they cannot be *private* or *protected* (*public*, *private* and *protected* are access specifiers and they would be discussed in Chapter 5).
- They cannot contain member functions.

On similar lines anonymous *enums* can be built as shown below:

```
enum { first, second, slleper, actwotier } ;
int t = second ;
```

2.3   Introducing Operators

All operators available in C can be used in C++ also. In addition to
them C++ has introduced some new operators listed in Table 2.3.

Operator	Known As
<<	Insertion Operator
>>	Extraction Operator
::	Scope Resolution Operator
::*	Pointer to Member Declarator
->*	Pointer to Member Operator
.*	Pointer to Member Operator
new	Memory Allocation Operator
delete	Memory Release Operator

Table 2.3. *New Operators Introduced In C++.*

In a complicated expression containing several operators the order
of evaluation of operators is decided by the precedence (or priority
or hierarchy) of operators.

There is another issue called *Associativity* that needs to be tackled
while evaluating some expressions. To understand this, consider
the following two expressions.

```
z = ( a + b ) * ( c + d ) ;
c = 3 / 2 * 5 ;
```

In the first expression the priority of both the + operators is same. Moreover, the order of evaluation of *(a + b)* and *(c + d)* is not going to alter the value of *z*. Hence, it is left to the compiler to decide which of the two is evaluated first.

In the second expression the compiler cannot guarantee same result if / is done before * or the other way round. Hence another concept called associativity comes into play. Both the operators * and / have an associativity of Left to Right. But * cannot be done earlier, because if done so, the right operand of / would be required for the multiplication to take place. Since the associativity of / is also L to R the right operand of / cannot be touched before left. Hence in this case / would be done before *.

2.3.1   Arithmetic Operators

C++ supports the same arithmetic operators of C and perform the same task. The arithmetic operators are +, -, /, *, %, -- and ++. The % operator is known as modulus operator. It works only on integral data types. The ++ and -- operators add or subtract 1 from the operand. Increment (++) and decrement (--) operator can either be postfix or prefix operators. If the operator appears after the operand, it is postfix operator. On the other hand, if it appears before the operand it is called prefix operator.

The precedence of arithmetic operators is given below:

```
++  --
-    (unary minus)
/ %
+ -
```

Operators on the same level of precedence are evaluated from left to right by the compiler. You can use parentheses to alter the order of evaluation. Parentheses are evaluated earlier than the arithmetic operators.

2.3.2   Relational Operators

The relational operators allow us to compare two values to see whether they are equal to each other, unequal, or whether one is greater than the other. The result is either true or false. In C++ also true means any non-zero value, whereas, false means zero. The relational operators are ==, !=, <, >, <= and >=. Their meaning and working remain the same as in C. The precedence of relational operators is given below:

```
<
<=
>
>=
==
!=
```

2.3.3   Logical Operators

C++ allows usage of all the three logical operators available in C. They are—&& (AND), || (OR), ! (NOT). The logical operators are used to connect the relational expressions created using the relational operators. The result of relational operators is true or false. Following is the truth table for logical operators.

p	q	p && q	p || q
0	0	0	0
0	1	0	1
1	1	1	1
1	0	0	1

The precedence of logical operators is given below:

```
!
&&
||
```

2.3.4 Manipulators

Manipulators are the operators that are used to format the data to be displayed. When we use manipulators the formatting instructions are inserted directly into a stream. Out of the several manipulators available, we have been using one quite often: *endl*. As we know, this manipulator sends a newline to the stream and flushes it.

Manipulators come in two flavors: those that take an argument and those that don't. Manipulators with no arguments are provided in 'iostream.h', whereas those that take arguments are provided in 'iomanip.h'. Table 2.4 gives a list of all manipulators along with their function.

Manipulator	Purpose
skipws	Skip whitespace on input
noskipws	Do not skip whitespace on input
dec	Convert to decimal
oct	Convert to octal
hex	Convert to hexadecimal
left	Left align, pad on right
right	Right align, pad on left
internal	Use padding between sign or base indicator and value
endl	Insert newline and flush the output stream
showpos	Shows plus sign for positive values
noshowpos	Do not show plus sign for positive values
uppercase	Display uppercase A-F for hex values, and E for scientific values
nouppercase	Do not display hex values in uppercase

showpoint	Show decimal point and trailing zeros for *float* values
noshowpoint	Do not show decimal point & trailing zeros for *float* values
scientific	Use scientific notation for printing *float* values
fixed	Use fixed notation for printing *float* values
ends	Insert null character to terminate an output string
flush	Flush the output stream
lock	Lock file handle
unlock	Unlock file handle
setw (int n)	Changes the field width for output to *n*
setfill (char n)	Changes the fill character to *n* (default is a space)
setprecision (int n)	Changes the precision to *n* places after decimal point
setbase (base n)	Changes base to *n*, where *n* is 8, 10 or 16. If *n* is zero, output is base 10, but input uses the C convention: 10 is 10, 010 is 8, and 0xC is 12
setiosflags (fmtflags n)	Sets format flags specified by *n*. Setting remains in effect until next change
resetiosflags (fmtflags n)	Clears only the format flags specified by *n*. Setting remains in effect until next change

Table 2.4 *List of Manipulators.*

The following program shows how to use these manipulators. It produces the same output as the previous program. However, you would find this program more compact and clean.

```
#include <iostream.h>
#include <conio.h>
#include <iomanip.h>

void main( )
{
    int i = 52 ;
    float a = 425.0 ;
    float b = 123.500328 ;
    char str[ ] = "Dream. Then make it happen!" ;

    clrscr( ) ;
    cout << oct << i << endl ;

    cout << setfill ( '0' ) ;
    cout << "Fill character:" << cout.fill( ) << endl ;

    cout << dec << setw ( 10 ) << i << endl ;
    cout << setiosflags ( ios::left )
        << dec << setw ( 10 ) << i << endl ;

    cout << setiosflags ( ios::internal )
        << dec << setw ( 10 ) << i << endl ;
    cout << i << endl ;

    cout.precision ( 6 ) ;
    cout << "Precision: " << cout.precision( ) ;
    cout << setiosflags ( ios::showpoint ) << resetiosflags ( ios::showpos )
        << endl << a ;
}
```

We can create our own manipulators. How this can be done would be discussed in Chapter 10.

2.3.5   Type Conversion

We are already aware that the = operator assigns a value from one variable to another in statements like

```
int a, b ;
a = b ;
```

We have also used the = operator in context of user-defined data types. Here, = assigns the value of one user-defined object to another, provided they are of the same type, in statements like

```
matrix3 = matrix1 + matrix2 ;
```

where the result of the addition is of the type *matrix*, and this result is assigned to another object *matrix3* of type *matrix*. Normally, when we assign the value of one object to another object of the same type, the values of all the data members are copied into the corresponding data members of the new object. The compiler doesn't need any special instructions to use = for the assignment of user-defined objects such as *matrix* objects.

Thus assignments between types, whether they are basic or user-defined, are handled by the compiler with no effort on our part, provided that the same data type is used on both sides of the assignment operator.

What if the variables on the two sides of the = are of different types? This is going to be a slightly complicated issue. Let us first see how the compiler handles the conversion of basic types, which it does automatically.

When we write a statement like

```
a = b ;
```

where *a* is of type *int* and *b* is of type *float*, the compiler calls a special routine to convert the value of *b*, which is expressed in floating-point format, to an integer format so that it can be assigned to *a*. There are many other such conversions possible: from *float* to *double*, *char* to *float*, and so on. Each such conversion has its own routine built into the compiler. These routines are called when the data types on either side of the assignment operator are different. These conversions are often known as implicit conversions since these conversions are not apparent in the listing of the program.

At times we may want to force the compiler to convert one type of data to another. This can be achieved by using typecasting. For instance, to convert a *float* to a *double* we can say

```
double a ;
float b = 3.14 ;
a = double ( b ) ;
```

Typecasting provides an explicit conversion. That is, in the listing it can be obviously seen that the *double( )* conversion function will convert *b* from *float* to a *double*. However, such explicit conversions use the same built-in routines as implicit conversions.

When we want to convert between user-defined data types and basic types, we can't rely on built-in conversion routines, since the compiler doesn't know anything about user-defined types besides what we tell it. Instead, we must write these conversion routines ourselves. How, we would see in Chapter 6.

2.3.6   Type Cast Operators

If we carry out an operation between an *int* and a *float* the *int* is promoted to a *float* before performing the operation. This conversion takes place automatically. A few more such automatic conversions are possible in C/C++. As against these automatic conversions, to carry out data conversions desired by the programmer typecasting is used. C++ provides a type cast operator for this purpose. Two different types of typecasting syntaxes are supported in C++. These are given below:

(type-name) expression
type-name (expression)

C supports only the first type of casting, whereas, C++ supports both. For example,

```
int y = 1001, j = 365, n ;
n = ( y - 1 ) * j ;  /* results in wrong answer since integer
                        range is exceeded on multiplication */

n = ( y - 1 ) * ( long ) j ;  // C style typecasting, also supported by C++
n = ( y - 1 ) * long ( j ) ;  // new C++ style typecasting
```

Instead of using typecasting we may as well have defined *j* as *long*. In this small fragment of code this would have worked. However, in a situation where we subsequently want to use *j* as an *int* there is no alternative to typecasting.

C++ also provides a new casting syntax using keywords *dynamic_cast*, *static_cast*, *const_cast*, and *reinterpret_cast*.

2.4 Control Statements

As the name suggests the 'Control Statements' enable us to specify the order in which the various instructions in a program are to be executed by the computer. In other words the control statements determine the 'flow of control' in a program. Let us discuss the control statements one by one.

2.4.1   If Statement

Like C, C++ uses the keyword *if* to implement the decision control instruction. The general form of *if* statement looks like this:

```
if ( this condition is true )
    execute this statement ;
```

The keyword *if* tells the compiler that what follows, is a decision control instruction. The condition following the keyword *if* is always enclosed within a pair of parentheses. If the condition is true, then the statement is executed. If the condition is not true then the statements given in the *else* block get executed. However, writing *else* block is optional. So, if *else* block does not exist, the control goes to the next statement in the program. Figure 2.3displays the flow of control in *if-else* statements.

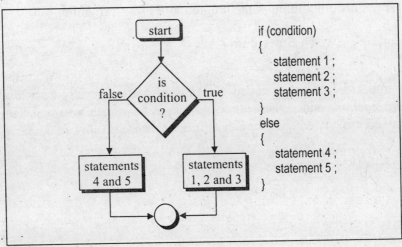

Figure 2.3 *if-else*.

Here is a simple program, which demonstrates the use of *if* and the relational operators.

```
/* Demonstration of if statement */

#include <iostream.h>

void main( )
```

```
{
    int num ;

    cout <<  "Enter a number less than 10 " ;
    cin >>  num ;

    if ( num <= 10 )
        cout << "What an obedient servant you are !" ;
}
```

On execution of this program, if you type a number less than or equal to 10, you get a message on the screen through *cout*. If you type some other number the program doesn't do anything.

2.4.2   Switch Statement

The control statement that allows us to make a decision from the number of choices is called a *switch*, or more correctly a *switch-case-default*, since these three keywords go together to make up the control statement. They most often appear as follows:

```
switch ( integer expression )
{
    case constant 1 :
        do this ;
    case constant 2 :
        do this ;
    case constant 3 :
        do this ;
    default :
        do this ;
}
```

The integer expression following the keyword *switch* is any expression that will yield an integer value. The keyword *case* is followed by an integer or a character constant. Each constant in each *case* must be different from all the others. The "do this" lines in the above form of *switch* represent any valid C++ statement.

What happens when we run a program containing a *switch*? First, the integer expression following the keyword *switch* is evaluated. The value it gives is then matched, one by one, against the constant values that follow the *case* statements. When a match is found, the program executes the statements following that *case*, and all subsequent *case* and *default* statements as well. If no match is found with any of the *case* statements, only the statements following the *default* are executed. Figure 2.4 shows the flow of control in switch-case control instructions.

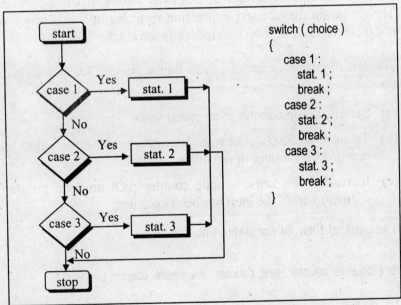

Figure 2.4. *Case.*

2.4.3   Loop Structures

There are three methods by way of which we can repeat a part of a program. They are:

(a) Using a *for* statement

(b) Using a *while* statement

(c) Using a *do-while* statement

We will discuss them in brief.

The *while* loop is ideally suited when we want to do something a fixed number of times. The syntax of while is given below:

```
while ( condition )
    statement ;
```

The *statement* can be a single statement or multiple statements. Multiple statements should be enclosed within a pair of braces. The *condition* may be any expression resulting into either zero or non-zero value. The loop iterates while the condition is true.

The *for* allows us to specify three things about a loop in a single line:

(a) Setting a loop counter to an initial value.

(b) Testing the loop counter to determine whether its value has reached the number of repetitions desired.

(c) Increasing the value of loop counter each time the program segment within the loop has been executed.

The general form of *for* statement is as under:

```
for ( initialise counter ; test counter ; increment counter )
{
    do this ;
    and this ;
    and this ;
}
```

At the time of execution in a *for* loop, firstly, the counter is initialized. Then the condition is tested. If the condition is true, the statements in the loop get executed. When control reaches the closing brace of the loop, it again goes back to the *for* statement to increment the counter. After the counter is incremented the condition is again tested. If true, statements get executed again. This goes on until the condition is true. The control comes out of the loop when the condition.fails.

The *do-while* loop looks like this:

```
do
{
    this ;
    and this ;
    and this ;
    and this ;
} while ( this condition is true ) ;
```

There is a minor difference between the working of *while* and *do-while* loops. This difference is the place where the condition is tested. The *while* tests the condition before executing any of the statements within the *while* loop. As against this, the *do-while* tests the condition after having executed the statements within the loop. This means that *do-while* would execute its statements at least once, even if the condition fails for the first time itself.

The flow of control in all the three loop statements is given in Figure 2.5.

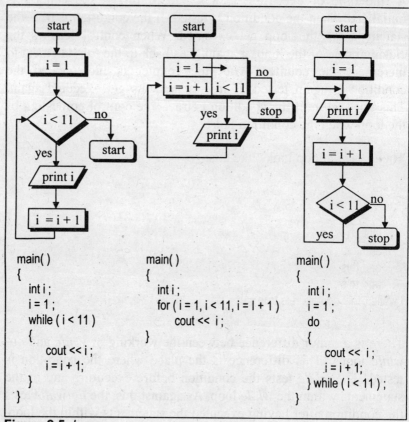

Figure 2.5. *Loop.*

2.4.4   Break Statement

We often come across situations where we want to jump out of a loop instantly, without waiting to get back to the conditional test. The keyword *break* allows us to do this. When the keyword *break* is encountered inside any loop or switch-case, control automatically passes to the first statement after the loop. A *break* is usually associated with an *if*. Let us see an example. This program determines whether a given number is prime or not.

```
#include <iostream.h>
void main( )
{
    int  num, i ;

    cout << "Enter a number " ;
    cin >> num ;

    i = 2 ;
    while ( i <= num - 1 )
    {
        if ( num % i == 0 )
        {
            cout <<  "Not a prime number" ;
            break ;
        }
        i++ ;
    }

    if ( i == num )
        cout << "Prime number" ;
}
```

In this program the moment *num % i* turns out to be zero, (i.e. *num* is exactly divisible by *i*) the message "Not a prime number" is printed and the control breaks out of the *while* loop. Why does the program require the *if* statement after the *while* loop at all? Well, there are two ways the control could have reached outside the *while* loop:

(a) It jumped out because the number proved to be not a prime.

(b) The loop came to an end because the value of *i* became equal to *num*.

When the loop terminates in the second case, it means that there was no number between 2 and *num - 1* that could exactly divide *num*. That is, *num* is indeed a prime. If this is true, the program should print out the message "Prime number".

One last thing about *break*. If used in a nested loops, *break* breaks only the nearest loop.

2.4.5   Continue Statement

In some programming situations we want to take the control to the beginning of the loop, bypassing the statements inside the loop, which have not yet been executed. The keyword *continue* allows us to do this. When the keyword *continue* is encountered inside any loop, control automatically passes to the beginning of the loop. Like *break*, *continue* is usually associated with an **if**. As an example, let's consider the following program.

```cpp
#include <iostream.h>
void main( )
{
    for ( int i = 1 ; i <= 2 ; i++ )
    {
        for ( int j = 1 ; j <= 2 ; j++ )
        {
            if ( i == j )
                continue ;

            cout << i << j ;
        }
    }
}
```

When the value of *i* equals that of *j*, the *continue* statement takes the control to the *for* loop (inner) bypassing rest of the statements pending execution in the *for* loop (inner).

2.4.6 Goto Statement

There is seldom a legitimate reason for using *goto*, and its use is one of the reasons that programs become unreliable, unreadable, and hard to debug. And yet many programmers (especially those coming from BASIC or FORTRAN background) find *goto* seductive.

In a difficult programming situation it seems so easy to use a *goto* to take the control where you want. However, almost always, there is a more elegant way of writing the same program using if, for, while and switch. These constructs are far more logical and easy to understand.

A *goto* statement can cause program control to end up almost anywhere in the program and it makes the program unreadable.

The general syntax of *goto* statement is given below:

```
goto label ;
...
...
label :
```

2.5 Console I/O Operations

I/O operations in C++ are carried out using streams. Streams allow I/O on a wide range of devices like terminals, disks and tape drives. Although every device is different, streams provide an interface that is independent of the device being accessed.

In this section firstly we would see the C-style console I/O functions and then C++-style stream I/O functions.

2.5.1 Unformatted Console I/O Functions

Console I/O functions are classified into two categories—formatted and unformatted console I/O functions. The basic difference between them is that the formatted functions allow the input read from the keyboard or the output displayed on the VDU to be formatted as per our requirements. For example, if values of average marks and percentage marks are to be displayed on the screen, then the details like where this output would appear on the screen, how many spaces would be present between the two values, the number of places after the decimal points, etc. can be controlled using formatted functions. On the other hand, unformatted functions do not allow formatting of data to be displayed.

In this section we would deal with the unformatted functions. There are several standard library functions available under the unformatted category—those that can deal with a single character and those that can deal with a string of characters.

We often want a function that will read a single character the instant it is typed without waiting for the Enter key to be hit. *getch( )* and *getche( )* are two functions which serve this purpose. These functions return the character that has been most recently typed. The 'e' in *getche( )* function means it echoes (displays) the character that you typed to the screen. As against this *getch( )* just returns the character that you typed without echoing it on the screen. *getchar( )* works similarly and echo's the character that you typed on the screen, but unfortunately requires Enter key to be typed following the character that you typed. The difference between *getchar( )* and *fgetchar( )* is that the former is a macro whereas the latter is a function.

putch( ) and *putchar( )* form the other side of the coin. They print a character on the screen. As far as the working of *putch( )* *putchar( )* and *fputchar( )* is concerned it's exactly same.

The limitation of *putch( )*, *putchar( )* and *fputchar( )* is that they can output only one character at a time.

gets( ) and puts( )

gets( ) receives a string from the keyboard. It is terminated when an Enter key is hit.

The *puts( )* function works exactly opposite to *gets( )* function. It outputs a string to the screen.

2.5.2   Unformatted Stream I/O Functions

A *stream* is a general name given to the flow of data. Different streams are used to represent different kinds of data flow. For example, the standard output stream flows to the screen display, the standard input stream flows from the keyboard (these streams can be redirected, if required). In C++ a stream is represented by an object of a particular class. For example, *cin* and *cout* that we have used so far are really objects of *istream_withassign* and *ostream_withassign* classes respectively. These classes have been derived from *istream* and *ostream* classes. We don't have to define these objects because they have already been defined for us in the 'iostream.h' file. Based on the nature of data flow the *iostream* library offers several classes arranged in a complex hierarchy.

An *iostream* system consists of three parts:

(a)   A buffer, which acts as an intermediary between the generalized input-output system and some particular source or sink for characters. This has been implemented in the *streambuf* class.

(b)   A specification system responsible for reporting errors and controlling formats. This has been implemented in the *ios* class.

(c)   A translation system that converts C++ language's typed objects to a sequence of characters or vice versa. This has been implemented in classes like *istream, ostream, iostream,* etc.

The *istream* class is derived from the *ios* class. It performs activities specific to input. One of the most commonly used member function of this class is the overloaded >> operator. It has been overloaded to extract values of all basic types. We can extract even a string using this operator:

```
char str [ 10 ] ;
cin >> str ;
```

However, in this case we have no control over the number of characters that would get extracted into the string. If the array overflows, it might be dangerous. Instead of this we can use the *get( )* member function. This function comes in several forms. These are as under:

Function	Purpose
get (ch)	Extracts one character into *ch*
get (str, MAX)	Extracts up to MAX characters into *str*
get (str, DELIM)	Extracts characters into array *str* until specified delimiter (typically '\n'). Leaves delimiting character in stream
get (str, MAX, DELIM)	Extracts characters into array *str* until MAX characters or the DELIM character. Leaves delimiting character in stream
getline (str, MAX, DELIM)	Extract characters into array *str*, until MAX characters or the DELIM character. Extracts delimiting character.

Table 2.5. *Overloaded get( ) function.*

In addition to these, the *istream* class supports a few miscellaneous functions. These are given below.

Function	Purpose
putback (ch)	Inserts last character read, back into input stream
peek (ch)	Reads one character, leaves it in stream
num = gcount( )	Returns number of character read by a (immediately preceding) call to *get( )*, *getline( )*, or *read( )*

Table 2.6. *Member functions of istream.*

The following program puts these functions to work.

```
#include <iostream.h>
void main( )
{
    char ch ;

    cout << endl << "Enter a character: " ;
    cin.get ( ch ) ;
    cout << ch ;
    cin.putback ( ch ) ;
    cin.get ( ch ) ;
    cout << endl << ch ;
    int count = cin.gcount( ) ;
    cout << endl << "Characters extracted in last get( ) = " << count ;

    // stuff stream with a Z
    cin.putback ( 'Z' ) ;
    ch = cin.peek( ) ;
    cout << endl << ch ;

    // Z is still in stream
    cin.get ( ch ) ;
    cout << endl << ch ;
```

}

The *ostream* Class

The *ostream* class handles output or insertion activities. Once again the most commonly used member function of this class is the overloaded << operator function. Two other useful member functions of this class are *put( )* and *flush( )*. The first one puts a character into the stream, whereas, the second flushes the buffer contents and inserts a newline.

We would work more with streams later in this book.

Exercises

[A] State True or False:

(a) In C++, a structure can contain data members, as well as functions that can operate upon the data members.

(b) In C++, a union can contain data members, as well as functions that can operate upon the data members.

(c) It is possible to create an array of references.

(d) Once a reference is tied with a variable it cannot be tied with another variable.

(e) A variable can be tied with several references.

(f) A reference to reference is allowed, whereas, a pointer to reference is not allowed.

(g) C++ permits the use of anonymous structures.

(h) A pointer of another type can be assigned to a void pointer without the need for typecasting.

(i) The following two definitions are same:

```
enum grade g ;
grade g ;
```

(j) A stream is represented by an object of a particular class.

(k) *cin* and *cout* are objects of *istream_withassign* and *ostream_withassign* classes respectively.

(l) The *istream* class is derived from the *ios* class.

(m) We can control the number of characters to be extracted using the *get( )* function.

(n) The *ostream* class handles input, whereas, the *istream* class handles output.

[B] Which of the following are invalid variable names and why?

```
InterestPaid
si-int
AVERAGE
percent.
123
dist in km
ot pay
Name
FLOAT
```

[C] What would be the output of the following programs:

```
int  i = 2, j = 3, k, l ;
float  a, b ;
k = i / j * j ;
l = j / i * i ;
a = i / j * j ;
b = j / i * i ;
printf( "%d %d %f %f", k, l, a, b ) ;
```

[D] Point out the errors, if any, in the following programs.

(a)
```
#include <iostream.h>
void main( )
{
    int i = 5 ;
    int &j = i ;
    int &k = j ;
    int &l = i ;

    cout << i << j << k << l ;
}
```

(b)
```
#include <iostream.h>
void main( )
{
    int a = 10, b = 20 ;
    long int c ;
    c = a * long int ( b ) ;
    cout << c ;
}
```

(c)
```
#include <iostream.h>
void main( )
{
    for ( int i = 0 ; i < 20 ; i++ )
    {
        for ( int j = 0 ; j < 5 ; j++ )
        {
            couf << i * j ;
        }
    }

    cout << i << j ;
}
```

(d)
```
#include <iostream.h>
```

```
        void main( )
        {
            for ( int i = 0 ; i < 20 ; i++ )
            {
                int j = 0 ;
                cout << "Always and never are two words..." ;
                cout << "...you should always remember never to use. " ;
            }
            cout << i ;
        }
```

(e)
```
        #include <iostream.h>
        void main( )
        {
            char *p = "Hello". ;
            p = "Hi" ;
            *p = 'G' ;
            cout << p ;
        }
```

(f)
```
        #include <iostream.h>
        void main( )
        {
            enum result { first, second, third } ;
            result a = first ;
            int b = a ;
            result c = 1 ;
            result d =  result ( 1 ) ;
        }
```

[E] What will be the output of the following programs:

(a)
```
        #include <iostream.h>
        void main( )
        {
            int i = 5 ;
            int &j = i ;
            int p = 10 ;
```

```
        j = p ;
        cout << endl << i << endl << j ;
        p = 20 ;
        cout << endl << i << endl << j ;
    }
```

(b)   ```
      #include <iostream.h>
      int i = 20 ;
      void main( )
      {
          int i = 5 ;
          cout << i << endl << ::i ;
      }
      ```

(c)   ```
      #include <iostream.h>
      int i = 20 ;
      void main( )
      {
          int i = 5 ;
          cout << i << endl << ::i ;
          {
              int i = 10 ;
              cout << i << endl << ::i ;
          }
      }
      ```

[F] Attempt the following:

(a) Any year is an input through keyboard. Write a program to determine whether the year is a leap year or not.

(b) If a sum is entered through keyboard, write a program to print the digits of the sum in words. For example, if Rs. 120 /- is entered, your program should print "One Two Zero". (Hint: use switch-case)

(c) Write a program to print all prime numbers from 1 to 300.
    (Hint: use loops, break and continue)

(d) If a five-digit number is input through the keyboard, write a
    program to reverse the number.

3
Functions

3.1 Introducing Functions

A function is a self-contained block of statements that perform a coherent task of some kind. Every C/C++ program can be thought of as a collection of these functions. Using a function is something like hiring a person to do a specific job for you.

The ways of supporting function has changed and improved in C++ as compared to C. Most of these changes are simple and straightforward. However, there are a few changes, which require you to adopt a new way of thinking and organising your program's code. Many of these requirements were driven by object-oriented facilities of C++. As we go along you would realise that these facilities were invented to make C++ programs *safer* and *more readable* than their C equivalents. Let us now see the various issues involved in C++ functions.

3.1.1   Declaring a Function

A function declaration is called function prototype. A function prototype indicates the name of the function, its return type and its parameters. General form of a function prototype is given below:

type function-name (argument-list) ;

Given below are a few examples of function prototypes:

float square (float) ;
char * strconvert (char *, int) ;
double nthroot (float, float) ;

Each of this declaration clearly specifies the number, order and the type of arguments each function is going to receive during a call, and the type of the value that each function would return when the control comes back from it.

The compiler uses the prototype to ensure that the types of actual arguments that you pass in a function call are the same as the types of the formal arguments in the function definition. No C++ function can be called unless its prototype is available to the compiler to crosscheck the argument type and the return value. This is known as strong type checking.

3.1.2 Defining a Function

Let's now see the style of defining functions in C++. The general form of a function definition is:

```
type function ( type arg1, type arg2, type arg3 )
{
    statement 1 ;
    statement 2 ;
    statement 3 ;
    statement 4 ;
}
```

Let us define a simple function.

```
void message( )
{
    cout << "Smile, and the world smiles with you..." ;
}
```

The function *message( )* doesn't have any arguments within the pair of parentheses, other functions may have them. We would discuss these arguments later in the chapter.

A C/C++ program must have at least one function. And if the program contains only one function, its name must always be *main( )*.

3.1.3   Calling a Function

To call a function we must write the function name followed by a pair of parenthesis. If the function takes parameters we must pass the parameters within pair of parenthesis. The parameters must be passed in the same sequence that is mentioned in the prototype of the function. The general syntax of calling a function is given below:

functionname (argument-list) ;

Let us now call the *message( )* function defined in the previous section.

```
void main( )
{
    message( ) ;
    cout << "\Cry, and you stop the monotony!" ;
}
```

And here's the output...

Smile, and the world smiles with you...
Cry, and you stop the monotony!

Here, through *main( )* we are calling the function *message( )*. When the function is called, the control passes to the first statement in the function *message( )*. Now the activity of *main( )* is temporarily suspended. When the *message( )* function runs out of statements to execute, the control returns to *main( )*, which comes to life again and begins executing its code at the exact point where it left off. Thus, *main( )* becomes the 'calling' function, whereas *message( )* becomes the 'called' function.

3.2 Passing Arguments and Returning Values

The mechanism used to convey information to the function is the 'argument'. We pass arguments to the functions while calling them. The arguments are sometimes also called 'parameters'. The parameters passed to the function are called as 'actual parameters' and the parameters given in function definition are called 'formal parameters'.

3.2.1   Passing and Returning Constants and Variables

Consider the following program. In this program, in *main( )* we have received the values of *a*, *b* and *c* through the keyboard and then output the sum of *a*, *b* and *c*. The calculation of sum is done in a different function called *calsum( )*. We have passed the values of *a*, *b* and *c* to the *calsum( )*.

```
#include <iostream.h>
void main( )
{
    int  a, b, c, sum ;
    int calsum ( int, int, int ) ; // prototype declaration

    cout << endl << "Enter any three numbers " ;
    cin >> a >> b >> c ;

    sum = calsum ( a, b, c ) ;
    cout << sum ;
    sum = calsum ( 12, 50, 34 ) ;
    cout << sum ;
}

int calsum ( int  x, int y, int z )
{
    int d ;

    d = x + y + z ;
```

```
    return d ;
}
```

In this program, from the function *main( )* the values of a, b and c are passed on to the function *calsum( )*, by making a call to the function *calsum( )* and mentioning a, b and c in the parentheses:

calsum (a, b, c) ;

In the *calsum( )* function these values get collected in three variables x, y and z. The sum gets calculated and is returned from the function using the *return* keyword.

The variables a, b and c are called 'actual arguments', whereas the variables x, y and z are called 'formal arguments'. Any number of arguments can be passed to a function being called. However, the type, order and number of the actual and formal arguments must always be same.

In the next call to the *calsum( )* function we have passed constants to it. The constants get collected in x, y and z respectively. Again the sum is calculated and returned.

The *return* statement serves two purposes:

- On executing the *return* statement it immediately transfers the control back to the calling program.
- It returns the value present in the parentheses after *return*, to the calling program. In the above program the value of sum of three numbers is being returned.

There is no restriction on the number of *return* statements that may be present in a function. Also, the *return* statement need not always be present at the end of the called function.

3.2.2   Passing and Returning Structure Variables

The way we pass primary data types to a function, we can also pass a derived data type like a structure variable to the function, or return a structure variable from it. This is shown in the following program.

```cpp
#include <iostream.h>
struct book
{
    char  name [ 25 ] ;
    char  author [ 25 ] ;
    int  callno ;
} ;

void main( )
{
    book get( ) ;
    void display ( book  b ) ;

    book b = get( ) ;
    display ( b ) ;
}

book get( )
{
    book t ;
    cin >> t.name >> t.author >> t.callno ;
    return t ;
}

void display ( book  b )
{
    cout << b.name << b.author <<  b.callno ;
}
```

The function *get( )* initialises the structure variable *t* using the values entered through keyboard and returns the entire structure variable. This variable is collected in *main( )* in another variable *b* of same type. We have passed *b* to the *display( )* function as a parameter. The *display( )* function displays the values stored in the structure variable.

If we declare the structure *book* inside *main( )* it will not be available to the other functions in the program. So, we have declared it globally.

3.2.3   Passing and Returning Reference Variables

When we pass variables or constants and collect them in simple variables, it is called a 'call by value'. If the function is called by value, a separate set of variables (formal arguments) is created thereby consuming more memory space. The function does not have access to the actual variables. This works fine as long as the function does not need to alter the values of the actual variables. However, sometimes a situation arises when a function needs to alter the values of actual variables. For example, if a function swaps the values of two variables that are being passed to it, the effect of swapping values must be felt in the calling function itself. This is not possible in a call by value. In such cases we must call a function by reference. When we pass arguments by reference, the 'formal' arguments in the called function refer to the actual arguments. It means that when the function works with its arguments, it is actually working with referents, i.e. with the actual arguments. In the following program the function *swap( )* is called by reference.

```
# include <iostream.h>
void main( )
{
    int a =10, b = 20 ;
    void swap ( int &, int & ) ;
```

```
        swap ( a, b ) ;  // call by reference
        cout << endl << a << "\t" << b ;
}

void swap ( int &i, int &j )
{
        int t ;
        t = i ;
        i = j ;
        j = t ;
}
```

We have seen how we can pass a reference to a function as a parameter. We can also return a reference from a function. When a function returns a reference, the function call can exist in any context where a reference can exist, including on the receiving side of an assignment. The following example would clarify this.

```
#include <iostream.h>
struct emp
{
        char name [ 20 ] ;
        int age ;
        float sal ;
} ;

emp e1 = { "Amol", 21, 2345.00 } ;
emp e2 = { "Ajay", 23, 4500.75 } ;

void main( )
{
        emp &fun( ) ;
        fun( ) = e2 ;
        cout << endl << e1.name << endl << e1.age << endl << e1.sal ;
}
```

```
emp &fun( )
{
    cout << endl << e1.name << endl << e1.age << endl << e1.sal ;
    return e1 ;
}
```

Here we have declared a structure *emp* and initialized two global variables *e1* and *e2* to some values. In *fun( )*, having printed the values stored in *e1* we have returned it by reference. What is strange is the call to the function *fun( )*. It has been written on the left-hand side of the assignment operator:

```
fun( ) = e2 ;
```

The result is that the variable returned by the function is assigned the value on the right hand side of the = sign. The following output of the *cout* statement in *main( )* verifies that the assignment has indeed taken place.

```
Ajay
23
4500.75
```

A word of caution! Do not try to return a local variable by reference. This is because the local variable goes óut of scope when the function returns. You would, therefore, be returning a reference for a variable that no longer exists, and the calling function would be referring to a variable that does not exist. Some C++ compilers issue a warning when they see code that returns references to automatic variables. If you ignore the warning, you get unpredictable results. Sometimes the program appears to work because the stack location where the automatic variable existed is intact when the reference is used. A program that appears to work in some cases can fail in others due to device or multitasking interrupts that use the stack.

3.3 Miscellaneous Features

In this section we would discuss few miscellaneous features of functions.

3.3.1 Function Overloading

Another significant addition made to the capabilities of functions in C++ is that of *function overloading.* With this facility you can have multiple functions with the same name. The following program illustrates this.

```
#include <iostream.h>

int abs ( int ) ;
long abs ( long ) ;
double abs ( double ) ;

void main( )
{
    int i = -25, j ;
    long l = -100000L, m ;
    double d = -12.34, e ;

    j = abs ( i ) ;
    m = abs ( l ) ;
    e = abs ( d ) ;

    cout << endl << j << endl << m << endl << e ;
}

int abs ( int ii )
{
    return ( ii > 0 ? ii : ii * -1 ) ;
}
```

```
long abs ( long ll )
{
      return ( ll > 0 ? ll : ll * -1 ) ;
}
double abs ( double dd )
{
      return ( dd > 0 ? dd : dd * -1 ) ;
}
```

How does the C++ compiler know which of the *abs( )s* should be called when a call is made? To solve this problem the C++ compiler changes the names of each and every function that you have defined and called. This process of changing the names of the functions is often called *name mangling*. Note that the names are mangled in the definition as well as the call. In either case the mangled name depends upon the type of the arguments. At run time there is no confusion as to which version of *abs( )* should be called, because by this time the non-unique function names in our source code have already been converted to unique mangled names.

Note that there is no standard way in which the name mangling is done. Each compiler uses its own method to do the name mangling. Thus the same function name would be mangled differently by Turbo C++ compiler and Visual C++ compiler. Also remember that name mangling is not only used for the overloaded functions, but every other function as well.

What if we make a call like,

ch = abs ('A') ;

We have not declared an *abs( )* function to handle a *char*. Hence the C++ compiler would implicitly convert the *char* to *int* and then call the *int* version of *abs( )*. Likewise, if we pass a *float* to *abs( )* then it would be converted to *double* and then the *double* version of *abs( )* would get called.

Sometimes implicit conversions are dangerous. If the conversion results into multiple matches then the compiler is not able to decide which version of the function it should call and hence reports an error. In such a case we can explicitly typecast the argument to call the desired version of the function. For example, if we drop the *int* version of *abs( )* from our program and then make the following call the compiler would report an error.

```
i = abs ( -35 ) ;
```

The error occurs because in absence of the *int* version the compiler doesn't know whether to convert *–35* to a *long int* and then call the *long int* version of *abs( )*, or to convert it to *double* and then call the *double* version of *abs( )*.

Overloaded functions must at least differ in the type, number or order of parameters they accept. Don't rely on the return values to differentiate them. Let us understand the reason for this with the help of an example.

```
int f( )
{
    return 9 ;
}

void f( )
{
}

void main( )
{
    f( ) ;
}
```

There is an ambiguity in the function call. This is because just by seeing the call we cannot figure out which version of *f( )* should get called (the version that returns a value or the version that does not return a value). Even if we are not collecting the value, we cannot assume that the function *f( )* that does not return a value would get called. This is because it is not necessary to collect the returned value even if the called function returns a value.

Can we fool the C++ compiler into believing that two same data types are different by renaming one of them using *typedef*? No. A *typedef* merely gives another name for an existing type and does not constitute an original type of its own. Hence, the following program segment would give an error:

```
typedef INT int ;
void display ( int ) ;
void display ( INT ) ;
```

The example above would not compile correctly because the compiler has no way of differentiating between the two versions of the function *display( )*. An *INT* is just another name for an *int*.

It's a bad programming idea to create overloaded functions that perform different types of actions; functions with the same name should have the same general purpose. For example, if we write an *abs( )* function that returns the square root of a number, it would be both silly and confusing. We must use overloaded functions judiciously. Their purpose is to provide a common name for several similar but slightly divergent functions. Overusing overloaded functions can make a program unreadable.

3.3.2   Function Overriding

Programmers often get confused with the terms 'function overloading' and 'function overriding'. They carry totally different meanings. We have already seen function overloading. Let us now see what does function overriding mean.

Function overriding means redefining an existing function. The redefined function must have the same prototype as the existing function. Function overriding is often used in inheritance. If a base class contains a member function the derived class can override it to add its own functionality to it. Similarly, a *virtual* function is often overridden in a derived class.

3.3.3 Constructors and Destructors

In the last chapter we had our first tryst with classes in C++. Just to reiterate, a class is a collection of data and functions that operate upon this data. A class has two special member functions called constructor and destructor. These functions are special because, we never call them, they are automatically called. The constructor gets called when an object of the class is created. On the contrary, destructor is called when the object dies.

We would see constructor and destructors in detail in Chapter 5.

3.3.4 Inline Functions

One of the important advantages of using functions is that they help us save memory space. As all the calls to the function cause the same code to be executed; the function body need not be duplicated in memory.

Imagine a situation where a small function is getting called several times in a program. As you must be aware, there are certain overheads involved while calling a function. Time has to be spent on passing values, passing control, returning value and returning control. In such situations to save the execution time you may instruct the C++ compiler to put the code in the function body directly inside the code in the calling program. That is, at each place where there's a function call in the source file, the actual code from the function would be inserted, instead of a jump to the function. Such functions are called *inline* functions. The in-line nature of the individual copy of the function eliminates the function-calling overhead of a traditional function. The following program shows *inline* function at work.

```
#include <iostream.h>
#include <stdlib.h>

inline void reporterror ( char *str )
{
    cout << endl << str ;
    exit ( 1 ) ;
}

void main ( )
{
    // code to open source file
    if ( fileopeningfailed )
        reporterror ( "Unable to open source file" ) ;

    // code to open target file
    if ( fileopeningfailed )
        reporterror ( "Unable to open target file" ) ;

    // code to copy contents of source file into target file
}
```

Note that the function must be declared to be *inline* before calling it. On compilation the contents of the *reporterror( )* function would get inserted at two places within our program. These obviously are the places where *reporterror( )* is being called.

One question that should occur to you is why ask the compiler to insert the code of the function in line with the other program code when we can easily do so ourselves? The trouble with repeatedly inserting the same code is that you lose the benefits of program organization and clarity that come with using functions. The program may run faster and take less space, but the listing is longer and more complex. Instead, if we write the code in a *inline* function the source file remains well organized and easy to read, since the function is shown as a separate entity. However, when the program is compiled, the function body is actually inserted into the program wherever a function call occurs.

You should use the *inline* function qualifier only when the function code is small. If the functions are large you should prefer the normal functions since the savings in memory space is worth the comparatively small sacrifice in execution speed.

Note that when we define the function *inline* there is no guarantee that its code would get inserted at the place where the call is being made. This is because we are just making a request to the compiler. The C++ language does not define under what conditions the compiler may choose to ignore our request. Because of this ambiguity in the language specification, compiler builders have flexibility in how they interpret the requirements. Given below is a list of common situations where even though we declarer the function *inline* the compiler ignores our request:

(a) If the function contains loop, a *switch* or a *goto*.

(b) If the function contains *static* variables.

Inline functions are similar to *#define* macros. However, they provide better type checking and do not have the side effects so typically associated with macros. For example consider the following program:

```
#include <iostream.h>

#define SQUARE( x )  x * x
inline float square ( float y )
{
    return y * y ;
}
```

```
void main ( )
{
    float a = 0.5, b = 0.5, c, d ;

    c = SQUARE ( ++a ) ;
    d = square ( ++b ) ;
}
```

During preprocessing the macro SQUARE gets expanded into

```
c = ++x * ++x ;
```

You can notice the undesirable side effect in this macro expansion: the variable is getting incremented twice even though we have used the incrementation operator only once. Such side effects would not occur in the *inline* function.

3.3.5   Default Arguments

In C if a function is defined to receive 2 arguments, whenever we call this function we have to pass 2 values to this function. If we pass one value then some garbage value is assumed for the last argument. As against this, functions in C++ have an ability to define default values for arguments that are not passed when the function call is made. Let us understand this with an example program.

```
#include <iostream.h>
#include <conio.h>

void box ( int sr = 1, int sc = 1, int er = 24, int ec = 80 ) ;

void main( )
{
    clrscr( ) ;
    box ( 10, 20, 22, 70 ) ;
    box ( 10, 20, 15 ) ;
```

```
    box ( 5, 10 ) ;
    box( ) ;
}

void box ( int sr, int sc, int er, int ec )
{
    int r, c ;

    gotoxy ( sc, sr ) ;
    cout << ( char ) 218 ;   // outputs a graphic character whose ascii
                             // value is 128
    gotoxy ( ec, sr ) ;
    cout << ( char ) 191 ;
    gotoxy ( sc, er ) ;
    cout << ( char ) 192 ;
    gotoxy ( ec, er ) ;
    cout << ( char ) 217 ;

    for ( r = sr + 1 ; r < er ; r++ )
    {
        gotoxy ( sc, r ) ;
        cout << ( char ) 179 ;
        gotoxy ( ec, r ) ;
        cout << ( char ) 179 ;
    }

    for ( c = sc + 1 ; c < ec ; c++ )
    {
        gotoxy ( c, sr ) ;
        cout << ( char ) 196 ;
        gotoxy ( c, er ) ;
        cout << ( char ) 196 ;
    }
}
```

When we call the function *box( )* with 4 arguments the box is drawn with the arguments passed. However, when we call it with 3 arguments the default value mentioned in the prototype of *box( )* is used for the last argument. Likewise, when we call it with two arguments default values are used for the last two arguments, and finally when we call it without any arguments, a box gets drawn with all the four default values mentioned in the prototype. Thus, the default arguments are used if the calling function doesn't supply the arguments when the function is called.

Note that if one argument is missing when the function is called, it is assumed to be the last argument. Thus, the missing arguments must be the trailing arguments (those at the end of the argument list). You can leave out last three arguments, but you cannot leave out the last but one and then put in the last. This is quite reasonable. After all, how would the compiler know which arguments you meant, if you left out some arguments in the middle. Not surprisingly, compiler will flag an error if you leave out some arguments for which the function you are calling doesn't provide default values.

The default arguments are given only in the function prototype and should not be repeated in the function definition. The compiler uses the prototype information to build a call, not the function definition. You can guess that there is an exception to this rule. If we are defining the function before the call, then we can drop the prototype and in such a case the default values are mentioned in the definition itself as shown below:

```
#include <iostream.h>
#include <conio.h>

void box ( int sr = 1, int sc = 1, int er = 24, int ec = 80 )
{
    // box drawing code
}
```

```
void main( )
{
    clrscr( ) ;
    box ( 10, 20, 22, 70 ) ;
    box ( 10, 20, 15 ) ;
    box( ) ;
}
```

Default arguments are useful in 2 cases:

(a) While making a function call if you don't want to take the trouble of writing arguments, which almost always have the same value.

(b) They are also useful in such cases where, after having written a program we decide to increase the capability of a function by adding another argument. Using default arguments means that the existing function calls can continue to use old number of arguments, while new function calls can use more.

Remember that the default value for an argument can be a global constant, a global variable, or even a function call. For example, such a function prototype is perfectly acceptable:

```
int myfunc ( flag = display( ) ) ;
```

In this case if *myfunc( )* is called without an argument, a default value will be obtained by making a call to the function *display( )*.

Exercises

[A] State True or False:

(a) Function is a self-contained block of statements performing a specific job.

(b) Two functions can be overloaded if their arguments are similar but their return values are different.

(c) Two functions can be overloaded only if their arguments differ in number, order or type.

(d) If function is defined before calling it, default arguments can be mentioned in the function definition itself.

(e) If default values are mentioned for the four arguments in the function prototype, we can call this function and pass it the first and the fourth argument.

(f) A function can be overloaded any number of times.

(g) C++ allows assigning of default values to function parameters while defining the function.

(h) On declaring a function inline the compiler replaces the function call with the actual function code.

(i) Declaring a function inline is only a request to the compiler to do the replacement. The request may or may not be granted.

(j) To return the control back to the calling function we must use the keyword *return*.

(k) The same variable names can be used in different functions without any conflict.

(l) Every called function must contain a *return* statement.

(m) A function may contain more than one *return* statements.

(n) If the function is defined before calling it, there is no need to mention its prototype.

(o) It is possible to return a value by reference.

(p) In C++ a function call can occur even on the left-hand side of an assignment operator.

(q) It is unsafe to return a local variable by reference.

[B] Point out the errors, if any, in the following programs.

(a)   void main( )

```
    {
        int a = 30 ;
        f( ) ;
    }

    void f( )
    {
        // some code
    }
```

(b)
```
    #include <iostream.h>
    void f( )
    {
        cout << "Hello" ;
    }

    void main( )
    {
        f( ) ;
    }
```

(c)
```
    #include <iostream.h>
    void f ( int, float ) ;

    void main( )
    {
        f( ) ;
    }

    void f ( int i = 10, float a = 3.14 )
    {
        cout << i << a ;
    }
```

(d)
```
    #include <iostream.h>
    void f ( int = 10, int = 20, int = 30 ) ;
    void f ( int, int ) ;
```

```
    void main( )
    {
        f ( 1, 2 ) ;
    }

    void f ( int x, int y, int z )
    {
        cout << endl << x << endl << y << endl << z ;
    }

    void f ( int x, int y )
    {
        cout << endl << x << endl << y ;
    }
```

[C] Answer the following:

(a) Complete the following program by defining the function
     swapb( ) and its prototype such that the output of the program
     is 20 10.

```
    #include <iostream.h>
    void swapa ( int &, int & ) ;
    void main( )
    {
        int a = 10, b = 20 ;

        swapa ( a, b ) ;
        cout << a << b ;
    }

    void swapa ( int &x, int &y )
    {
        swapb ( x, y ) ;
    }
```

[D] Attempt the following:

(a) A 5-digit positive integer is entered through the keyboard, write a function to calculate sum of digits of the 5-digit number.

(b) Write a function to calculate the factorial value of any integer entered through the keyboard.

(c) Write a function *power (a, b)*, to calculate the value of *a* raised to *b*.

(d) A positive integer is entered through the keyboard. Write a function to obtain the prime factors of this number.

For example, prime factors of 24 are 2, 2, 2 and 3, whereas prime factors of 35 are 5 and 7.

4
Classes and Objects

4.1 Introducing Classes and Objects

A class is the most important feature in C++. We are now familiar with the terms classes and objects. Just to reiterate, a class is a collection of data and functions that operate upon this data. An object is a specific instance of the class.

There is almost no difference in the syntax of a structure and a class, hence at least in principle they can be used interchangeably. But most C++ programmers use structures to exclusively hold data and classes to hold both data and functions.

4.1.1   Declaring a Class

A class declaration specifies its data members, member functions and their scope. The general syntax of a class declaration is given below:

```
class class_name
{
    private:
        data members declaration
        member functions definition
    public :
        data members declaration
        member functions definition
} ;
```

The keyword *class* specifies that what follows is the declaration of the data type called *class-name*. Like a structure, the body of a class is delimited by braces and terminated by a semicolon.

The class body contains declaration of data members and member functions. They together are called 'class members'.

The body of the class contains two unfamiliar keywords: *private* and *public*. They are used in C++ to implement a concept called *data hiding*. It means that data is concealed within a class, so that it cannot be accessed by functions outside the class even by mistake. The mechanism used to hide data is to put it in a class and make it *private*. *private* data members and member functions can be accessed from within the class. *public* data members and member functions on the other hand, are accessible from outside the class. By default, the class members are *private*. The keywords *private* and *public* are called 'access specifiers. The scope of the access specifier is applicable to all the members defined after specifying it.

To begin with, let us take a program that demonstrates the syntax and general features of classes in C++.

```
#include <iostream.h>

class rectangle
{
    private :

        int len, br ;

    public :

        void getdata( ) ;
        void setdata ( int l, int b ) ;
        void displaydata( ) ;
        void area_peri ( ) ;
};
```

The keyword *class* is followed by the class name *rectangle*. Thus, here, we are creating a new data type *rectangle*. The class *rectangle* specified in this program contains two data members *len* and *br* representing the length and breadth respectively and four functions *setdata( ), getdata( ), displaydata( )* and *area_peri( )*. As their names suggest, the first function sets the data items (length and breadth) to given values, the second function receives the values of data items, the third displays these values, whereas the fourth calculates and prints the area and perimeter.

In the class the data items *len* and *br* follow the keyword *private*, so they can be accessed from within the class, but not from outside it. The above mentioned four member functions would provide access to the data members of class.

Usually the data within a class is *private* and the functions are *public*. This is a result of how classes are used. The data is hidden so it will be safe from accidental manipulation, while the functions that operate on the data are *public* so they can be accessed from outside the class. However, there is no rule that data must be *private* and functions *public*. In fact in some cases you may be required to use *private* functions and *public* data.

4.1.2   Creating Class Instances

In the above section we have created only a new data type called *rectangle*, we have not created any variables of the type *rectangle*. A class variable is known as an object of the class.

An object is an *instance* of a class, and the process of creating an object is called *instantiation*. To create an object, we have to mention the class name and the object name as shown below:

rectangle r1, r2 ;

You would appreciate that creating a class object is just like creating any other variable.

When we declare an integer variable, 2 bytes (4 bytes under Windows) get reserved for it in memory. Likewise, when we create an object of a class memory gets allocated for it. But how many bytes an object would occupy? An object would occupy as many bytes as the sum of sizes of its data members. Note that the class declaration does not occupy any memory. It is only when we create the object that memory gets allocated.

4.1.3   Accessing Class Members

Since the data members of the *rectangle* class are *private* we cannot access them in *main( )*, they are accessible only inside the member functions of the class. So, to initialise the data members or to obtain the values from them, we must use the member functions. The class members can be accessed only through the object of the class. The syntax is shown below:

object_name.function_name (argument-list) ;

So, we would call the member functions using the objects *r1* and *r2* as shown below.

r1.setdata (10, 20) ;
r2.setdata (5, 8) ;

Member functions are always called using an object because a member function is always called to act on a specific object, not on the class in general. To use a member function, the dot operator connects the object name and the member function. The dot operator is also called 'class member access operator'. We can also access the *public* data members using the dot operator.

The first call to *setdata( )* function executes the *setdata( )* member function of the *r1* object. This function sets the variables *len* and *br* to values *10* and *20* respectively. Likewise, the second call to *setdata( )* sets the values for variables in the second object.

The in-memory representation of objects *r1* and *r2* is shown in Figure 4.1.

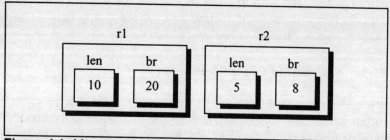

Figure 4.1. *Memory representation of objects.*

On similar grounds we can call the other member functions.

```
r1.displaydata( ) ;      // display the data set by setdata( )
r1.area_peri( ) ;        // calculate and print area and perimeter

r2.displaydata( ) ;
r2.area_peri( ) ;
```

Some languages refer to calls to member functions as *messages*. Thus the call

```
r1.setdata ( 10, 20 ) ;
```

can be thought of as sending a message to *r1* telling it to set up values in variables. The term *message* is not a formal part of C++, but is a useful idea to keep in mind when we discuss member functions.

One last thing, one member function can call the other member function. In this case the function is called directly, without using the dot operator.

4.1.4   Defining Member Functions of the Class

The member functions can be defined either inside the class or
outside the class.

The class *rectangle* after defining the member functions inside the
class is given below:

```
class rectangle
{
    private :

        int len, br ;

    public :

        void getdata( )
        {
            cout << endl << "Enter length and breadth " ;
            cin >> len >> br ;
        }

        void setdata ( int l, int b )
        {
            len = l ;
            br = b ;
        }

        void displaydata( )
        {
            cout << endl << "length = " << len ;
            cout << endl << "breadth = " << br ;
        }

        void area_peri ( )
        {
            int a, p ;
```

```
            a = len * br ;
            p = 2 * ( len + br ) ;
            cout << endl << "area = " << a ;
            cout << endl << "perimeter = " << p ;
        }
};
```

The functions defined inside a class are *inline* functions.

Generally, member functions are defined outside the class to separate declaration and implementation of the class. The declaration of the class is placed in a header (.h) file and its implementation in the source file (.cpp). This separation is useful while creating large sized classes or the classes that are meant for distribution. The syntax to define functions outside the class is given below:

```
return-type class_name :: function_name ( argument list )
{
    // statement 1 ;
    // statement 2 ;
    // statement 3 ;
}
```

This is how we could have defined the member functions of *rectangle* class.

```
void rectangle::getdata( )
{
    cout << endl << "Enter length and breadth " ;
    cin >> len >> br ;
}

void rectangle::setdata ( int l, int b )
{
```

```
        len = 1 ;
        br = b ;
}

void rectangle::displaydata( )
{
        cout << endl << "length = " << len ;
        cout << endl << "breadth = " << br ;
}

void rectangle::area_peri( )
{
        int a, p ;
        a = len * br ;
        p = 2 * ( len + br ) ;
        cout << endl << "area = " << a ;
        cout << endl << "perimeter = " << p ;
}
```

The operator *::* tells the compiler that the function belongs to the *rectangle* class. Failure to mention *rectangle::* would lead the compiler to believe that the function is an ordinary function and not a member function of the class *rectangle*.

Although the functions are defined outside the class, they should be declared in the class as shown below:

```
#include <iostream.h>

class rectangle
{
        private :

                int len, br ;
        public :
```

```
            void getdata( ) ;
            void setdata ( int l, int b ) ;
            void displaydata( ) ;
            void area_peri ( ) ;
};
```

The functions defined outside the class are not *inline*. However, we can make them inline by using the keyword *inline* as shown below:

```
inline void rectangle::area_peri( )
{
    ...
}
```

4.2 Objects and Functions

A class object can be passed to a function as an argument. This section describes how.

4.2.1   Passing Objects as Function Arguments

Like a variable of other data types, an object can also be passed to a function either by value, by reference or by address (passing address and collecting in pointer). In the following program we have defined a member function that concatenates the values of two objects passed to it. It demonstrates how to pass an object by value.

```
#include <iostream.h>
#include <string.h>

class str
{
    private:
```

```
            char s [ 50 ] ;
    public :

        void set ( char *ss )
        {
            strcpy ( s, ss ) ;
        }

        void print( )
        {
            cout << s << endl ;
        }

        void concat ( str s2 )
        {
            strcat ( s, s2.s ) ;
        }
} ;

void main( )
{
    str s1, s2 ;
    s1.set ( "hand in " ) ;
    s2.set ( "hand" ) ;
    s1.concat ( s2 ) ;
    s1.print( ) ;
}
```

The class *str* has a data member *s*, three member functions—*set( )* that initialises the data member *s*, *print( )* that displays the value of *s* and *concat( )* that concatenates the values of objects. When we say 'concatenates values of objects' we mean concatenating the values of data members of the object. So, the *concat( )* function actually concatenates the strings stored in *s* of the two objects.

In *main( )* we have created two objects of *str* and called the *set( )* member function using them. We have passed a string to it. In the *set( )* function we have stored this string in *s*. Next, we have called the *concat( )* function passing to it *s2*. The function concatenates the s2's s at the end of *s1*'s *s*. When we use *s* in this function, it is *s1's* s since we have called the function using the object *s1*. We have then called the *print( )* function to display the concatenated string.

Note that an object can also be passed to a non-member function. However, this function cannot access *private* members using the object.

4.2.2   Passing Array of Objects as Function Arguments

We can create an array of objects using the same syntax that we use to create an array of integers or floats. Let us now see a program that creates an array of objects and passes it to a non-member function.

```
#include <iostream.h>

class sample
{
    private :

        int i ;

    public :

        void set ( int ii )
        {
            i = ii ;
        }

        void print( )
        {
            cout << endl << i ;
        }
```

```
};

void show ( sample *p )
{
    for ( int j = 0 ; j < 5 ; j++ )
        p [ j ].print( ) ;
}

void main( )
{
    sample s [ 5 ] ;

    for ( int j = 0 ; j < 5 ; j++ )
        s [ j ].set ( j ) ;

    show ( s ) ;
}
```

Here, we have created an array *s* of five *sample* objects. We have called the *set( )* member function using each object in the array to set a value in the data member *i*. Then we have called the *show( )* function and passed to it the base address of the array. We have collected this address in a pointer *p*. This pointer points to the zeroth element of the array. Next, using this pointer we have called the *print( )* member function for individual object in the array to print the value of *i* for each object.

4.2.3   Returning Objects from Functions

There is nothing special about returning an object from a function. It is just like returning any other variable. For example, the following function *concat( )* returns the object of type *str*.

```
str concat ( str s2 )
{
    str t ;
```

```
        strcpy ( t.s, s ) ;
        strcat ( t.s, s2.s ) ;
        return t ;
}
```

When the control returns from *concat( )* we would collect the object returned by it in another object *s3* as shown below.

```
str s3 ;
s3 = s1.concat ( s2 ) ;
```

4.3 Structures in C++

C++ extends the reach of structures by allowing the inclusion of even functions within structures. In fact, you can use structures in almost exactly the same way that you use classes. The only formal difference between a class and a structure is that in a class the members are *private* by default, while in a structure they are *public* by default.

C++ has also incorporated an important feature of inheritance in structures.

Though in principle we can use a structure at every place where a class is used, in most situations programmers prefer to use structures to group data, and classes to group both data and functions.

4.3.1   Declaring Structures

The general form of a structure declaration statement is given below:

```
struct <structure name>
{
```

```
    private:

        structure elements declaration ;

    public:

        Member function definitions
};
```

Here is the declaration of a structure that contains both data member and member function.

```
struct sample
{
    private :

        int data ;

    public :

        void fun( )
        {
            // some code
        }
};
```

In a structure all members are by default *public*. Still here we can't afford to drop the keyword *public*. On doing so the *private* clause would become applicable even to the function *fun( )*. If we are still keen on dropping the keyword *public* we will have to define the function before the data members as shown below:

```
struct sample
{
```

```
void fun( )
{
    // some code
}
```

private :

```
        int data ;
};
```

4.3.2   Defining Structure

Like class declaration, structure declaration is also a blueprint and does not occupy memory. Memory gets allocated only when we create a structure variable. Unlike C, while creating a variable a structure name is used without the keyword *struct*. For example, a structure variable can be created only by writing

struct_name variable_name ;

The variable can also be created while declaring the structure as shown below:

```
struct struct_name
{
    // structure elements
} variable1 ;
```

To access the structure elements and member functions the . and the -> operators can be used. A structure variable can also be a data member of a class.

4.3.3 Nested Structures

One structure can be nested within another structure. Using this facility complex data types can be created. The following program shows nested structures at work.

```
main( )
{
    struct address
    {
        char  phone [ 15 ] ;
        char  city [ 25 ] ;
        int  pin ;
    } ;

    struct emp
    {
        char  name [ 25 ] ;
        struct address  a ;
    } ;
    emp  e = { "jeru", "531046", "nagpur", 10 } ;

    cout <<  "\nname = " << e.name << "phone = " << e.a.phone ;
    cout <<  "\ncity = " << e.a.city  << "pin = " << e.a.pin ;
}
```

And here is the output...

```
name = jeru phone = 531046
city = nagpur pin = 10
```

Notice the method used to access the element of a structure that is part of another structure. For this the dot operator is used twice, as in the expression,

e.a.pin or e.a.city

Exercises

[A] State True or False:

(a) Generally, structures are used to exclusively hold data and classes to hold both data and functions.

(b) The access specifiers are used to implement the concept of data hiding.

(c) Declaring a class occupies memory.

(d) The size of an object is equal to the sum of sizes of all the data members.

(e) Class members can be accessed using its object only.

(f) Objects are to classes as variables are to data types.

(g) We need to create an object of a class in a member function to call another member function from it.

(h) If member functions are defined outside the class, there is no need to declare them inside the class.

(i) In C++, a structure can contain data members, as well as functions that can operate upon the data members.

(j) By default members of a structure are *public* and that of a class are *private*.

(k) In a class data members are always *private*, whereas, member functions are always *public*.

[B] Answer the following:

(a) What is the difference between a class and structure in C++?.

(b) Given the statement,

maruti.engine.bolts = 25 ;

which of the following is True?

1. structure bolts is nested within structure engine
2. structure engine is nested within structure maruti
3. structure maruti is nested within structure engine
4. structure maruti is nested within structure bolts

[C] Attempt the following:

(a) Design a class to store information of an employee such as employee code, name and salary. The class should have member functions to store and display this information. Give proper access specifiers to the member functions as well as data members of a class.

(b) Write a menu driven program to perform following operations on the private data members of class sample

1. Add two numbers
2. Multiply two numbers
3. Check whether the number is even or odd

Write separate function for each operation.

(c) Create a structure named *india* with structure elements as *cityname, population, tot_literate*. Create a variable *city* that contains 50 elements of type *india*. Populate it with values and display only those city names where literacy is 80% or more.

5
Constructors & Destructors

5.1 Constructors

We had an introduction to constructors in Chapter 3. In this chapter we would learn more about them. Consider the following program.

```
#include <iostream.h>

class stack
{
    private :

        int i ;
        int a [ 10 ] ;

    public :

        void init( )
        {
            i = 0 ;
        }

        void push ( int d )
        {
            a [ i ] = d ;
            i++ ;
        }

        void print( )
        {
            for ( int j = 0 ; j < i ; j++ )
                cout << endl << a [ j ] ;
        }
} ;

void main( )
{
```

```
stack s ;
s.init( ) ;
s.push ( 10 ) ;
s.push ( 20 ) ;

s.print( ) ;
}
```

The member function *push( )* pushes the data in the array *a* at i^{th} location. *i* is initialised to *0* in the *init( )* member function. Hence, it becomes necessary to call the *init( )* member function before calling *push( )* function. If the user fails to call *init( )* the program would fire.

It would be a better idea if data members of an object get initialised with some default value at the time of object creation itself. C++ provides a special function called constructor for this purpose. Using constructors we can initialise data members of an object when it is created. Let us modify the above program by writing constructor in it.

5.1.1   Declaring and Defining Constructors

A constructor is defined as shown below:

```
stack( )
{
    i = 0 ;
}
```

If we want, we can declare the constructor inside the class and define it outside the class. This is shown below:

```
class stack
{
```

```
    private :

        int i ;

    public :

        stack( ) ;
};
stack::stack( )
{
    i = 0 ;
}
```

Now when we create an object as

```
stack s ;
```

the constructor would get called. It is now guaranteed that the data member *i* would be initialised to *0* when an object of class *stack* is created.

Let us now compare the initialization of an object through a constructor with initialization of normal variables. If we are to initialize variables of intrinsic data types we do so through statements like,

```
int age = 23 ;
float salary = 4500.50 ;
```

C++ allows one more way to initialise the intrinsic data types. This is shown below.

```
int age ( 23 ) ;
float salary ( 4500.50 ) ;
```

This notation of initialising variables is known as a class constructor notation.

5.1.2 Characteristics of Constructors

The characteristics of constructor are listed below:

(a) The constructor is a special member function that allows us to set up values while defining an object.

(b) The constructor is called automatically whenever an object is created.

(c) Name of the constructor is same as the class name.

(d) Constructors have no return type, not even *void*.

(e) Constructors are usually *public*.

(f) An object with constructor cannot be used as an element of union.

(g) Constructor cannot be declared as *virtual*.

(h) Constructor can be a zero-argument constructor or parameterized constructor (constructor with one or more arguments).

(i) We can specify default values for the arguments in the constructor.

(j) Like normal function constructors can be overloaded.

5.1.3 Order of Constructor Invocation

At the time of object creation firstly memory for the object gets allocated and then constructor gets called. The constructor for global objects gets called in order of their declaration. Following program illustrates when constructors get called.

```
#include <iostream.h>
class sample
```

```
{
    private:

        int i ;

    public :

        sample ( int ii )
        {
            i = ii ;
            cout << endl << "Constructed " << i ;
        }
};

sample s1 ( 1 ) ;
sample s2 ( 2 ) ;

void main( )
{
    sample s3 ( 3 ) ;
    sample s4 ( 4 ) ;
}
```

The output of the program would be

Constructed 1
Constructed 2
Constructed 3
Constructed 4

The objects are destructed (refer section 5.3) in the reverse order of construction of objects.

5.1.4   Nameless Objects

All objects that we created so far had user-defined names. At times we may prefer to create nameless objects. For example, we can create nameless objects for the integer class as follows:

```cpp
#include <iostream.h>

class integer
{
    private :

        int i ;

    public :

        integer( )
        {
        }

        integer ( int j )
        {
            i = j ;
        }
} ;
void main( )
{
    integer( ) ;
    integer ( 10 ) ;
}
```

Note the way to create nameless objects:

```cpp
integer( ) ;
integer ( 10 ) ;
```

When we create the first nameless object zero-argument constructor of the *integer* class gets called. Likewise, while creating the second nameless object the one-argument constructor gets called.

This facility of creating nameless objects is very useful while building an array of objects as shown below:

```
integer a [ 3 ] = {
                integer( ),
                integer-( 5 ),
                integer ( 10 )
        };
```

Had we not been permitted to create nameless objects we would have been required to create the array in the following manner:

```
integer i, j ( 5 ), k ( 10 ) ;
integer a[ ] = { i, j, k } ;
```

Of these the first method is better. This is because in the second method space would be consumed by the array as well as by the objects *i, j* and *k*.

As against this, when we create nameless objects they die as soon as assignment of the objects to the array is over. This is good since when the objects die the memory occupied by them is vacated.

5.1.5   Constraints on Constructors

Constructors suffer from two constraints. These are as under:

(a) A constructor cannot return a value. So, we cannot do error checking in constructor like this.

```
bool stack ( int i )
{
    if ( i > 10 )
        return false ;
    else
        return true ;
}
```

(b)ˆ We cannot invoke constructor for the same object twice. So, if we want to set up different values for an existing object we have to either call a member function using this object or create a new object with the new values and assign it to the existing object.

5.2 Types of Constructors

Various types of constructors are discussed here.

5.2.1   Default Constructors

We say that when an object is created, constructor gets called. But in the classes we saw in the previous chapter we had not defined constructor. Why didn't compiler report an error? This is because, if we don't define a constructor in a class, compiler provides one for us. This constructor is called *default constructor*. Default constructor is a zero-argument constructor. If we ourselves define a constructor (either zero-argument or parameterized constructor) this default constructor is not provided by the compiler.

5.2.2   Parameterized Constructors

Often we would require that data members of different objects should get initialised with different values. At such times, we can define parameterized constructors i.e. constructors that accept parameters. Let us take an example.

```
#include <iostream.h>
```

```cpp
class sample
{
    private :

        int i ;
        float f ;

    public :

        sample( )
        {
            i = 0 ;
            f = 0.0 ;
        }

        sample ( int ii, float ff )
        {
            i = ii ;
            f = ff ;
        }

        void print( )
        {
            cout << endl << i << endl << f ;
        }
} ;

void main( )
{
    sample s1 ;
    sample s2 ( 10, 16.78f ) ;

    s1.print( ) ;
    s2.print( ) ;
}
```

Look at the statement

sample s2 (10, 16.78f) ;

Here, the object *s2* would get created and the two-argument constructor would get called.

If you notice carefully, you would find that there are two constructors with the same name *sample( )*. Hence we call these constructors as *overloaded constructors*. Which of the two constructors gets called when an object is created depends on how many arguments are used in the definition of the object. This is shown below:

```
sample s1 ;  // calls zero-argument constructor
sample s2 ( 100, 34.78 ) ;  // calls two-argument constructor
```

The overloaded constructors are useful when we want some objects to be initialised during definition and some not to be initialised.

Remember that if we provide a parameterized constructor we won't be able to create an object by writing

sample s1 ;

unless we provide a zero-argument constructor too.

The statement

sample s (10) ;

is equivalent to

sample s = 10 ;

Both these statements would invoke one-argument constructor of class *sample*.

5.2.3 Copy Constructors

The C++ compiler is a fatherly old chap who doesn't nag you with small little details. It understands the pulls and pressures that the C++ programmer has to contend with and does things on your behalf. It carries out several small little tasks in its own way unless you order to do it some other way. An important example of this process is the *copy constructor*.

Consider the following statements:

```
circle c1 ;
circle c2 = c1 ;
```

Here *c1* and *c2* are objects of the type *circle*, which is a predefined class. The statement

In the statement

```
circle c2 = c1 ;
```

we have initialised one object with another object during declaration. The compiler creates a new object *c2* and copies the data from *c1* member-by-member, into *c2*. This is what the *copy constructor* does by default.

The compiler provides a copy constructor by default. However, should you want that the copy constructor should do something more complex, then you can always override these default actions. Before we see when it would be necessary to override this default actions let us first confirm through a program that it really takes place.

```
#include <iostream.h>
class circle
{
```

```
    private :

        int radius ;
        float x, y ;

    public :

        circle( )
        {
        }

        circle ( int rr, float xx, float yy )
        {
            radius = rr ;
            x = xx ;
            y = yy ;
        }

        circle ( circle& c )
        {
            cout << endl << "Copy constructor invoked" ;
            radius = c.radius ;
            x = c.x ;
            y = c.y ;
        }

        void showdata( )
        {
            cout << endl << endl << "Radius = " << radius ;
            cout << endl << "X-Coordinate = " << x ;
            cout << endl << "Y-Coordinate = " << y ;
        }
} ;

void main( )
{
    circle c1 ( 10, 2.5, 2.5 ) ;
    circle c2 = c1 ;
```

```
        c1.showdata( ) ;
        c2.showdata( ) ;
}
```

Most of the program is straightforward. What is important here is the statement *circle c3 = c1*. When this statement gets executed the overloaded copy constructor gets called.

Notice the definition of the copy constructor. The copy constructor takes one argument, an object of the type *circle*, passed by reference. Here's its prototype:

circle (circle &)

Is it necessary for us to use a reference in the argument to the copy constructor? Can we not pass a value instead? No. Because, if we pass the argument by value, its copy is constructed using the copy constructor. This means the copy constructor would call itself to make this copy. This process would go on and on until the compiler runs out of memory. Hence in the copy constructor the argument must always be passed by reference.

A copy constructor also gets invoked when objects are passed by value to functions and when objects are returned from functions. When an object is passed by value the copy that the function operates on is created using a copy constructor. If we pass the address or reference of the object the copy constructor would of course not be invoked, since in these cases the copies of the objects are not to be created.

When an object is returned from a function the copy constructor is invoked to create a copy of the value returned by the function.

5.2.4 Dynamic Constructors

If data members of a class include a pointer and is used in its member functions, then we must initialise it in the constructor instead of leaving this responsibility on member functions. Thus, memory is allocated for the data member of object at the time of its creation. This is known as dynamic creation of object. Following is an example of dynamic construction of object.

```cpp
#include <iostream.h>

class array
{
    private :

        int *a ;
        int dim, i ;

    public :

        array( )
        {
            a = new int [ 10 ] ;
            dim = 10 ;
            i = 0 ;
        }

        array ( int I )
        {
            a = new int [ I ] ;
            dim = I ;
            i = 0 ;
        }

        void add ( int d )
        {
            if ( i >= dim )
```

```
            {
                    cout << endl << "Array bounds exceed" ;
                    return ;
            }
            a [ i ] = d ;
            i++ ;
        }
};

void main( )
{
    array a1, a2 ( 5 ) ;

    a1.add ( 100 ) ;
    a1.add ( 200 ) ;

    a2.add ( 1 ) ;
    a2.add ( 2 ) ;
    a2.add ( 3 ) ;
    a2.add ( 4 ) ;
    a2.add ( 5 ) ;
}
```

Here, the size of array pointed to by data member *a* can be different for different objects of the class. To allocate memory dynamically we have used the *new* keyword. (Refer Chapter 8 for more information about *new*). The statement

```
a = new int [ 10 ] ;
```

allocates memory for ten integers and store pointer to the memory in *a*. If an object is created without passing an argument to it, array of ten integers get created. Otherwise, we can specify the size of the array by passing one argument to the constructor. The *add( )* member function adds an element to the array and reports an error if the number of elements exceed the dimension of the array.

5.3 Destructors

We've seen that a special member function—the constructor—is called automatically when an object is created. Similarly, when an object is destroyed a function called destructor automatically gets called. Let us see how destructor is declared and defined.

5.3.1 Declaring and Defining Destructors

A destructor has the same name as the constructor (which is same as the class name) but is preceded by a tilde (~) character. The following program shows how destructor is defined.

```
#include <iostream.h>
class example
{
    public:

        example( )  // contstuctor
        {
            cout << endl << "Inside the constructor" ;
        }

        ~example( )  // destructor
        {
            cout << endl << "Inside the destructor" ;
        }
};

void main( )
{
    example e ;
}
```

When the object *e* gets created the constructor gets called. When control goes outside *main( )* the object *e* gets destroyed. This invokes the destructor function. Like constructors, destructors do not have a return value. They also take no arguments (the assumption being that there's only one way to destroy an object).

The most common use of destructors is to deallocate memory that was allocated for the object by the constructor. We can define a destructor outside the class and define it inside the class as shown below:

```
class example
{
    public:

        ~example( ) ;
};
example::~example( ) ;
{
}
```

5.3.2   Characteristics of Destructors

The features of a destructor are listed below:

(a) The destructor gets called automatically when an object goes out of scope. If the object is a local object then it goes out of scope when the control returns from the function. If the object is a global object then it goes out of scope when execution of the program comes to an end.

(b) The destructor neither takes any arguments nor returns any value.

(c) Destructors cannot be overloaded.

(d) Destructors can be declared as *virtual*.

5.3.3   Constraints on Destructors

Since destructors can't return any value we cannot check for the successful execution of destructor. Secondly, we cannot invoke a destructor explicitly to destroy an object.

Exercises

[A] State True or False:

(a) Constructor and destructor are member functions of a class.

(b) It is necessary that a constructor in a class should always be *public*.

(c) If a class contains a 3-argument constructor then it is necessary to define explicitly a zero-argument, a 1-argument and a 2-argument constructor.

(d) Member functions of a class have to be called explicitly, whereas, the constructor gets called automatically.

(e) A constructor gets called whenever an object gets instantiated.

(f) Constructors can be overloaded.

(g) The return type of a constructor is always *void*.

(h) We can call destructor of a class explicitly.

(i) Compiler provides a default destructor if we don't write one in a class.

(j) Destructors can be overloaded.

[B] Answer the following:

(a) What is a constructor? When is it called?

(b) State the characteristics of constructor and destructor.

(c) What do you mean by dynamic construction of an object?

(d) When does the copy constructor get called?

(e) What is the difference between the following statements
```
circle s1 ( 10 ) ;
circle s2 = s1 ;
```

[C] What would be the output of the following programs:

(a)
```cpp
#include <iostream.h>
class user
{
    private :
        int i ;
        float f ;
        char c ;
    public :
        void displaydata( )
        {
            cout << endl << i << '\n' << f << "\n" << c ;
        }
};

void main( )
{
    cout << sizeof ( user ) ;
    user u1 ;
    cout << endl << sizeof ( u1 ) ;
    u1.displaydata( ) ;
}
```

(b)
```cpp
#include <iostream.h>
```

```
class date
{
    private :
        int dd, mm, yy ;
    public :
        date( )
        {
            cout << endl << "Reached here" ;
        }
} ;
void main( )
{
    date today ;
    date *p = &today ;
    cout << endl << p ;
}
```

(c)
```
#include <iostream.h>
class student_rec
{
    private :
        int m1, m2, m3 ;
        float percentage ;
    public :
        student_rec( )
        {
            m1 = m2 = m3 = 0 ;
            percentage = 0.0 ;
        }
        void calc_perc ( int x, int y , int z )
        {
            m1 = x ; m2 = y ; m3 = z ;
            percentage = ( m1 + m2 + m3 ) / 3.0 ;
            display_perc( ) ;
        }
        void display_perc( )
        {
            cout << endl << "Percentage = " << percentage << "%" ;
```

```
            }
        };

    void main( )
    {
        student_rec s1 ;
        s1.display_perc( ) ;
        s1.calc_perc( 35, 35, 35 ) ;
        s1.display_perc( ) ;
    }
```

(d)
```
    #include <iostream:h>
    class control
    {
        public :
            control( )
            {
                calculate( ) ;
                cout << endl << "Constructor" ;
            }
            void calculate( )
            {
                display( ) ;
                cout << endl << "Calculator" ;
            }
            void display( )
            {
                cout << endl << "displayed" ;
            }
    };

    void main( )
    {
        control c1 ;
    }
```

6

Operator Overloading

6.1 Operator Overloading

Operator overloading is one of the most fascinating features of C++. It can transform complex, obscure program listings into intuitively obvious ones. By overloading operators we can give additional meaning to operators like +, *, -, <=, >=, etc. which by default are supposed to work only on standard data types like *int*s, *float*s, etc. For example, if *str1* and *str2* are two character arrays holding strings "Bombay" and "Nagpur" in them then to store "BombayNagpur" in a third string *str3*, in C we need to perform the following operations:

```
char str1 [ 20 ] = "Nagpur" ;
char str2[ ] = "Bombay" ;
char str3 [ 20 ] ;
strcpy ( str3, str1 ) ;
strcat ( str3, str2 ) ;
```

No doubt this does the desired task but don't you think that the following form would have made more sense:

```
str3 = str1 + str2 ;
```

Such a form obviously would not work with C, since we are attempting to apply the + operator on non-standard data types (strings) for which addition operation is not defined. That's the place where C++ scores over C, because it permits the + operator to be overloaded such that it knows how to add two strings.

Operator overloading is one form of polymorphism, in the sense that we can overload an operator to perform a new job in addition to its predefined job.

6.1.1   Overloading Unary operators

As you know, a unary operator acts on only one operand. Examples of unary operators are the increment and decrement operators ++ and --, and the unary minus, as in -45. Let us now implement an overloaded unary operator for a class called *index*. Here is the program...

```
#include <iostream.h>

class index
{
    private :

        int count ;

    public :

        index( )
        {
            count = 0 ;
        }

        index ( int i )
        {
            count = i ;
        }

        void operator ++ ( )
        {
            ++count ;
        }

        void showdata( )
        {
            cout << count ;
        }
```

```
};

void main( )
{
    index c ;

    cout << endl << "c = " ;
    c.showdata( ) ;

    ++c ;
    cout << endl << "c = " ;
    c.showdata( ) ;

    ++c ;
    cout << endl << "c = " ;
    c.showdata( ) ;
}
```

Operator overloading really speaking teaches a normal C++ operator to act on a user-defined operand. In our case the operator ++ is taught to operate on a user-defined data type *index*. This is achieved by declaring a function using the keyword *operator* and the actual operator to be overloaded. For example, look at the following declaration,

```
void operator ++ ( )
```

Here, *operator* is a keyword, and is followed by the operator (++) which is to be overloaded.

In this program the *count* of object *c* is initially set to *0*. On encountering the expression ++*c* it is incremented by *1*. The program output looks like this:

```
c = 0
c = 1
c = 2
```

Internally, the expression ++c is treated as:

c.operator ++ ( ) ;

While calling this function no value is passed to it and no value is returned from it. The compiler can easily distinguish between the expression ++c and an expression, say ++j, where j might be an integer variable. It can make this distinction by looking at the data type of the operands. If the operand is a basic type like an *int*, as in ++j then the compiler will use its built-in routine to increment an *int*. But if the operand is an *index* variable, then the compiler will now use our *operator++( )* function instead.

Can you guess in which situation our *operator ++( )* function flop? Suppose we you use a statement like this in *main ( )*:

d = ++c ;

The compiler will complain. Why? Because we have defined the ++ operator to have a return type of *void* in the *operator ++( )* function, while in the assignment statement it is being asked to return a variable of type *index*. That is, the compiler is being asked to return whatever value c has after being operated on by the ++ operator, and assign this value to *d*. So, in its existing form we can't use ++ to increment *index* objects in assignments. Of course the normal ++ operator, applied to basic data types like *int*, would not have this problem.

To make it possible to use our *operator ++ ( )* in assignment expressions, we must provide a way for it to return a value. The next program shows how this can be achieved.

```
#include <iostream.h>
class index
{
    private :
```

```
            int count ;

        public :

            index( )
            {
                count = 0 ;
            }

            index operator ++ ( )
            {
                ++count ;
                index temp ;
                temp.count = count ;
                return temp ;
            }

            void showdata( )
            {
                cout << count ;
            }
} ;

void main( )
{
    index c, d ;

    cout << endl << "c = " ;
    c.showdata( ) ;

    ++c ;
    cout << endl << "c = " ;
    c.showdata( ) ;
    d = ++c ;
    cout << endl << "c = " ;
    c.showdata( ) ;
    cout << endl << "d = " ;
    d.showdata( ) ;
```

```
}
```

Here the *operator ++( )* function increments the *count* in its own object as before, then creates the new *temp* object and assigns *count* in the new object the same value as in its own object. Finally it returns the *temp* object. This has the desired effect. Expressions like *++c* now return a value, so they can be used in other expressions, such as

```
d = ++c ;
```

In this case the value returned from *++c* is assigned to *d*. Program's output would now look like this:

```
c = 0
c = 1
c = 2
d = 2
```

In our program we created a temporary object called *temp*. Its sole purpose was to provide a return value for the ++ operator. We could have achieved the same effect using the following the approach:

```
#include <iostream.h>

class index
{
    private :

            int count ;
    public :

            index( )
            {
                count = 0 ;
```

```
                }

                index ( int i )
                {
                    count = i ;
                }

                index operator ++ ( )
                {
                    ++count ;
                    return index ( count ) ;
                }

                void showdata( )
                {
                    cout << count ;
                }
        } ;

void main( )
{
        index c, d ;
        cout << endl << "c = " ;
        c.showdata( ) ;

        ++c ;
        cout << endl << "c = " ;
        c.showdata( ) ;

        d = ++c ;
        cout << endl << "c = " ;
        c.showdata( ) ;
        cout << endl << "d = " ;
        d.showdata( ) ;
}
```

Note that the *operator ++( )* function has changed now. In this function the statement,

```
return index ( count ) ;
```

creates an object of type *index*. This object has no name. It won't need one since it is anyway going to die soon. This unnamed object is initialised to the value provided by the argument *count*.

But to carry out this initialisation don't we need a one-argument constructor? We certainly do. And if you observe the program carefully you would notice that now we have provided one in our program.

Once the unnamed object is initialised to the value of *count*, it can then be returned. The output of this program would be same as that of the previous one.

Postfix Notation

So far we've used the overloaded increment operator in its prefix form:

```
++c ;
d = ++c ;
```

What about postfix, where the variable is incremented after its value is used in the expression, as in

```
c++ ;
d = c++ ;
```

To make both versions of the increment operator work, we must define two overloaded ++ operators, as shown in the following program:

```cpp
#include <iostream.h>

class index
{
    private :

        int count ;

    public :

        index( )
        {
            count = 0 ;
        }

        index ( int i )
        {
            count = i ;
        }

        index operator ++ ( )
        {
            return index ( ++count ) ;
        }

        index operator ++ ( int )
        {
            return index ( count++ ) ;
        }

        void showdata( )
        {
            cout << count ;
        }
} ;

void main( )
{
```

```
        index c, d, e, f ;
        e = ++c ;
        cout << endl << "c = " ;
        c.showdata( ) ;
        cout << endl << "e = " ;
        e.showdata( ) ;

        f = d++ ;
        cout << endl << "d = " ;
        d.showdata( ) ;
        cout << endl << "f = " ;
        f.showdata( ) ;
    }
```

Now there are two different functions for overloading the ++ operator. The one we've seen before, for prefix notation, is

```
index operator ++ ( )
{
    return index ( ++count ) ;
}
```

The new one, for postfix notations, is

```
index operator ++ ( int )
{
    return index ( ++count ) ;
}
```

The only difference is the *int* in the parentheses. This *int* isn't really an argument, and it doesn't mean integer. It's simply a signal to the compiler to create the postfix version of the operator. Here's the output from the program:

```
c = 1
e = 1
d = 1
f = 0
```

The last two lines of the output show the result of the statement

f = d++ ;

Here *d* is incremented to *1*, but *f* is assigned the value of *d* before it is incremented, so *f* contains the value *0*.

On similar lines we can implement the pre and post decrement operators as well.

6.1.2   Overloading Binary Operators

Let us now take an example where we would overload binary operators. Suppose we want to perform complex number arithmetic. A complex number consists of a real part and an imaginary part. Here is the program which implements complex number addition and multiplication using overloaded operators rather than through member functions like *add_complex( )* and *mul_complex( )*.

```
#include <iostream.h>
class complex
{
    private :

        float real, imag ;
    public :

        complex( )
        {
        }
```

```
complex ( float r, float i )
{
    real = r ;
    imag = i ;
}

void getdata( )
{
    float r, i ;
    cout << endl << "Enter real and imaginary part " ;
    cin >> r >> i ;
    real = r ;
    imag = i ;
}

void setdata ( float r, float i )
{
    real = r ;
    imag = i ;
}

void displaydata( )
{
    cout << endl << "real= " << real ;
    cout << endl << "imaginary= " << imag ;
}

complex operator + ( complex c )
{
    complex t ;
    t.real = real + c.real ;
    t.imag = imag + c.imag ;
    return t ;
}

complex operator * ( complex c )
{
```

```
            complex t ;

            t.real = real * c.real - imag * c.imag ;
            t.imag = real * c.imag + c.real * imag ;
            return t ;
        }
};

void main( )
{
    complex c1, c2 ( 1.5, -2.5 ), c3, c4 ;

    c1.setdata ( 2.0, 2.0 ) ;
    c3 = c1 + c2 ;
    c3.displaydata( ) ;

    c4.getdata( ) ;
    complex c5 ( 2.5, 3.0 ), c6 ;
    c6 = c4 * c5 ;

    c6.displaydata( ) ;

    complex c7 ;
    c7 = c1 + c2 * c3 ;
    c7.displaydata( ) ;
}
```

You would agree that the statement

c7 = c1 + c2 * c3 ;

is more intuitive than the statement

c7.add_complex (c1, c2.mul_complex (c3)) ;

In the statement $c7 = c1 + c2 * c3$ the multiplication operator function is called before the addition operator function. The hierarchy of operators remains same even when they are overloaded.

Let us examine the call and the definition of the overloaded '+' operator more closely.

```
// definition
complex operator + ( complex c )
{
    complex t ;
    t.real = real + c.real ;
    t.imag = imag + c.imag ;
    return t ;
}

// call
c3 = c1 + c2 ;
```

When the *operator +( )* function is called, the object *c2* is passed to it and is collected in the object *c*. As against this, the object *c1* gets passed to it automatically. This becomes possible because the statement *c3 = c1 + c2* is internally treated by the compiler as

```
c3 = c1.operator + ( c2 ) ;
```

That should give you an idea why the first operand in case of an overloaded binary operator function becomes available automatically, whereas, the second operand needs to be passed explicitly.

In the definition of the overloaded + operator function when we use the statement

```
t.real = real + c.real ;
```

real refers to the one that belongs to the object using which the operator function has been called. That is, if the function has been called through the statement

```
c3 = c1 + c2 ;
```

then *real* represents *c1*'s *real*, since the statement *c3* = *c1* + *c2* is internally treated as *c3* = *c1.operator* + *(c2)*. That should be an acceptable explanation for the time being. The real mechanism that makes this possible is a pointer called *this* pointer. It is time to understand the *this* pointer.

The *this* Pointer

The member functions of every object have access to a pointer named *this*, which points to the object itself. When we call a member function, it comes into existence with the value of *this* set to the address of the object using which it was called. The *this* pointer can be treated like any other pointer to an object.

Using a *this* pointer any member function can find out the address of the object using which it is called. It can also be used to access the data in the object it points to. The following program shows the working of the *this* pointer.

```
#include <iostream.h>

class example
{
    private :

        int i ;

    public :

        void setdata ( int ii )
        {
            i = ii ;  // one way to set data
            cout << endl << "my object's address is " << this ;
            this->i = ii ;  // another way to set data
        }
```

```
        void showdata( )
        {
                cout << i ;  // one way to display data
                cout << endl << "my object's address is " << this ;
                cout << this->i ;  // another way to display data

        }
} ;

void main( )
{
        example e1 ;
        e1.setdata ( 10 ) ;
        e1.showdata( );
}
```

Here is the output of the program...

```
my object's address is 0x8fabfff410
my object's address is 0x8fabfff410
10
```

From the output we can confirm that each time the address of the same object *e1* got printed. Since the *this* pointer contains the address of the object, using it we can reach the data member of the *example* class through statements like:

```
this -> i = ii ;  // another way to set data
cout << this -> i ;  // another way to display data
```

Let us now get back to our overloaded *operator +( )* function of the last section. In it we had a statement,

```
t.real = real + c.real ;
```

This statement internally is treated as:

t.real = this -> real + c.real ;

When the *operator +( )* function is called through the statement

c3 = c1.operator + (c2) ;

the *this* pointer would contain the *c1* object's address. As a result, *this -> real* would refer to *c1*'s *real*.

6.1.3   Overloading Comparison Operators

We would now enhance the *complex* class so that we can compare two objects of the *complex* class. Here is the overloaded < operator function.

```
int operator < ( complex c )
{
    if ( ( real < c.real ) && ( imag < c.imag ) )
        return 1 ;
    else
        return 0 ;
}
```

The *operator<( )* function would get invoked when the following condition would get executed.

```
if ( c1 < c3 )
    // do something
```

6.1.4   Overloading Arithmetic Assignment Operators

The compiler provides overloaded assignment operator function by default. This function does the copying of the member data from one object to another. Should we want to do something more complex then we can override this default function. Following definition shows the assignment operator function for the *complex* class.

```
complex operator = ( complex &c )
{
    cout << endl << "assignment operator reached" ;
    real = c.real ;
    imag = c.imag ;
    return *this ;
}
```

If you add this function to the *complex* class and run the program the message "assignment operator reached" would get printed thrice on the screen. This is because the following statements of the program would invoke the *overloaded =( )* function.

```
c3 = c1 + c2 ;
c6 = c4 * c5 ;
c7 = c1 + c2 * c3 ;
```

Note that we have passed the argument to overloaded operator function by reference. This is often desirable, though not absolutely necessary. Had the argument been passed by value it would have created another local object in the function. In our program it would not have mattered much, but in case of large objects this would lead to considerable wastage of memory.

The *operator = ( )* function in our program returns a value using the *this* operator. Returning a value makes it possible to chain = operators in *c4 = c2 = c1*.

Consider the statement,

```
c4 = c2 = c1 ;
```

As we know, during execution firstly *c2 = c1* will get executed. This internally becomes,

```
c2.operator = ( c1 ) ;
```

The argument *c1* passed to the assignment operator gets collected in the object *c*. Now data of *c* is copied into *c2's* data members. At this stage the *this* pointer contains *c2*'s address. Hence on returning **this* we are simply returning *c2*.

Before we close this section let me answer three most frequently asked questions about operator overloading.

(a) Which operators cannot be overloaded?

The operators that cannot be overloaded are *sizeof, ., .*, ::,* and *?:.*

If an operator has unary and binary forms (such as operators + or &), both can be overloaded.

(b) What is the precedence of operator functions?

The operator functions have the same precedence as the intrinsic operations that use the same operator. For example, the * operator always has a higher priority over the + operator. There is no way to change operator precedence and its associativity.

(c) Is it possible to redefine intrinsic operators?

What you are really asking is, is it possible to create your own operator for adding a pair of *ints*? The answer is no. Allowing you to change the behavior of intrinsic operations would make any program virtually unreadable.

6.2 Data and Type Conversions

We had an introduction to type conversion in Chapter 2. In this chapter we would see few complex issues related with type conversion. There are three types of conversion that we may wish to perform. These are:

−   Conversion between basic types
−   Conversion between objects and basic types

– Conversion between objects of different classes

Let us now discuss each one of these conversion types.

6.2.1 Conversion between Basic Types

We have already dealt with conversion between basic types in Chapter 2. So we would not discuss it here again.

6.2.2 Conversion between Objects and Basic Types

The following program shows how to convert between a basic type and a user-defined type and vice versa. In this program the user-defined type is a *string* class and the basic type is *int*. The program shows conversion from *string* to *int* and from *int* to *string*. Here's the program...

```
// conversions: string to int, int to string
#include <iostream.h>
#include <stdlib.h>
#include <string.h>

class string
{
    private :
        char str [ 20 ] ;

    public :

        string( )
        {
            str [ 0 ] = '\0' ;
        }

        string ( char *s )
        {
            strcpy ( str, s ) ;
```

```
            }
            string ( int a )
            {
                itoa ( a, str, 10 );
            }

            operator int( )
            {
                int i = 0, l, ss = 0, k = 1 ;

                l = strlen ( str ) - 1 ;
                while ( l >= 0 )
                {
                    ss = ss + ( str[l] - 48 ) * k ;
                    l-- ;
                    k *= 10 ;
                }
                return ( ss ) ;
            }

            void displaydata( )
            {
                cout << str ;
            }
    } ;
void main( )
{
        string s1 = 123 ;
        cout << endl << "s1 = " ;
        s1.displaydata( ) ;

        s1 = 150 ;
        cout << endl << "s1 = " ;

        s1.displaydata( ) ;

        string s2 ( "123" ) ;
        int i = int ( s2 ) ;
```

```
    cout << endl << "i = " << i ;

    string s3 ( "456" ) ;
    i = s3 ;
    cout << endl << "i = " << i ;
}
```

Here, to convert an *int* to a user-defined type *string* we have used a constructor with one argument. It is called when an object of type *string* is created with a single argument. The function assumes that this argument represents an *int* which it converts to a *string* and assigns it to *str* using the *itoa( )* function. Thus the conversion from *int* to *string* is carried out when we create an object in the statement

```
string s1 = 123 ;
```

A similar conversion is carried out when the statement

```
s1 = 150 ;
```

is executed. Here we are converting an *int* to a *string*, but we are not creating a new object. The one argument constructor is called even in this case. When the compiler comes across a statement that needs a conversion, it looks for any tool that can carry out this work for it. In our program it finds a constructor that converts an *int* to a *string*, so it uses it in the assignment statement by first creating an unnamed temporary object with it's *str* holding the value corresponding to the integer *150* and then assigns this object to *s1*. Thus if the compiler doesn't find an overloaded = operator it looks for a constructor to do the same job.

To convert a *string* to an *int* the overloaded cast operator is used. This is often called a conversion function. This operator takes the value of the *string* object of which it is a member, converts this value to an *int* value and then returns this *int* value. This operator gets called in two cases:

```
i = int ( s2 ) ;
```

and

i = s3 ;

In the second assignment the compiler first searches for an overloaded assignment operator. Since this search fails the compiler uses the conversion function to do the job of conversion.

6.2.3   Conversion between Objects of Different Classes

In the last section we saw how data conversion takes place from user-defined objects to intrinsic data types and vice versa. Let us now see how do we go about converting data between objects of different user-defined classes? The same two methods used for conversion between basic types and user-defined types apply to conversions between two user-defined types. That is, we can use a one-argument constructor, or we can use a conversion function. The choice depends on where we want to put the conversion routine: in the class declaration of the source object or of the destination object. We propose to examine both the cases here.

Conversion Routine in Source Object

When the conversion routine is in the source class, it is commonly implemented as a conversion function as shown in the following program. The two classes used in the program are *date* and *dmy*. Both classes are built to handle dates, the difference being the *date* class handles it as a string, whereas the *dmy* class handles it as three integers representing day, month and year. Here is the listing of the program...

```
#include <iostream.h>
#include <stdlib.h>
#include <string.h>
```

```
class date
{
    private :

        char dt [ 9 ] ;

    public :

        date( )
        {
            dt [ 0 ] = '\0' ;
        }

        date ( char *s )
        {
            strcpy ( dt, s ) ;
        }

        void displaydata( )
        {
            cout << dt ;
        }
} ;

class dmy
{
    private :

        int day, mth, yr ;

    public :

        dmy( )
        {
            day = mth = yr = 0 ;
        }

        dmy ( int d, int m, int y )
```

```
              {
                  day = d ;
                  mth = m ;
                  yr = y ;
              }

              operator date( )
              {
                  char temp [ 3 ], str [ 9 ] ;

                  itoa ( day, str, 10 ) ;
                  strcat ( str, "/" ) ;
                  itoa ( mth, temp, 10 ) ;
                  strcat ( str, temp ) ;
                  strcat ( str, "/" ) ;
                  itoa ( yr, temp, 10 ) ;
                  strcat ( str, temp ) ;

                  return ( date ( str ) ) ;
              }

              void displaydata( )
              {
                  cout << day << "\t" << mth << "\t" << yr ;
              }
} ;

void main( )
{
      date d1 ;
      dmy d2 ( 17, 11, 94 ) ;

      d1 = d2 ;

      cout << endl << "d1 = " ;
      d1.displaydata( ) ;
      cout << endl << "d2 = " ;
      d2.displaydata( ) ;
```

}

In *main( )* we have defined an object *d1* of the type *date*, which is not initialized. We have also defined an object *d2* of the type *dmy*, which has been initialised. Next an assignment is carried out through the statement *d1 = d2*.

Since *d1* and *d2* are objects of different classes, the assignment involves a conversion, and as we specified, in this program the conversion function *date( )* is a member of the *dmy* class. This function transforms the object of which it is a member to a *date* object, and returns this object, which *main( )* then assigns to *d1*.

Conversion Routine in Destination Object

Let's now see how the same conversion is carried out when the conversion routine is present in the destination class. In such cases usually a one-argument constructor is used. However, things are complicated by the fact that the constructor in the destination class must be able to access the data in the source class to perform the conversion. That is, since the data *day*, *mth* and *yr* in the *dmy* class is *private*. we must provide special functions like *getday( )*, *getmth( )* and *getyr( )* to allow direct access to it. Here's a program that implements this.

```
#include <iostream.h>
#include <stdlib.h>
#include <string.h>

class dmy
{
    private :

        int day, mth, yr ;

    public :
```

```
            dmy( )
            {
                day = mth = yr = 0 ;
            }

            dmy ( int d, int m, int y )
            {
                day = d ;
                mth = m ;
                yr = y ;
            }

            int getday( )
            {
                return ( day ) ;
            }
            int getmth( )
            {
                return ( mth ) ;
            }

            int getyr( )
            {
                return ( yr ) ;
            }

            void displaydata( )
            {
                cout << day << "\t" << mth << "\t" << yr ;
            }
};

class date
{
    private :

        char dt [ 9 ] ;
```

```
public :
    date( )
    {
        dt [ 0 ] = '\0' ;
    }

    date ( char *s )
    {
        strcpy ( dt, s ) ;
    }

    void displaydata( )
    {
        cout << dt ;
    }

    date ( dmy t )
    {
        int d = t.getday( ) ;
        int m = t.getmth( ) ;
        int y = t.getyr( ) ;
        char temp [ 3 ] ;
        itoa ( d, dt, 10 ) ;
        strcat ( dt, "/" ) ;
        itoa ( m, temp, 10 ) ;
        strcat ( dt, temp ) ;
        strcat ( dt, "/" ) ;
        itoa ( y, temp, 10 ) ;
        strcat ( dt, temp ) ;
    }
} ;

void main( )
{
    date d1 ;
    dmy d2 ( 17, 11, 94 ) ;

    d1 = d2 ;
```

```
cout << endl << "d1 = " ;
d1.displaydata( ) ;
cout << endl << "d2 = " ;
d2.displaydata( ) ;
}
```

When we execute the statement *d1 = d2* the one-argument constructor in the *date* class (whose argument is a *dmy* object) gets called. This constructor function gets the access to the data of *d2* by calling the *getday( ), getmth( )* and *getyr( )* functions. Finally it converts this data into a string. The output of this program is similar to the earlier one. The difference is behind the scenes. Here a constructor in the destination object, rather than a conversion function in the source object, handles the conversion.

That brings us to the important question: when should we use a one-argument constructor in the destination class, and when should we use a conversion function in the source class? Often this choice is simple. If you have a library of classes, you may not have access to its source code. If you use an object of such a class as the source in a conversion, then you'll have access only to the destination class, and you'll need to use a one-argument constructor. Or, if the library class object is the destination, then you must use a conversion function in the source. What if we use a conversion function as well as a one-argument constructor? The compiler would of course flash an error since this becomes an ambiguous situation.

6.2.4   Constraints on Type Conversion

The constraints on type conversion are as follows:

(a) Although type conversion provides flexibility, it may encourage making mistakes by allowing mixing of data types.

(b) If we use an object of a library class as the source, we can't write a conversion function in the library class as its source code may not be available.

(c) If the library class object is the destination, then it becomes compulsory to use a conversion function in the source class, as once again the source code of library class may not be available.

(d) Providing a conversion function as well as a one-argument constructor in a class results in the compile-time error.

Exercises

[A] State True or False:

(a) Operator overloading is one form of polymorphism.

(b) We can use the overloading feature to add the objects of two different user-defined types.

(c) If we don't provide an assignment operator in a class declaration then the compiler automatically adds one to our class.

(d) To carry out conversion from an object to a basic type or vice versa it is necessary to provide the conversion functions.

(e) To carry out conversion from object of one type to another it is necessary to provide the conversion functions.

(f) If the ++ operator has been overloaded then the expressions *j*++ and ++*j* would call the same overloaded function.

(g) If the binary + operator is overloaded inside a class then while calling it only one argument needs to be passed.

(h) The *this* pointer always contains the address of the object using which the member function/data is being accessed.

(i) The *this* pointer can be used even outside the class.

[B] Answer the following:

(a) If we wish to provide an assignment operator function within a class called *rectangle* what would be its prototypes?

(b) How many arguments are required to define an overloaded unary operator function and overloaded binary operator function?

[C] Attempt the following:

(a) Write a program that consists of two classes *time12* and *time24*. The first one maintains time on a 12-hour basis, whereas the other one maintains it on a 24-hour basis. Provide conversion functions to carry out the conversion from object of one type to another.

(b) Write a program that implements a *date* class containing data members *day*, *month* and *year*. Implement assignment operator and copy constructor in this class.

7

Derived Classes & Inheritance

7.1 Derived Classes and Base Classes

Now that we have familiarized ourselves with classes—the building blocks of object oriented programming—let us now deal with another important C++ concept called *inheritance*. Inheritance is probably the most powerful feature of object-oriented programming after classes themselves. Inheritance is the process of creating new classes, called *derived classes*, from existing classes. These existing classes are often called *base classes*. The derived class inherits all the capabilities of the base class but can add new features and refinements of its own. By adding these refinements the base class remains unchanged.

Inheritance is one of the corner stones of object-oriented programming. It has several advantages to offer. Most important amongst these is that it permits code reusability. Once a base class is written and debugged, it need not be touched again but at the same time it can be adapted to work in different situations. Reusing existing code saves time and money and increases a program's reliability. Inheritance can also help in the original conceptualization of a programming problem, and in the overall design of the program.

The code reusability is of great help in the case of distributing class libraries. A programmer can use a class created by another person or company, and, without modifying it, derive other classes from it that are suited to particular programming situations.

Suppose that we have designed a class called *index* that serves as a general-purpose index (counter). Assume that we have worked long and hard to make the *index* class operate just the way we want, and we're pleased with the results, except for one thing. The *index* class can only increment the counter and not decrement it. To achieve this we can insert a decrement routine directly into the source code of the *index* class. However, there are several reasons why we might not want to do this. Firstly, the *index* class works well and has been thoroughly tested and debugged. This is an exaggeration in this case, but it would be true in a larger and more complex class. Now if we start modifying the source code of the *index* class, the testing process will need to be carried out again. And then there always exists a possibility that at the end of the entire process the original class itself may not work satisfactorily.

Sometimes there might be another reason for not modifying the *index* class: We might not have access to its source code, especially if it had been distributed as part of a class library.

To avoid these problems we can use inheritance to create a new class based on *index*, without modifying *index* itself. Let us now understand the concept of inheritance using a program.

7.1.1   Defining a Derived Class

The derived class is declared by specifying the base class along with the new members that the derived class requires for implementation. The syntax for declaring a derived class is:

```
class derived_class : visibility-mode base_class
{
     // Derived class member functions and data
};
```

The colon in the first line of the above code shows that the class, *derived_class* is derived from the *base_class*. The visibility mode is an optional access specifier that specifies whether the features are inherited in *public* mode, *protected* mode or *private* mode. We would learn more about these modes later in the chapter.

Let us now implement the *index* class.

```
#include <iostream.h>
```

```cpp
class index  // base class
{
    protected :

        int count ;

    public :

        index( )  // zero argument constructor
        {
            count = 0 ;
        }

        index ( int c )  // one argument constructor
        {
            count = c ;
        }

        void display( )
        {
            cout << endl << "count = " << count ;
        }

        void operator ++ ( )
        {
            count++ ;
        }
} ;

class index1 : public index  // derived class
{
    public :

        void operator -- ( )
        {
            count-- ;
        }
} ;
```

```
void main( )
{
    index1 i ;
    i++ ;
    i++ ;
    i.display( ) ;
    i-- ;
    i.display( ) ;
}
```

Here we have first declared a base class called *index* and then derived a class called *index1* from it. *index1* inherits all the features of the base class *index*. *index1* doesn't need a constructor or the *operator ++( )* functions, since they are already present in the base class.

The first line of the *index1* class,

```
class index1 : public index
```

specifies that the class *index1* has been derived from the base class *index*. Instead of the *base - derived* terminology some authors tend to use the *parent - child* terminology. Figure 7.1 shows the relationship between the base class and the derived class. Note that the arrow in the figure means *derived from*. The direction of the arrow says that the derived class refers to the functions and data in the base class, while the base class has no access to the derived class data or functions.

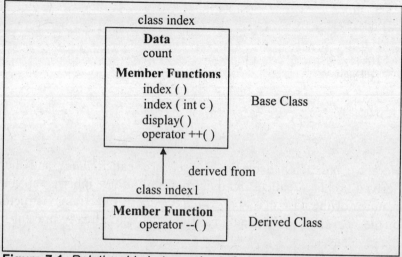

Figure 7.1. *Relationship between base & derived classes.*

A program can declare objects of both the base and derived classes. The two objects are independent of one another.

The data members in the classes that we've created so far used the *private* access specifier. As against this, in the above program the data has been given a new specifier—*protected*. Had we used *private* specifier for *count* it would not have been accessible in *index1*. We don't want to make *count public*, since that would allow it to be accessed through any function anywhere in the program, and thereby eliminate the advantages of data hiding. A *protected* member, on the other hand, can be accessed by member functions in its own class or in any class derived from its own class. It can't be accessed from functions outside these classes, such as *main( )*. This is just what we want. Hence the *protected* access specifier.

7.1.2　Accessing the Base Class Members

In the above program the object *i* uses the function *operator ++( )* from the base class to increment *count*. It also uses the *display( )* function to print the value of *i*. It means that using an object of the derived class we can call member functions of the base class.

Can member functions of the derived class access members of the base class? In other words, can *operator --( )* in *index1* access *count* in *index*? The answer is that members of a derived class can access members of the base class if the base class members are *public* or *protected*. They can't access *private* members. This rule holds good for data members as well as member functions.

Figure 7.2 clearly indicates who can access what in a base class–derived class relationship.

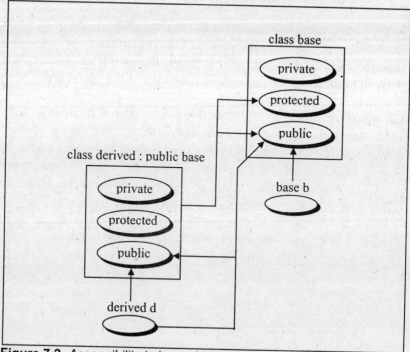

Figure 7.2. *Accessibility in base-derived classes.*

Table 7.1 shows the accessibility of the base class members.

Visibility Mode	Access from the derived class	Access from the outside functions and classes
private	No	No
protected	Yes	No
public	Yes	Yes

Table 7.1. *Accessibility of base class members.*

One last thing. When a base class and a derived class have *public* member functions with the same name and parameter list types, the function in the derived class gets a priority when the function is called as a member of the derived class object.

7.1.3 Accessing Protected Members

As we saw in section 7.1.1 the *protected* members of the base class are accessible to the member functions of the derived class. However, the *protected* members are not available outside the class. Suppose from the derived class if we derive one more class the protected members of the base class would also be available to the member functions of this new class. Thus, once a member is declared *protected* it is available to all the classes inherited from it.

7.1.4 Derived Class Constructors

When we define an object of a derived class, the compiler executes the constructor function of the base class followed by the constructor function of the derived class. Following program will prove this.

```cpp
#include <iostream.h>
class base
{
    public :

        base( )
        {
            cout << "\nzero-argument base constructor" ;
        }

        base ( int i )
        {
            cout << "\none-argument base constructor" ;
        }
};

class der : public base
{
    public :
```

```
            der( )
            {
                cout << "\nzero-argument derived constructor" ;
            }

            der ( int i )
            {
                cout << "\none-argument derived constructor" ;
            }
    } ;

void main( )
{
    cout << "\nCreating zero-argument object" ;
    der d ;

    cout << "\nCreating one-argument object" ;
    der d1 ( 0 ) ;
}
```

The output of the program would be as follows:

```
Creating zero-argument object
zero-argument base constructor
zero-argument derived constructor
Creating one-argument object
zero-argument base constructor
one-argument derived constructor
```

From the above output we can draw a conclusion that whenever an object of derived class is created, zero-argument constructor of the base class is called first and then appropriate constructor of the derived class gets called.

Suppose we created a derived class object by passing one argument to its constructor and we want that the one-argument constructor, not the zero-argument constructor of base class should get called. In such a case we need to call the one-argument constructor of base class explicitly using the following syntax.

```
der ( int i ) : base ( i )
{
    cout << "\none-argument derived constructor" ;
}
```

Functions That Are Not Inherited

All functions do not get inherited. For example, the constructor and the destructor functions never get inherited. This would make sense if we look at a small example.

```
class base
{
    private :

        int i ;

    public :

        base( )
        {
            i = 10 ;
        }
};

class derived : public base
{
    // ...
};
```

Since *i* has been defined as *private* in the *base* class it is not available to the *derived* class. Had the constructor been inherited then in the *derived* class the initialisation of *i* would not have been possible. For the same reason the destructors are also not inherited.

In general, constructors and destructors deal with creation and destruction of an object, and they know what to do with the aspects of the object only at their particular level in the class hierarchy. Hence they are not inherited. Another function that is not inherited is the *operator = ( )* function as it performs a constructor-like activity.

If we have a zero-argument constructor, a destructor, an assignment operator function and a copy constructor in the base class, they do not get inherited in the derived class. However, if we do not provide their definitions in the derived class the compiler adds them automatically.

7.2 Inheritance

We have already seen the inheritance mechanism once. In this section we would see advanced issues of inheritance.

7.2.1   Types of Inheritance

There are five types of inheritance. They are as follows:

–   Single Inheritance: When a class is derived from a single class, it is called 'Single Inheritance'.

–   Multiple Inheritance: A class can be derived from more than one class. Such a derivation is called 'Multiple Inheritance'. For example,

```
class A : public B, public C
{
};
```

- Multilevel Inheritance: When a class is derived from base class, which in turn is derived from another class, then the inheritance is called 'Multilevel Inheritance'. For example

```
class A {    } ; ;
class B : public A {    } ;
class C : public B {    } ;
```

- Hybrid Inheritance: When a base class is derived from two or more classes, which in turn are derived from the same base class is called 'Hybrid Inheritance'. For example

```
class A {    } ; ;
class B : public A {    } ;
class C : public A {    } ;
class D : public B, public C {    } ;
```

- Hierarchical Inheritance: A class may be inherited by several other classes. This is called 'Hierarchical Inheritance'. For example

```
class A {    } ; ;
class B {    } ;
class C {    } ;
class D : public A, public B, public C {    } ;
```

The essence of these different types of inheritance has been captured in Figure 7.3.

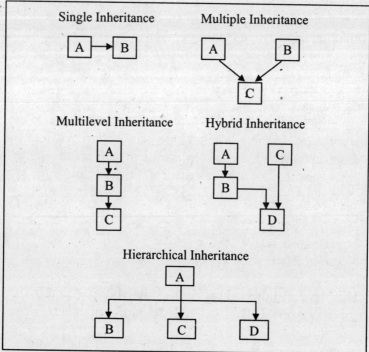

Figure 7.3. *Types of Inheritance.*

7.2.2   Access Control in Protected Derived Class

So far we have used *public* inheritance. We are also allowed to use *protected* inheritance. It's something that you don't use often, but it's there in the language for the sake of completeness.

If a class *derived1* is derived *public*ly from a class called *base* then the *protected* and *public* members of *base* remain *protected* and *public* members for *derived1*.

Similarly, if a class *derived1* is derived *protected*ly from a class called *base* then the *protected* and *public* members of base become *protected* members for *derived1*.

The following program shows *protected* inheritance at work.

```
class base
{
    protected :

        int i ;

    public :

        int j ;
};

class derived1 : protected base
{
    protected :

        int ii ;

    public :

        int jj ;
};

class derived2 : public derived1
{
    public :

        f( )
        {
            i = 10 ;  // works
            j = 10 ;  // works
            ii = 10 ;  // works
            jj = 10 ;  // works
        }
};
void main( )
```

```
{
    derived2 d1 ;

    d1.i = 10 ;  // error
    d1.j = 10 ;  // error
    d1.ii = 10 ;  // error
    d1.jj = 10 ;  // works
}
```

Here we have derived the class *derived2* *public*ly from *derived1*. The *derived1* class in turn has been derived from the class *base* using the *protected* specifier. As a result, now *i* and *j* have become *protected* members of the class *derived1*. Since *derived2* has been *public*ly derived from *derived1* *i* and *j* remain as *protected* members of *derived2*. Hence *i* and *j* can be accessed in the function *f( )*. However, they cannot be accessed from *main( )*.

7.2.3   Access Control in Private Derived Class

When we inherit *private*ly we create a new class that has all the data and the functionality of the base class, but that functionality is hidden; i.e. the members of the base class (*private, protected* or *public*) can be accessed in the derived class but not outside it.

If a class *derived1* is derived *private*ly from a class called *base* then the *protected* and *public* members of *base* become *private* members for *derived1*.

You may wonder what purpose such an inheritance may serve. There may occasionally be situations where you want to hide part of the functionality of the base class. By default, when we inherit privately all *public* members of the base class become *private* for the derived class. If you want only some of them to remain *private* and the rest to be accessible from outside the class it can be done as shown in the following program.

```
#include <iostream.h>

class base
{
    public :

        void display( )
        {
            cout << endl << "in display" ;
        }

        void show( )
        {
            cout << "in show" ;
        }
} ;

class derived : private base
{
    public :

        base :: display ;
} ;

void main( )
{
    derived d ;
    d.display( ) ;  // works
    d.show( ) ;    // error
}
```

Here we wanted *base::display( )* to be accessible in spite of *private* inheritance. We achieved this just by mentioning the name (no arguments or return values) in the *public* section of the *derived* class. As a result, *display( )* is accessible from *main( )*, whereas *show( )* is not. In other words we have been able to hide part of the functionality of the base class.

Figure 7.4 depicts the accesses if a class is derived *privately* or *protected*ly from a base class.

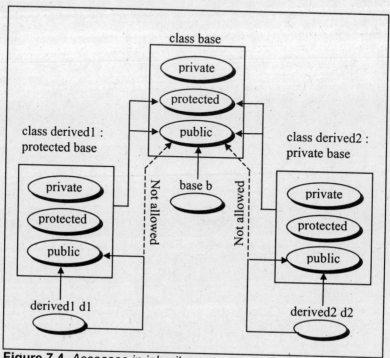

Figure 7.4. *Accesses in inheritance.*

7.3 Multiple Inheritances

In the last section we saw how to derive a class from a base class which itself has been derived from another base class. We called this as multiple levels of inheritance. Let us now see another aspect of inheritance, where a class can be derived from more than one base class. This is called *Multiple Inheritance*. The syntax for multiple inheritance is similar to that for single inheritance.

Let us understand multiple inheritance, with a simple example. Imagine a company that markets both hardware and software.

Suppose we create a base class *item* that stores the title of the item (a string) and its price (a *float*). Suppose we have another base class called *sales* that holds an array of three *floats* so that it can record the sale in rupees of a particular item for the last three months. Now we derive two classes *hwitem* (hardware item) and *switem* (software item) from both *item* and *sales*. The *hwitem* class holds category of the item and its original equipment manufacturer, whereas the *switem* class holds the type of the software item and the OS under which it works. Each class has its own *getdata( )* and *displaydata( )* functions to input and output data respectively. The program, which implements these classes, is given below.

```cpp
#include <iostream.h>

class item
{
    private :

        char title [ 20 ] ;
        float price ;

    public :

        void getdata( )
        {
            cout << endl << "Enter title and price " ;
            cin >> title >> price ;
        }

        void displaydata( )
        {
            cout << endl << "Title and price " ;
            cout << title << "\t" << price ;
        }
} ;
```

```
class sales
{
    private :

        float salesfig [ 3 ] ;

    public :

        void getdata( )
        {
            cout << endl << "Enter sales figures for 3 months " ;
            for ( int i = 0 ; i < 3 ; i++ )
                cin >> salesfig [ i ] ;
        }

        void displaydata( )
        {
            cout << endl << "sales figures for 3 months " ;
            for ( int i = 0 ; i < 3 ; i++ )
                cout << salesfig [ i ] << "\t" ;
        }
} ;

class hwitem : private item, private sales
{
    private :

        char category [ 10 ] ;
        char oem [ 10 ] ;

    public :

        void getdata( )
        {
            item :: getdata( ) ;
            cout << endl << "Enter category and oem " ;
            cin >> category >> oem ;
            sales :: getdata( ) ;
```

```
        }

        void displaydata( )
        {
            item :: displaydata( ) ;
            cout << endl << "category and oem " ;
            cout << category << "\t" << oem ;
            sales :: displaydata( ) ;
        }
} ;

class switem : private item, private sales
{
    private :

        char category [ 10 ] ;
        char os [ 10 ] ;

    public :

        void getdata( )
        {
            item :: getdata( ) ;
            cout << endl << "Enter category and os " ;
            cin >> category >> os ;
            sales :: getdata( ) ;
        }

        void displaydata( )
        {
            item :: displaydata( ) ;
            cout << endl << "category and os " ;
            cout << category << "\t" << os ;
            sales :: displaydata( ) ;
        }
} ;
```

```
void main( )
{
    hwitem h1, h2 ;

    h1.getdata( ) ;
    h1.displaydata( ) ;
    h2.getdata( ) ;
    h2.displaydata( ) ;

    switem s1, s2 ;

    s1.getdata( ) ;
    s1.displaydata( ) ;
    s2.getdata( ) ;
    s2.displaydata( ) ;
}
```

Figure 7.5 shows the hierarchy of classes used in the program.

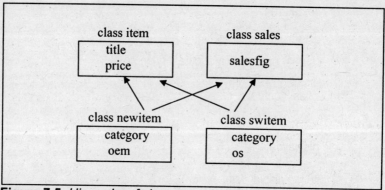

Figure 7.5. *Hierarchy of classes.*

7.3.1 Member Functions in Multiple Inheritance

In multiple inheritance the derived class can access all the *public* and *protected* members of the base classes. If the base classes are designed by different programmers, it may happen that name of a member function of these classes coincide. Now, if the function is called using derived object, an ambiguous situation would arise. We would see how to deal with this situation in section 7.3.3.

7.3.2 Constructors in Multiple Inheritance

Let us now go one step further. Let us see how constructors are handled in multiple inheritance. For the sake of convenience we would use the same classes (except for the *switem* class) developed in the last section. The only addition that we would make is the definition of constructors in each class. The program, which implements these classes, is given below.

```
#include <iostream.h>
#include <string.h>

class item
{
    private :

        char title [ 20 ] ;
        float price ;

    public :

        item( )
        {
            strnset ( title, 0, 20 ) ;
            price = 0 ;
        }

        item ( char *t, float p )
```

```
        {
            strcpy ( title, t ) ;
            price = p ;
        }

        void getdata( )
        {
            cout << "\nEnter title and price " ;
            cin >> title >> price ;
        }

        void displaydata( )
        {
            cout << endl << "Title and price " ;
            cout << title << "\t" << price ;
        }
} ;
class sales
{
    private :

        float salesfig [ 3 ] ;

    public :

        sales( )
        {
            for ( int i = 0 ; i < 3 ; i++ )
                salesfig [ i ] = 0 ;
        }

        sales ( float a, float b, float c )
        {
            salesfig [ 0 ] = a ;
            salesfig [ 1 ] = b ;
            salesfig [ 2 ] = c ;
        }
```

```
        void getdata( )
        {
            cout << "\nEnter sales figures for 3 months " ;
            for ( int i = 0 ; i < 3 ; i++ )
                cin >> salesfig [ i ] ;
        }

        void displaydata( )
        {
            cout << endl << "sales figures for 3 months " ;
            for ( int i = 0 ; i < 3 ; i++ )
                cout << salesfig [ i ] << "\t" ;
        }
} ;

class hwitem : private item, private sales
{
    private :

        char category [ 10 ] ;
        char oem [ 10 ] ;

    public :

        hwitem( ) : item( ), sales( )
        {
            strnset ( category, 0, 10 ) ;
            strnset ( oem, 0, 10 ) ;
        }

        hwitem ( float a, float b, float c, char *t, float p,
                char *cat, char *o ) : item ( t, p ), sales ( a, b, c )
        {
            strcpy ( category, cat ) ;
            strcpy ( oem, o ) ;
        }

        void getdata( )
```

```
        {
            item :: getdata( ) ;
            cout << endl << "Enter category and oem " ;
            cin >> category >> oem ;
            sales :: getdata( ) ;
        }

        void displaydata( )
        {
            item :: displaydata( ) ;
            cout << endl << "category and oem " ;
            cout << category << "\t" << oem ;
            sales :: displaydata( ) ;
        }
};

void main( )
{
    hwitem h1 ;
    hwitem h2 ( 50000.00, 125000.00, 170000.00, "IBM PC/AT", 25000,
                "FG", "IBM" ) ;
    h1.displaydata( ) ;
    h2.displaydata( ) ;
}
```

The new feature in this program is the use of constructors in the derived class *hwitem*. These constructors call the appropriate constructors in base classes *item* and *sales*.

The zero-argument constructor of the *item* class looks like this:

```
item( )
{
    strnset ( title, 0, 20 ) ;
    price = 0 ;
}
```

This constructor fills 0s for the *title*, so the user will be made aware if an attempt is made to display data for an uninitialised *item* object. You're already familiar with the zero-argument constructor in the *sales* class. The zero-argument constructor in *hwitem* calls both these constructors through the statement:

hwitem( ) : item( ), sales( )

The names of the base-class constructors follow the colon (and not *::*) and are separated by commas. These base class constructors will be called in order when the *hwitem( )* constructor is invoked.

The situation in multi-argument constructors is more complex. The constructor for *hwitem* calls the multiple argument constructors of *sales* and *item*, so it must supply values for their arguments. In addition it has two arguments of its own: the category of item and the oem manufacturer. So this constructor has seven arguments. It calls the constructors of its base classes. Here's how it looks like:

```
hwitem ( float a,float b,float c,char *t, float p,
         char *cat, char *o )  : item ( t, p ), sales ( a, b, c )
{
    strcpy ( category, cat ) ;
    strcpy ( oem, o ) ;
}
```

As before, a colon signals the start of the list of constructors to be called, with the members of the list being separated by commas. Of the first five arguments passed to *hwitem( )*, two are passed on to *item( )* and three to *sales( )*. The last two arguments are used to initialise the *category* and *oem* manufacturer of the hardware item, within the body of the constructor function.

Another small issue. If we change the order of the constructors in the list following the colon would the calling sequence also change? No. In fact the order in the list has no bearing on the order of calling. Then how is the order decided? It is decided from the order used in the declaration of the class. In our program the class declaration looked like this:

```
class hwitem : private item, private sales
{
    // code
};
```

Hence, even if the constructor definition is as follows

```
hwitem( ) : sales( ), item( )
{
}
```

the constructors would still get called in the order *item( )* followed by *sales( )*.

Note that the destructors in case of multiple inheritance are called in exactly the reverse order of the constructors. Why is the order of calling constructors governed by the order in the class declaration? This is because if you change the order of constructor calls while defining the constructor, you may have two different call sequences in two different constructors, but the poor destructor wouldn't know how to properly reverse the order of calls for destruction.

7.3.3   Ambiguity in Multiple Inheritance

In the above program both the classes *sales* and *item* contain a member function *displaydata( )* having same name and prototype. When we call the *displaydata( )* function from the *displaydata( )* functions of the *hwitem* (derived class), the compiler would not know the *displaydata( )* function of which base class (*sales* or *item*) should be called. This ambiguity is easily eliminated by preceding the *displaydata( )* function with the class name and the scope resolution operator as shown below:

```
item :: displaydata( ) ;
sales :: displaydata( ) ;
```

A Word of Caution

Imagine a situation where a class has been derived from two base classes. The two base classes have functions with the same name, say *f( )*, while the derived class has no function with this name. Now what would happen if the derived class object tries to call the base class function *f( )*? An error would occur since the compiler can't figure out *f( )* of which base class you wish to call. This problem can be resolved using the scope resolution operator to specify the function from which base class you wish to call. This is shown below:

```
// base1 and base2 are base classes
// Both base classes contain the function f( )
// The class derived has been derived from base1 and base2
derived d ;
d.f( ) ;  // Error
d.base1::f( ) ;
d.base2::f( ) ;
```

Exercises

[A] State True or False:

(a) We can derive a class from a base class even if the base class's source code is not available.

(b) Multiple inheritance is different from multiple levels of inheritance.

(c) The way a derived class member function can access base class *protected* and *public* members, the base class member functions can access *protected* and public *member* functions of derived class.

(d) It is possible to derive a derived class through *public* derivation, *private* derivation or *protected* derivation.

(e) A derived class member function has an access to *protected* and *public* members of base class, irrespective of whether the derived class has been derived *public*ly or *private*ly.

(f) If the derived class has been derived *public*ly then a derived class object, can access *public* members of base class.

(g) An object of a derived class (however derived) cannot access *private* or *protected* members of base class.

(h) *private* members of base class cannot be accessed by derived class member functions or objects of derived class.

(i) In *public* inheritance the *protected* members of the base class become *public* for the functions outside the derived class.

(j) There is no difference between *private* and *protected* inheritance.

(k) In *private* inheritance part of the base class interface can be made available to the functions outside the derived class.

(l) The size of a derived class object is equal to the sum of sizes of data members in base class and the derived class.

(m) Creating a derived class from a base class requires fundamental changes to the base class.

(n) If a base class contains a member function *func( )*, and a derived class does not contain a function with this name, an object of the derived class cannot access *func( )*

(o) If no constructors are specified for a derived class, objects of the derived class will use the constructors in the base class.

(p) If a base class and a derived class each include a member function with the same name, the member function of the derived class will be called by an object of the derived class

(q) A class D can be derived from a class C, which is derived from a class B, which is derived from a class A.

(r) It is illegal to make objects of one class, members of another class.

[B] What would be the output of the following programs:

(a)
```cpp
#include <iostream.h>
class base
{
    private :
        int i ;
} ;

class derived : public base
{
    private :
        int j ;
} ;

void main( )
{
    cout << endl << sizeof ( derived ) << endl << sizeof ( base ) ;
    derived o1 ;
    base o2 ;
    cout << endl << sizeof ( o1 ) << endl << sizeof ( o2 ) ;
}
```

(b)
```cpp
#include <iostream.h>

class base1
{
    private :
        int b1 ;
```

```cpp
};
class base2
{
    private :
        int b2 ;
};

class derived : public base1, public base2
{
    private :
        int d1 ;
};

void main( )
{
    cout << endl << sizeof ( base1 ) << endl << sizeof ( base2 )
        << endl << sizeof ( derived ) ;
}
```

(c)   ```cpp
       #include <iostream.h>

       class base
       {
           protected :
               int i ;

           public :
               base( )
               {
                   cout << endl << &i ;
               }
       };

       class derived: public base
       {
           public :
               derived( ) : base( )
       ```
       ```

```
                 {
                      cout << endl << &i ;
                 }
        } ;

        void main( )
        {
             derived d1 ;
             base b1 ;
        }
```

(d)   #include <iostream.h>

```
        class base
        {
             protected :
                  int i ;

             public :
                  void funct( )
                  {
                       cout << endl << &i ;
                  }
        } ;

        class derived : public base
        {
             private :
                  ini i ;

             public :
                  derived( )
                  {
                       cout << endl << &i ;
                       funct( ) ;
                  }
        } ;
```

```
    void main( )
    {
        derived d1 ;
    }
```

(e)   #include <iostream.h>

```
    int top = 3 ;

    class base
    {
        protected :
            int top ;

        public :
            base( )
            {
                top = 2 ;
                cout << endl << top ;
            }
    } ;

    class derived : public base
    {
        private :
            int top ;
        public :
            derived( ) : base( )
            {
                top = 1 ;
                cout << endl << top ;
                cout << endl << base::top ;
                cout << endl << ::top ;
            }
    } ;

    void main( )
    {
```

```
        derived d1 ;
    }

(f)  #include <iostream.h>

    class index
    {
        protected :
            int count ;

        public :
            index( )
            {
                count = 0 ;
            }

            void operator ++( )
            {
                count++ ;
            }

            void display( )
            {
                cout << endl << count ;
            }
    } ;

    void main( )
    {
        index c ;
        c++ ;
        c.display( ) ;
        ++c ;
        c.display( ) ;
    }

(g)  #include <iostream.h>
```

```
class base
{
    public :
        base( )
        {
            cout << endl << "third" ;
        }
} ;

class derived1 : public base
{
    public :
        derived1( ) : base( )
        {
            cout << endl << "second" ;
        }
} ;

class derived2 : public derived1
{
    public :
        derived2( ) : derived1( )
        {
            cout << endl << "first ;
        }
} ;

void main( )
{
    derived2 object ;
}
```

[C] Answer the following:

(a)   What does inheritance mean? What are its advantages.

(b)   What are the different types of inheritance?

(c) How does *protected* specifier is different than *private* specifier?

(d) Suppose there is a base class *B* and a derived class *D* derived from *B*. *B* has two *public* member functions *b1( )* and *b2( )*, whereas *D* has two member functions *d1( )* and *d2( )*. Write these classes for the following different situations:

  – *b1( )* should be accessible in *main( )*, *b2( )* should not be.

  – Neither *b1( )*, nor *b2( )* should be accessible in *main( )*.

  – Both *b1( )* and *b2( )* should be accessible in *main( )*.

(e) If a class *D* is derived from two base classes *B1* and *B2*, then write these classes each containing a zero-argument constructor. Ensure that while build an object of type *D* firstly the constructor of *B2* should get called followed by that of *B1*. Also provide a destructor in each class. In what order would these destructors get called?

(f) Assume a class *D* that is *privately* derived from class *B*. Which of the following can an object of class *D* located in *main( )* access?

  - *public* members of *D*
  - *protected* members of *D*
  - *private* members of *D*
  - *public* members of *B*
  - *protected* members of *B*
  - *private* members of *B*

8
Pointers

8.1 Addresses and Pointers

Consider the declaration,

int i = 3 ;

This declaration tells the C compiler to:

(a) Reserve space in memory to hold the integer value.

(b) Associate the name **i** with this memory location.

(c) Store the value 3 at this location.

We may represent i's location in the memory by the following memory map:

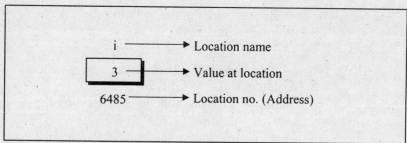

Figure 8.1. *In memory view of variables.*

We see that the computer has selected memory location 6485 as the place to store the value 3. This location number 6485 is not a number to be relied upon, because some other time the computer may choose a different location for storing the value 3. The important point is, i's address in memory is a number.

We can print this address through the following program:

```
#include <iostream.h>
void main( )
{
```

```
    int i = 3 ;

    cout << "\nAddress of i = " << &i ;
    cout << "\nValue of i = " << i ;
}
```

The output of the above program would be:

```
Address of i = 0x8fc4fff4
Value of i = 3
```

The address is displayed in hex because by default *cout* prints addresses in hex. Look at the first *cout* statement carefully. The '&' operator used in this statement is the. The expression *&i* returns the address of the variable *i*, which in this case happens to be 0x8fc4fff4.

The other pointer operator available is '*', called 'value at address' operator. It returns the value stored at a particular address. The 'value at address' operator is also called an 'indirection' operator.

8.1.1 · Static and Dynamic Memory Allocation

Memory can be allocated statically or dynamically to store information used by an application. C++ uses static memory allocation for allocating memory for all the variables (local as well as global) declared in a program. For dynamic memory allocation and deallocation C++ uses *new* and *delete* operators.

Whether static or dynamic, memory allocation is always done only at the time of execution. Then what is the difference between static and dynamic allocation? In static allocation arrangement is made at compile time (through an entity known as symbol table) indicating how much memory to allocate for each variable used in the program when the execution of the program begins. The space allocated for each variable cannot be increased or decreased during execution. As against this, how much memory is to be allocated is decided at the time of execution. Moreover, once the memory is allocated for an entity this memory can be de-allocated on the fly when the execution is going on. Also, if required the allocated memory can be increased or decreased as per the requirement of the program. As a result, applications using dynamic memory allocation make optimal use of memory and increases efficiency of application. On the other hand, applications using static memory allocation may result into wastage of memory since they tend to allocate too much or too less memory.

8.1.2   Declaring and Initializing Pointers

Let us now see what are pointers and how they can be used in various expressions. We have seen that the expression &*i* returns the address of *i*. If we so desire, this address can be collected in a variable by saying,

j = &i ;

But remember that *j* is not an ordinary variable like any other integer variable. It is a variable, which contains the address of another variable (*i* in this case).

Since *j* is a variable the compiler must provide it space in memory. Once again, the following memory map would illustrate the contents of *i* and *j*.

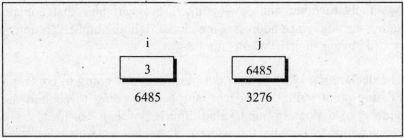

Figure 8.2. *Contents of i and j.*

As you can see, *i*'s value is 3 and *j*'s value is *i*'s address.

But wait, we can't use *j* in a program without declaring it. And since *j* is a variable, which contains the address of *i*, it is declared as,

int *j ;

This declaration tells the compiler that *j* will be used to store the address of an integer value-in other words *j* points to an integer. How do we justify the usage of * in the declaration,

int *j ;

Let us go by the meaning of *. It stands for 'value at address'. Thus, *int *j* would mean, the value at the address contained in *j* is an *int*.

Look at the following declarations,

int *alpha ;
char *ch ;
float *s ;

Here, *alpha*, *ch* and *s* are declared as pointer variables, i.e. variables capable of holding addresses. Remember that, addresses (location nos.) are always going to be whole numbers, therefore pointers always contain whole numbers. Now we can put these two facts together and say—pointers are variables that contain addresses, and since addresses are always whole numbers, pointers would always contain whole numbers.

The declaration *float* *s* does not mean that *s* is going to contain a floating-point value. What it means is, *s* is going to contain the address of a floating-point value. Similarly, *char* *ch* means that *ch* is going to contain the address of a *char* value. Or in other words, the value at address stored in *ch* is going to be a *char*.

8.1.3   Accessing the Variable Pointed to by Pointer

We can access the variable pointed to by a pointer using the value at address (*) operator. For example,

```
int i = 35 ;
int *p = &i ;
cout << *p ;
```

The *cout* statement would print 35. Suppose the address of *i* is *1000*. The value *35* would get stored at address *1000*. We have stored this address in *p*. The expression **p* would access the value at address stored in *p*. That is, the value at address *1000*, which happens to be *35*.

Let us now see a program that demonstrates the relationships we have been discussing.

```
#include <iostream.h>
void main( )
{
    int i = 3 ;
    int *j ;
    j = &i ;
```

```
        cout <<  "\nAddress of i = " << &i ;
        cout << "\nAddress of i = " << j ;
        cout << "\nAddress of j = " << &j ;
        cout << "\nValue of j = " << j ;
        cout << "\nValue of i = " << i ;
        cout << "\nValue of i = " << *( &i ) ;
        cout << "\nValue of i = " << *j ;
}
```

The output of the above program would be:

```
Address of i = 0x1240fff4
Address of i = 0x1240fff4
Address of j = 0x1240fff2
Value of j = 0x1240fff4
Value of i = 3
Value of i = 3
Value of i = 3
```

Note that printing the value of *(&i) is same as printing the value of *i*.

Work through the above program carefully, taking help of the memory locations of *i* and *j* shown earlier. This program summarises everything we have discussed so far.

8.2 Memory Management

While creating an application, we must ensure that our application should consume optimum amount of memory without loosing the flexibility. For example, suppose we are to allocate space for storing the percentage marks obtained by students in a class. If we do this using an array then we are required to make a commitment to the size of the array while writing the program. When we do so we may end up committing either too much or too less memory.

Moreover, we have to mention the size of the array as a positive non-aero integer constant. We do not have the flexibility of mentioning the size using a variable. This can be overcome by allocating the space for storing marks dynamically rather than statically. This calls for usage an operator called *new* that has been introduced in C++. What is so great about this? After all, we have been allocating memory dynamically using *malloc( )* in C programming as well? That's the beauty of it. *new* goes a step further than *malloc( )* as you would see in section 8.2.2. Before that let us get familiar with *new* and its counterpart the *delete* operator.

8.2.1   Using *new* and *delete* Operators

While doing dynamic memory allocation in C *the* memory is allocated from *heap*. Thus heap is a pool of memory from which standard library C functions like *malloc( )* and *calloc( )* allocate memory. The memory allocated from system heap using *malloc( )*, *calloc( )* and *realloc( )* is vacated (deallocated) using the function *free( )*.

C++ offers a better way to accomplish the same job through the use of the *new* and *delete* operators. The *new* operator allocates memory from free store (in the C++ lexicon, heap is called *free store*), whereas, the *delete* operator returns the allocated memory back to the free store. Thus the *new* and *delete* operators perform the job of *malloc( )* and *free( )*. These operators associate the allocation of memory with the way we use it.

The *new* operator, when used with the pointer to a data type, a structure, or an array, allocates memory for the item and assigns the address of that memory to the pointer. The *delete* operator does the reverse. It returns to the free store the memory owned by the object.

The following code snippet shows the *new* and *delete* operators at work.

```
int *p1 ;
struct employee
{
    char name [ 20 ] ;
    int age ;
    float sal ;
} *p2 ;

p1 = new int ;           // allocates 2 bytes
p2 = new employee ;  // allocates 26 bytes

// some code

delete p1 ;
delete p2 ;
```

Instead of using the *new* operator to allocate memory had we used *malloc( )* the allocation statements would have looked like this:

```
p1 = ( int * ) malloc ( sizeof ( int ) ) ;
p2 = ( stuct employee * ) malloc ( sizeof ( struct employee ) ) ;
```

Note that since *malloc( )* returns a *void* pointer it is necessary to typecast it into an appropriate type depending on the type of pointer we have on the left hand side of the assignment operator. This gets completely avoided when we are using the *new* operator.

Can we *free( )* the memory allocated with *new* or *delete* the pointers allocated with *malloc( )*? No. They are incompatible with one another. Memory allocated using *new* should be freed only using *delete*. Similarly, memory allocated using *malloc( )* should be freed only using *free( )*.

The advantages of *new* and *delete* over the C functions *malloc( )* and *free( )* are not immediately obvious. They appear to do the same job. However, *new* and *delete* provide a more readable syntax than *malloc( )* and *free( )*. When you read the section after the next you would be able to appreciate their advantages over traditional memory allocation used in C.

8.2.2   Using Pointer to Object

We saw how to create a pointer to an *int*, pointer to a *float* and pointer to a *char*. In this section we would see how to create a pointer to an object. We would also see an important point about *new* and *delete* operators. Here is a program...

```
#include <iostream.h>
#include <string.h>

class employee
{
    private :

        char name [ 20 ] ;
        int age ;
        float sal ;

    public :

        employee ( )
        {
            cout << endl << "reached zero-argument constructor" ;
            strcpy ( name, "" ) ;
            age = 0 ;
            sal = 0.0 ;
        }

        employee ( char *n, int a, float s )
        {
```

```
            cout << endl << "reached three-argument constructor" ;
            strcpy ( name, n ) ;
            age = a ;
            sal = s ;
        }

        void setdata ( char *n, int a, float s )
        {
            strcpy ( name, n ) ;
            age = a ;
            sal = s ;
        }

        void showdata( )
        {
            cout << endl << name << "\t" << age << "\t" << sal ;
        }

        ~employee( )
        {
            cout << endl << "reached destructor" ;
        }
} ;

void main( )
{
    employee *p ;
    p = new employee ;
    p -> setdata ( "sanjay", 23, 4500.50 ) ;

    employee *q ;
    q = new employee ( "ajay", 24, 3400.50 ) ;

    p -> showdata( ) ;
    q -> showdata( ) ;

    delete p ;
    delete q ;
```

}

The output of the program looks like this...

```
reached zero-argument constructor
reached three-argument constructor
sanjay    23    4500.5
ajay 24    3400.5
reached destructor
reached destructor
```

In this program we have created *p* and *q* as pointers to objects of the *employee* class. We have declared *p* as

employee *p ;

The expression *employee** indicates that *p* is going to point to an object of type *employee*. The statement

p = new employee ;

creates a new object of the *employee* class on heap and stores its address in *p*. In addition to this, the statement also causes the constructor to be called. Thus, the *new* operator creates an object dynamically and also calls the constructor for it. Which constructor to call is decided depending upon the number of arguments passed. For example in this program the statement

q = new employee ("ajay", 24, 3400.50) ;

would call three argument constructor since we have mentioned three arguments while creating the object.

Look at the way we have called the member functions of *employee* class.

p -> setdata ("sanjay", 23, 4500.50) ;
p -> showdata( ) ;

We have used the -> operator to call the functions.

The way *new* creates an object and calls a constructor, *delete* calls the destructor of the class and then destroys the object. Destruction involves de-allocation of memory for that object.

We can also declare a pointer that points to the object created on stack. For example,

```
employee e ;
employee *p = &e ;
```

We cannot use the *delete* operator to delete the memory allocated for the object *e*.

8.2.3   Using Pointer to Pointer

Pointer we know is a variable, which contains address of another variable. Now this variable itself could be another pointer. Thus, we now have a pointer, which contains another pointer's address. The following example should make this point clear.

```
#include <iostream.h>
void main( )
{
    int i = 3 ;
    int *j ;
    int **k ;

    j = &i ;
    k = &j ;

    cout << "\nAddress of i = " << &i ;
    cout << "\nAddress of i = " << j ;
    cout << "\nAddress of i = " << *k ;
    cout << "\nAddress of j = " << &j ;
```

```
        cout << "\nAddress of j = " << k ;
        cout << "\nAddress of k = " << &k ;

        cout << "\n\nValue of j  = " << j ;
        cout << "\nValue of k  = " << k ;
        cout << "\nValue of i  = " << i ;
        cout << "\nValue of i  = " << *( &i ) ;
        cout << "\nValue of i  = " << *j ;
        cout << "\nValue of i  = " << **k ;
}
```

The output of the above program would be:

```
Address of i = 0x1240fff4
Address of i = 0x1240fff4
Address of j = 0x1240fff2
Value of j = 0x1240fff4
Value of i = 3
Value of i = 3
Value of i = 3
```

The following memory map would help you in tracing out how the program prints the above output.

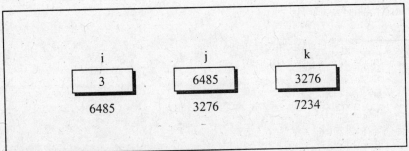

Figure 8.3. *Showing a pointer to pointer.*

Observe how the variables *i*, *j* and *k* have been declared,

```
int i ;
int *j ;
int **k ;
```

Here, *i* is an ordinary *int*, *j* is a pointer to an *int*, whereas *k* is a pointer to a pointer.

8.3 Pointers and Arrays

Arrays and pointers are very closely related. So, discussing pointers without discussing arrays or vice versa would make the discussion incomplete and wanting.

8.3.1   Array of Pointers

The way there can be an array of *ints* or an array of *floats*, similarly there can be an array of pointers. Since a pointer variable always contains an address, an array of pointers would be nothing but a collection of addresses. The addresses present in the array of pointers can be addresses of isolated variables or addresses of array elements or any other addresses. All rules that apply to an ordinary array apply in Toto to the array of pointers as well. I think a program would clarify the concept.

```
void main( )
{
    int *arr [ 4 ] ;  /* array of integer pointers */
    int i = 31, j = 5, k = 19, l = 71 ;

    arr [ 0 ] = &i ;
    arr [ 1 ] = &j ;
    arr [ 2 ] = &k ;
    arr [ 3 ] = &l ;
    for ( int m = 0 ; m <= 3 ; m++ )
        cout << *( arr [ m ] ) ;
}
```

And here is the output...

31
5
19
71

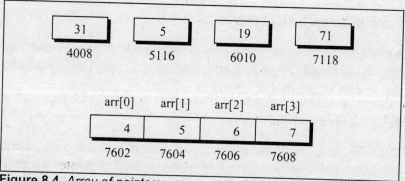

Figure 8.4. *Array of pointers.*

Figure 8.4 shows the contents and the arrangement of the array of pointers in memory. As you can observe, *arr* contains addresses of isolated *int* variables *i, j, k* and *l*. The *for* loop in the program picks up the addresses present in *arr* and prints the values present at these addresses.

8.3.2   Dynamic Arrays

Consider the array declaration,

int marks [100] ;

Such a declaration would typically be used if 100 student's marks were to be stored in memory. The moment we make this declaration 200 bytes are reserved in memory for storing 100 integers in it. However, it may so happen that when we actually run the program we might be interested in storing only 60 student's marks. Even in this case 200 bytes would get reserved in memory, which would result in wastage of memory.

Other way round there always exists a possibility that when you run the program you need to store more than 100 student's marks. In this case the array would fall short in size. Moreover, there is no way to increase or decrease the array size during execution of the program. In other words, when we use arrays static memory allocation takes place. What if we want to allocate memory only at the time of execution? This can be achieved using the *new* operator. Following statements show how to create an array dynamically.

int *p3 ;
p3 = new int [30] ; // allocates memory for storing 30 integers

Here the *new* operator accepts a data type with an array dimension. The dimension that we have given is a constant 30, representing the number of integers. You can, however, supply a variable dimension, and the *new* operator allocates the correct amount of memory as shown below:

```
int n ;
cin >> n ;

int *p = new int [ n ] ;
```

When you run this code you can type in the size of the array. The *new* operator uses the value that you enter to decide the size of memory to be allocated.

For creating an array of objects of the *employee* class dynamically, we can write the following statement.

```
employee *p = new employee [ 10 ] ;
```

We can access the array elements using the usual subscript notation like *p [0], p [1]*, etc.

Memory allocated for the dynamic array must be deallocated using *delete* operator. Here is the syntax for using the *delete* operator for freeing a dynamically created array:

```
delete [ ] p3 ;
```

It indicates that we are not deleting a *thing* but an array of *things* (*thing*s being integers in this case) pointed to by the pointer *p3*. Would a simple

```
delete p3 ;
```

not work in this case? Well, it deletes the complete array. But if the array is an array of objects, then the destructor would be called only for the first object in the array. The statement, *delete[ ] p3*, deletes the complete array and calls the destructor for each object in the array.

8.4 Pointers and Functions

Let us now see pointers in conjunction with functions.

8.4.1   Invoking Functions by Passing the Values

We have already seen what is a call by value in Chapter 3. Just to reiterate, when a function is called by value, a copy of arguments gets created. Changes made in the values of these arguments do not get reflected in the actual arguments.

8.4.2   Invoking Functions by Passing the References

Instead of passing a variable by value we can also pass it by reference as shown in the following program.

```
#include <iostream.h>
class item
{
    private :

        char category ;
        int code ;
        int price ;

    public:

        item( )
        {
        }

        item ( char c, int cd, int pr )
        {
            category = c ;
            code = cd ;
            price = pr ;
        }
```

```
          void filldata ( item &i )
          {
               i.category = category ;
               i.code = code ;
               i.price = price ;
          }

          void show( )
          {
               cout << category << "\t" << code << "\t" << price ;
          }
};

void main( )
{
     item i1 ( 'E', 10, 125 ) ;
     item i2 ;

     i1.filldata ( i2 ) ;
     i2.show( ) ;
}
```

The *item* class holds information like category, code and price of
an item. The *filldata( )* function copies the information of the
calling object into the object passed to it. We have collected the
object passed to it in a reference. In a call to the *filldata( )* function
a copy of the object does not get created. This works out better
than the call by value since the entire object (all its data members)
does not get copied into another object.

8.4.3   Invoking Functions by Passing the Pointers

Arguments are generally passed to functions in one of the
following ways:

(a) sending the values of the arguments

(b) sending the references of the arguments

(c) sending the addresses of the arguments

we have already dealt with the first two ways. Let us now see the third way of passing arguments. If the function is called by passing to it the addresses of arguments, it is called 'call by address'. In call by address, the addresses of actual arguments in the calling function are copied into formal arguments of the called function. This means that using the formal arguments in the called function we can make changes in the actual arguments of the calling function. The following program illustrates this fact.

```
#include <iostream.h>
void main( )
{
    int a = 10 ;
    int b = 20 ;
    void swapa ( int *x, int *y ) ;

    swapa ( &a, &b ) ;
    cout << endl << a << endl b ;
}

void swapa ( int *x, int *y )
{
    int t ;

    t = *x ;
    *x = *y ;
    *y = t ;
}
```

The output of the above program would be:

a = 20
b = 10

Using 'call by address' intelligently we can make a function return more than one value at a time, which is not possible in call by value. This is shown in the program given below.

```
#include <iostream.h>
void main( )
{
    int radius ;
    float area, perimeter ;
    void areaperi ( int r, float *a, float *p ) ;

    cout << "\nEnter radius of a circle " ;
    cin >> radius ;
    areaperi ( radius, &area, &perimeter ) ;
    cout << "Area = " << area ;
    cout << "\nPerimeter = " << perimeter ;
}

void areaperi ( int r, float *a, float *p )
{
    *a = 3.14 * r * r ;
    *p = 2 * 3.14 * r ;
}
```

And here is the output...

```
Enter radius of a circle 5
Area = 78.5
Perimeter = 31.4
```

Here, we are making a mixed call, in the sense, we are passing the value of *radius* but, addresses of *area* and *perimeter*. And since we are passing the addresses, any change that we make in values stored at addresses contained in the variables *a* and *p*, would make the change effective even in *main( )*. That is why when the control returns from the function *areaperi( )* we are able to output the values of *area* and *perimeter*.

Thus, we have been able to return two values from a called function. This helps us to overcome the limitation of the *return* statement, which can return only one value from a function at a time.

What is the difference between a call by reference and a call by address? In a call by reference, we can access the members of the using the . operator, whereas in call by address we are required to do the same using a slightly clumsy -> operator.

8.4.4 Function Returning by Reference

We have seen how to return a reference from a function in chapter 3. You must be remembering that we cannot return a reference to the local variable from a function. Similarly, if a function returns a reference its call can appear at the left hand side of the assignment operator.

8.4.5 Function Returning by Pointer

The way functions return an *int*, a *float*, a *double* or any other data type, it can even return a pointer. However, to make a function return a pointer it has to be explicitly mentioned in the calling function as well as in the function definition. The following program illustrates this.

```
#include <iostream.h>
void main( )
{
    int *p ;
    int *fun( ) ;  /* prototype declaration */
    p = fun( ) ;
    cout << p ;
    cout << endl << *p ;
```

```
}

int *fun( ) /* function definition */
{
    int *i = new int ;
    *i = 20 ;
    return ( i ) ;
}
```

This program shows how a pointer can be returned from a function. Note that the prototype declaration tells the compiler that *fun( )* is a function which receives nothing but returns an integer pointer. The first *cout* would output the address contained in *p* (address returned by *fun( )*). The second *cout* would output the value *20*.

8.5 Pointers and Strings

Strings are a special kind of array. It contains a collection of characters terminated by '\0'. In this section we would see how pointers and strings are related.

8.5.1 Defining Pointers to String Constants

Suppose we wish to store "Hello". We may either store it in a string or we may ask the compiler to store it at some location in memory and assign the address of the string in a *char* pointer. This is shown below:

```
char str[ ] = "Hello" ;
char *p = "Hello" ;
```

There is a subtle difference in usage of these two forms. For example, we cannot assign a string to another, whereas, we can assign a *char* pointer to another *char* pointer. This is shown in the following program.

```
void main( )
{
    char str1[ ] = "Hello" ;
    char str2 [ 10 ] ;

    char *s = "Good Morning" ;
    char *q ;

    str2 = str1 ; /* error */
    q = s ; /* works */
}
```

Also, once a string has been defined it cannot be initialised to another set of characters. Unlike strings, such an operation is perfectly valid with *char* pointers.

```
void main( )
{
    char str1[ ] = "Hello" ;
    char *p = "Hello" ;

    str1 = "Bye" ; /* error */
    p = "Bye" ; /* works */
}
```

8.5.2   Defining Arrays of Pointers to Strings

As we know, a pointer variable always contains an address. Therefore, if we construct an array of pointers it would contain a number of addresses. Let us see how the names in the earlier example can be stored in the array of pointers.

```
char *names[ ] = {
```

```
                        "akshay",
                        "parag",
                        "raman",
                        "srinivas",
                        "gopal",
                        "rajesh"
              };
```

In this declaration *names[ ]* is an array of poii.ters. It contains base addresses of respective names. That is, base addresses of "akshay" is stored in *names[0]*, base addresses of "parag" is stored in *names[1]* and so on. This is depicted in the Figure 8.5.

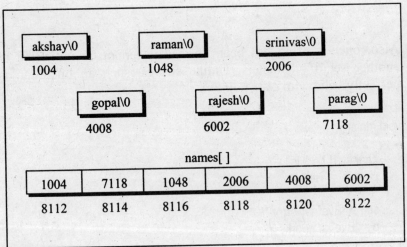

Figure 8.5. *Array of pointers to string.*

In the two-dimensional array of characters, the strings were occupying a total of 60 bytes. As against this by using the array of pointers to strings the same strings can now be stored using only 53 bytes, 41 bytes for the actual strings and 12 for the array of pointers. A substantial saving that goes on increasing with the number of names being stored.

Thus, one reason to store strings in an array of pointers is to make more efficient use of available memory.

Another reason to use array of pointers to store strings is to obtain greater ease in the manipulation of the strings. The following program shows this. The purpose of the program is very simple. We want to exchange the positions of the names "raman" and "srinivas".

```cpp
#include <iostream.h>
main( )
{
    char *names[ ] = {
                        "akshay",
                        "parag",
                        "raman",
                        "srinivas",
                        "gopal",
                        "rajesh"
                    };
    char *temp ;

    cout << "\nOriginal: " << names [ 2 ] << names [ 3 ] ;
    temp = names [ 2 ] ;
    names [ 2 ] = names [ 3 ] ;
    names [ 3 ] = temp ;

    cout << "\nNew: " << names [ 2 ] << names [ 3 ] ;
}
```

And here is the output...

```
Original: raman srinivas
New: srinivas ramam
```

In this program all that we are required to do is exchange the addresses of the names stored in the array of pointers, rather than the names themselves. Thus, by effecting just one exchange we are able to interchange names. This makes managing strings very convenient.

Thus, from the point of view of efficient memory usage and ease of programming, an array of pointers to strings definitely scores over a two-dimensional character array. That is why, even though in principle strings can be stored and handled through a two-dimensional array of characters, in actual practice it is the array of pointers to strings which is more commonly used.

Limitation of Array of Pointers to Strings

When we are using a two-dimensional array of characters we are at liberty to either initialise the strings where we are declaring the array, or receive the strings using *cin*. However, when we are using an array of pointers to strings we can initialise the strings at the place where we are declaring the array, but we cannot receive the strings from keyboard using *cin*. This is because when we declare the array it contains garbage addresses. And it would be definitely wrong to store the input strings at these addresses.

Exercises

[A] State True or False:

(a) If memory is allocated using *new [ ]* it must be deallocated using *delete [ ]*.

(b) *new* not only allocates memory but also calls the object's constructor.

(c) Heap and free store are two different things.

(d) In C++ to reallocate memory we should use the *renew* operator.

(e) The *new* operator always returns a pointer of appropriate type, whereas, *malloc( )* returns a *void* pointer which needs to be typecasted explicitly.

(f) It is unsafe to deallocate the memory using *delete* if it has been allocated using *malloc( )*.

[B] Answer the following:

(a) What is the difference in the following two statements?

delete a ;
delete [ ] a ;

(b) Point out the reasons why using *new* is a better idea than using *malloc( )*?

(c) What does the *delete* operator do in addition to deallocating the memory used by the object?

(d) Replace the following code using the *new* operator.

```
#include <alloc.h>
#define MAXROW 3
#define MAXCOL 4
void main( )
{
    int ( *p )[ MAXCOL ] ;
    p = ( int ( * ) [ MAXCOL ] ) malloc ( MAXROW * sizeof ( *p ) ) ;
}
```

(e) Replace the following code using the *new* operator.

```
#include <alloc.h>
#define MAXROW 3
#define MAXCOL 4
void main( )
{
    int ( *p )[ MAXCOL ][ MAXROW ] ;
    p = ( int ( * ) [ MAXROW ][ MAXCOL ] ) malloc ( sizeof ( *p ) ) ;
```

}

[C] Attempt the following:

(a) Write a program that will allocate memory dynamically for a 1-D, 2-D and a 3-D array of integers. Store some values in these arrays and then print them out. We must be able to access elements of these arrays using forms *a[i]*, *b[i][j]* and *c[i][j][k]*.

(b) Write a program to count the number of 'e' in the following array of pointers to strings:

```
char *s[ ] = {
                "We will teach you how to...",
                "Move a mountain",
                "Level a building",
                "Erase the past",
                "Make a million",
                "...all through C!"
        };
```

(c) Write a program to reverse the strings stored in the following array of pointers to strings:

```
char *s[ ] = {
                "To err is human...",
                "But to really mess things up...",
                "One needs to know C!!"
        };
```

9
Virtual Functions

9.1 Introducing Virtual Functions

Many programmers carry a wrong impression that since they have started using classes, objects, function overloading, operator overloading and inheritance they have graduated to the object-oriented world. Though on the face of it everything may appear nice, neat and clean don't get fooled. If you stop here, you're missing out on the greatest part of the language, which is the jump to true object-oriented programming. You can do this only with polymorphism implemented through *virtual* functions.

Overloading of functions or operators is called static polymorphism (one thing with several distinct forms). We have already dealt with this type of polymorphism. The other type of polymorphism simplifies the syntax of performing the same operation with a hierarchy of classes. Thus, you can use polymorphism to keep the interface to the classes clean, because you do not have to define unique function names for similar operations on each derived class. This kind of Polymorphism is supported by the *virtual* keyword.

Virtual means existing in appearance but not in reality. When virtual functions are used, a program that appears to be calling a function of one class may in reality be calling a function of a different class. But why on earth would we want this? Suppose we have three different classes called *line*, *circle* and *triangle*. Each class contains a *draw( )* function to draw the relevant shape on the screen. If we are to draw a picture containing numerous lines, circles and triangles we can create an array of pointers, which would hold addresses of all the objects in the picture. The array definition may look like,

shape *arr [50] ;

When it is time to draw the picture we can simply run the loop,

```
for ( i = 0 ; i < 50 ; i++ )
    arr[ i ]->draw( ) ;
```

When *arr[i]* contains address of the *line* object it would call the *line::draw( )* function. Similarly, when it contains the address of the *circle* object it would call the *circle::draw( )* function. This is amazing for two reasons:

(a) Functions from different classes are executed through the same function call.

(b) The array *arr[ ]* has been defined to contain *shape* pointers and not *line* or *circle* pointers.

This concept is called polymorphism. The functions have the same appearance, the *draw( )* function, but different actual functions are used. Which *draw( )* function would get used depends on the contents of *arr[i]*. However, for this polymorphic approach to work, several conditions must be met. These are:

(a) The classes *line*, *circle* and *triangle* all must be derived from the same base class, *shape*.

(b) The *shape* base class must contain a *draw( )* function which has been declared *virtual*.

All this would be too much to digest at one shot. So let us break it into pieces and try to understand it part by part through simple programs.

9.1.1   Accessing Normal Member Functions using Pointers

First of all we would see a program that calls member functions using pointers. Here is the program...

```
#include <iostream.h>
```

```
class one
{
    public :

            void display( )
            {
                    cout << endl << "In base class" ;
            }
} ;

class oneofone : public one
{
    public :

            void display( )
            {
                    cout << endl << "In oneofone class" ;
            }
} ;

class twoofone : public one
{
    public:

            void display( )
            {
                    cout << endl << "In twoofone class" ;
            }
} ;

void main( )
{
    one *ptr ;
    oneofone o1 ;
    twoofone o2 ;

    ptr = &o1 ;
    ptr -> display( ) ;
```

```
    ptr = &o2 ;
    ptr -> display( ) ;
}
```

Here *oneofone* and *twoofone* are classes derived from the base class *one*. Each of these three classes has a member function *display( )*. In *main( )* having created the objects *o1*, *o2* (from the two derived classes) and a pointer *ptr* to base class, we have assigned the address of a derived class object to the base class pointer through the statement, .

ptr = &o1 ;

Should this not give us an error, since we are assigning an address of one type to a pointer of another? No, since in this case the compiler relaxes the type checking. The rule is that pointers to objects of a derived class are type-compatible with pointers to objects of the base class. Taking the address of a derived class object and treating it as the address of the base class object is called *upcasting*.

When we execute the statement,

ptr -> display( ) ;

which function gets called—*display( )* of *oneofone* or *display( )* of *one*? The function in the base class gets called. This is because the compiler ignores the contents of the pointer *ptr* and chooses the member function that matches the *type* of the pointer. Here, since *ptr*'s type matches the base class, the *display( )* of base class gets called. Same thing happens when we call *display( )* for the second time.

Sometimes this is what we want, but it doesn't provide the facility discussed at the beginning of this discussion—accessing functions of different classes using the same statement. How this can be achieved is shown in the next section.

9.1.2   Accessing Virtual Member Function using Pointers

We would now make a small change in our program. We would declare the *display( )* function in the base class as *virtual* and call it using pointers.

```
class one
{
    public :

        virtual void display( )  // virtual function
        {
            cout << endl << "In Base class" ;
        }
} ;
```

If we execute the program now the output would be:

```
In oneofone class
In twoofone class
```

As can be seen from the output, this time instead of the base class, the member functions of the derived classes are executed. Thus the same function call,

```
ptr -> display( ) ;
```

executes different functions, depending on the contents of *ptr*. The rule here is that the compiler selects the function to be called based on the *contents* of the pointer *ptr*, and not on the *type* of the pointer. Problem is how does the compiler know which function to compile, when it doesn't know which object's address *ptr* may contain. It could be the address of an object of the *oneofone* class or of the *twoofone* class. Which version of *display( )* does the compiler call?

In fact the compiler doesn't know what to do, so it arranges for the decision to be deferred until the program is running. At run time, when it is known what object is pointed to by *ptr*, the appropriate version of *display( )* gets called. This is called *late binding* or *dynamic binding*. (Choosing functions in the normal way, during compilation, is called early, or static binding.) Late binding requires some overhead but provides increased power and flexibility.

Instead of pointers had we used references the effect would have been same. The following code shows use of references instead of pointers in *main( )*.

```
void main( )
{
    oneofone o1 ;
    twoofone o2 ;
    one &ref1 = o1 ;
    one &ref2 = o2 ;
    ref1.display( ) ;
    ref2.display( ) ;
}
```

9.1.3   Late Binding & Working of Virtual Mechanism

Using virtual functions is only part of the story. Knowing how compiler implements them completes the other part. We have seen the first part. Before we take up the second and the more interesting part let me reiterate a few facts that we have learnt in the last section. A clear understanding of them is utmost necessary for you to follow the subsequent discussion.

(a) The term binding refers to the connection between a function call and the actual code executed as a result of the call.

(b) If the function invoked in response to each call is known at compile-time, it is called static or early binding, because the compiler can figure out the function to be called before the program is run.

(c) Dynamic binding is so named because the actual function called at run-time depends on the contents of the pointer. It is also known as late binding, because the connection between the function call and the actual code executed by the call is determined *late* during the execution of the program and not when the program is compiled.

(d) The keyword *virtual* tells the compiler that it should not perform early binding. Instead, it should automatically install all the mechanisms necessary to perform late binding.

(e) Unlike C++, in C language there is only one kind of binding—early binding.

Consider the following simple program.

```
#include <iostream.h>
class sample
{
    private :

        int i ;

    public :

        virtual void display( )
        {
            cout << endl << "In sample class" ;
        }
};
```

```
class example
{
    private :

        int i ;

    public :

        void display( )
        {
            cout << endl << "In example class" ;
        }
} ;

class trial
{
    public :

        void display( )
        {
            cout << endl << "In trial class" ;
        }
} ;

void main( )
{
    sample s ;
    example e ;
    trial t ;

    cout << endl << sizeof ( s )
         << endl << sizeof ( e )
         << endl << sizeof ( t ) ;
}
```

Here is the output that you would get if you run the program...

2
1

To say the least you would find the output surprising. We had only an *int* in the object *s* still the size is being reported as 4 bytes. With the same *int* in the object *e* its size is being reported only as 2 bytes. Lastly, even though we didn't have any data in the object *t* its size has turned out to be 1 byte. Let us try to find why this so happens.

With no virtual functions, the size of the object *e* is exactly what you'd expect—the size of a single *int*. With a single virtual function in *sample*, the size of the object *s* is the size of *int* plus the size of a *void* pointer. The compiler inserts this pointer (called VPTR, as we would soon see) if you have one or more virtual functions. As there are no data member in *trial* the C++ compiler forces the object *t* to be of nonzero size (in our case 1 byte) because each object must have a distinct address. If you imagine indexing into an array of zero-sized objects, you'll be able to appreciate why the size has to be nonzero. Nonzero is fine, but why *1*? Because the smallest nonzero positive integer is *1*.

Having established the fact that the compiler silently adds a void pointer to an object of a class which contains virtual functions let us see what this pointer points to and when is it set up.

To accomplish late binding, the compiler creates a table called VTABLE for each class that contains virtual functions and for the classes derived from it. The compiler places the addresses of the virtual functions for that particular class in the VTABLE. If you don't redefine a function that was declared virtual in the base class, the compiler uses the address of the base-class version in the derived class.

When objects of the base class or the derived class are created it secretly places a pointer, called the *vpointer* (abbreviated as

VPTR), which points to the class's VTABLE. When you make a virtual function call through a base-class pointer the compiler quietly inserts code to fetch the VPTR and look up the function address in the VTABLE, thus calling the right function and causing late binding to take place.

The VPTR must be initialized to point to the starting address of the appropriate VTABLE. (This happens in the constructor, as we will see later in more detail.)

Once the VPTR is initialized to the proper VTABLE, the object in effect "knows" what type it is. But this self-knowledge is worthless unless it is used at the point a virtual function is called.

Suppose a pointer to the base class object contains address of the derived class object and you call a virtual function using this pointer. Now something special happens. Instead of performing a typical function call, which is simply an assembly language CALL to a particular address, the compiler generates different code to perform the function call. The compiler starts with the contents of the base-class pointer. These contents are address of the derived class object. Using this address the VPTR of the derived class object is fetched. Using VPTR the VTABLE of the derived class is accessed. From this table the address of the function being called is extracted. Lastly using this address the function of the derived class is called.

All of this—setting up the VTABLE for each class, initializing the VPTR, inserting the code for the virtual function call—happens automatically, so you don't have to worry about it.

I am sure what we said here would seem pretty abstract unless we see it working in a program. So let us write one. Figure 9.1 shows the hierarchy of classes that we propose to implement in the program.

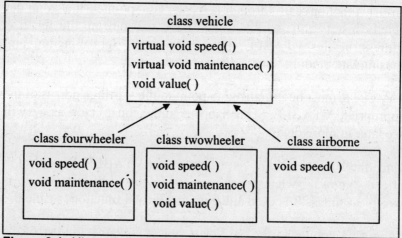

Figure 9.1. *Hierarchy of classes.*

Given below is the code for the program that implements this class hierarchy.

```
#include <iostream.h>
#include <conio.h>

class vehicle
{
    public :

        virtual void speed( )
        {
            cout << endl << "In speed of Vehicle" ;
        }

        virtual void maintenance( )
        {
            cout << endl << "In maintenance of Vehicle" ;
        }
```

```
        void value( )
        {
            cout << endl << "In value of Vehicle" ;
        }
} ;

class fourwheeler : public vehicle
{
    , public :

        void speed( )
        {
            cout << endl << "In speed of fourwheeler" ;
        }

        void maintenance( )
        {
            cout << endl << "In maintenance of fourwheeler" ;
        }
} ;

class twowheeler : public vehicle
{
    public :

        void speed( )
        {
            cout << endl << "In speed of twowheeler" ;
        }

        void maintenance( )
        {
            cout << endl << "In maintenance of twowheeler" ;
        }

        void value( )
        {
            cout << endl << "In value of twowheeler" ;
```

```
            }
};

class airborne : public vehicle
{
    public :

        void speed( )
        {
            cout << endl << "In speed of airborne" ;
        }
};

void main( )
{
    vehicle *ptr1 ;
    vehicle v ;

    ptr1 = &v ;
    ptr1 -> speed( ) ;
    ptr1 -> maintenance( ) ;
    ptr1 -> value( ) ;

    vehicle *ptr2, *ptr3, *ptr4 ;
    fourwheeler maruti ;
    twowheeler bajaj ;
    airborne jumbo ;

    ptr2 = &maruti ;
    ptr3 = &bajaj ;
    ptr4 = &jumbo ;
    ptr2 -> speed( ) ;
    ptr2 -> maintenance( ) ;
    ptr3 -> speed( ) ;
    ptr3 -> maintenance( ) ;

    ptr4 -> speed( ) ;
    ptr4 -> maintenance( ) ;
```

```
    ptr2 -> value( ) ;
    ptr3 -> value( ) ;

    vehicle w ;
    w.speed( ) ;

    fourwheeler f ;
    f.speed( ) ;

    airborne a ;
    a.maintenance( ) ;
}
```

Here is the output of the program...

```
In speed of vehicle
In maintenance of vehicle
In value of vehicle
In speed of fourwheeler
In maintenance of fourwheeler
In speed of twowheeler
In maintenance of twowheeler
In speed of airborne
In maintenance of vehicle
In value of vehicle
In value of vehicle
In speed of vehicle
In speed of fourwheeler
In maintenance of vehicle
```

As we saw earlier a VTABLE is created for every class that contains virtual functions and for the classes derived from it. It means in our program a VTABLE would be built for all the four classes: *vehicle, twowheeler, fourwheeler* and *airborne*. Each of these VTABLEs would contain addresses of the virtual functions. For all the objects built from these classes the compiler would automatically insert a VPTR, which would point to the class's VTABLE. This is shown in Figure 9.2.

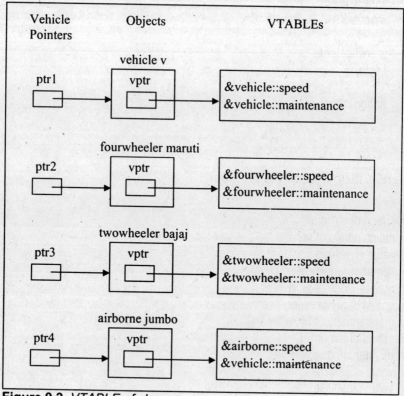

Figure 9.2. *VTABLE of classes.*

Note that the class *airborne* doesn't contain the definition of the *maintenance( )* function. Hence its VTABLE contains the address of the base class's *maintenance( )* function.

Let us now understand the working of the program a step at a time. To begin with, we have stored the address of the base class object in a pointer to the base class through the statements

```
vehicle *ptr1 ;
vehicle v ;
ptr1 = &v ;
```

Next we call the member functions of the base class through the statements

```
ptr1 -> speed( ) ;
ptr1 -> maintenance( ) ;
ptr1 -> value( ) ;
```

Though these calls appear similar, behind the screen they are built differently. This is because the first two functions have been declared as *virtual* in the base class, whereas the third has not been. Since *value( )* is not *virtual*, irrespective of the whether the base class object's or derived class object's address is stored in *ptr1* it is always the base class's *value( )* that would get called.

Since *speed( )* has been defined *virtual* in the base class, which of its implementation (of vehicle, *twowheeler*, *fourwheeler* or *airborne*) would be called depends upon whose address is stored in *ptr1*. In our case this turn's out to be *vehicle* object's address. So while calling *speed( )* firstly the *vptr* is retrieved from the vehicle object *v*. Using this pointer the VTABLE of the vehicle class is accessed. From this VTABLE the address of *speed( )* (of *vehicle*) is retrieved. Using this address *vehicle::speed( )* is ultimately called. Exactly same argument applies to calling *maintenance( )*. Because the fetching of the *vptr* and the determination of the actual function address occurs at run-time, you get the desired late binding.

The next case is more interesting. Consider the statements

```
vehicle *ptr2 ;
fourwheeler maruti ;
```

```
ptr2 = &maruti ;

ptr2 -> speed( ) ;
ptr2 -> maintenance( ) ;
```

Here we have stored the address of the derived class object in a pointer to the base class object. Now when we call *speed( )* the *vptr* of the object *maruti* would be used to access the VTABLE of the *fourwheeler* class. From this VTABLE the address of *fourwheeler::speed( )* would be retrieved. Using this address the function *fourwheeler::speed( )* would then get called.

If you think on these lines you can understand the subsequent calls made using *ptr2*, *ptr3* and *ptr4*.

Now consider the calls

```
ptr2 -> value( ) ;
ptr3 -> value( ) ;
```

Since *value( )* has not been defined as *virtual* in the base class VTABLEs are not involved in generating a call to *vehicle::value( )*. In our program we have not overridden *value( )* in the derived class. Had we done so still it is the base class implementation that would have been called.

The next three calls are interesting:

```
vehicle w ;
w.speed( ) ;

fourwheeler f ;
f.speed( ) ;

airborne a ;
```

a.maintenance( ) ;

Here the *vptr* or VTABLEs are not involved at all. While calling *f.speed( )* there is no ambiguity. As the compiler has an object (rather than its address) it knows the exact type and therefore it will not use late binding for any function calls. In general, for efficiency's sake, most compilers will perform early binding when they are making a call to a virtual function for an object because they know the exact type.

Now that we are through with the program let us look at a few more subtle issues related to virtual functions:

(a) Because of the vital role played by *vptr* while calling virtual functions it is critical that the *vptr* is always pointing to the proper VTABLE. You don't ever want to be able to make a call to a virtual function before the *vptr* is properly initialized. So the best place where this automatic initialisation can take place is the constructor. However, in our program, we didn't have a constructor in any class. That is why the compiler always adds a zero-argument constructor to our class when we don't define one—to initiate the *vptr*, if necessary.

(b) How does the compiler manage to obtain the value of *vptr* from the object? All objects have their *vptr* in the same place (often at the beginning of the object), so the compiler can pick it out of the object easily.

9.1.4 Pure Virtual Function

We can add another refinement to the virtual function declared in the base class of the last program. Since the function *display( )* in the base class never gets executed we can easily do away with the body of this virtual function and add a notation =*0* in the function declaration, as shown below:

```
class base
{
    public :

        virtual void display( ) = 0 ;
} ;
```

The *display( )* function is now known as a *pure* virtual function. Thus, a pure virtual function is a virtual function with no body and a *= 0* in its declaration. The = sign here has got nothing to do with assignment; the value 0 is not assigned to anything. It is used to simply tell the compiler that a function will be pure, i.e. it will not have any body.

If we can remove the body of the virtual function can we not remove the function altogether. That would be too ambitious and moreover it doesn't work. Without a function *display( )* in the base class, statements like

```
ptr -> display( ) ;
```

would be invalid.

Since *display( )* of the base class was never getting called we made it a pure virtual function. There is another side to it. At times we may want that a user should never be able to create an object of the base class. For example, if there is base class called *shape* from which three classes *line*, *circle* and *triangle* have been derived. We would never make an object of the *shape* class; we would only make objects of the derived classes to draw specific shapes. A class from which we would never want to create objects is called an *abstract* class. Such a class exists only as a parent for the derived classes. Now how do we communicate to users who are going to use our classes that they should never create an object of the base class. One way is to document this fact and rely on the users to remember it. That's a sloppy way. Instead, a better way would be to write the base class such that any object creation from it becomes impossible. This can be achieved by placing at least one pure virtual function in the base class. Now anybody who tries to create an object from such a base class would be reported an error by the compiler. Not only will the compiler complain that you are trying to create an object of the abstract class, it will also tell you the name of the virtual function that makes the base class an abstract class.

Whenever a pure virtual function is placed in the base class, you must override it in all the derived classes from which you wish to create objects. If you don't do this in a derived class then the derived class becomes an abstract class.

9.1.5   Virtual Base Classes

Let us look at one more subtlety of virtual functions. Consider the situation where there is one parent class called *base* and two classes derived from it, *derived1* and *derived2*. Suppose we derive a class *derived3* from *derived1* and *derived2*. Now suppose a member function of *derived3* class wants to access data or functions in the *base* class. Since *derived1* and *derived2* are derived from *base* each inherits a copy of *base*. This copy is referred to as a *subobject*. Each subobject contains its own copy of *base*'s data. This is shown in Figure 9.3.

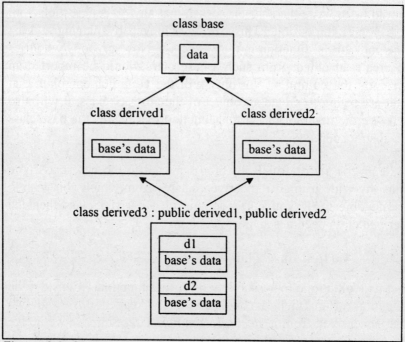

Figure 9.3. *Showing copy of subobjects in each class.*

Now when *derived3* refers to the data in the *base* class, which of the two copies will it access? This is an ambiguous situation for the compiler, hence it reports an error. To get rid of this ambiguity, we should make *derived1* and *derived2* as *virtual* base classes as shown in the following program.

```
#include <iostream.h>

class base
{
    protected :

        int data ;
```

```
    public :

        base( )
        {
            data = 500 ;
        }
} ;

class derived1 : virtual public base
{
} ;

class derived2 : virtual public base
{
} ;

class derived3 : public derived1, public derived2
{
    public :

        int getdata( )
        {
            return data ;
        }
} ;

void main( )
{
    derived3 ch ;
    int a ;

    a = ch.getdata( ) ;
    cout << a ;
}
```

Using the keyword *virtual* in the two base classes causes them to
share the single subobject of the *base* class, which eliminates the

ambiguity. Since there is only one subobject there is no ambiguity when it is referred in the *derived3* class. Here *derived1* and *derived2* are known as *virtual base classes*.

The ambiguity that we discussed occurs not only in the case of member data but also in case of member functions. This is shown in the following program.

```
#include <iostream.h>

class base
{
    public :

        void fun( )
        {
            cout << endl << "In base::fun( )" ;
        }
};

class derived1 : public base
{
};

class derived2 : public base
{
};

class derived3 : public derived1, public derived2
{
};

void main( )
{
    derived3 d ;
    d.fun( ) ;
}
```

On compilation the compiler reports an error since *derived3* inherits two copies of *fun( )*, one via *derived1* and another via *derived2*. Hence when we attempt to call *d.fun( )* the compiler would not know whether we intend to call the copy of *derived1* or that of *derived2*. Again the error can be overcome by using the *virtual* keyword in derivation of *derived1* and *derived2* as shown below:

```
class derived1 : virtual public base
{

};

class derived2 : virtual public base
{

};
```

9.1.6   Defining Run-Time Polymorphism

So, from the discussion we did in this chapter we can define run-time polymorphism as 'calling an appropriate member function while the program is running'. Run-time polymorphism is achieved by virtual mechanism.

9.2 Other Functions

Apart from usual member functions, a class can also have *friend* functions and *static* functions. The working and usage of these functions are discussed in this section.

9.2.1   Friend Functions

So far we have learnt that that only member functions can access *private* data of a class. This is the essence of data encapsulation. However, sometimes we have to make an exception to this rule to avoid programming inconvenience. At such times we have to allow functions outside a class to access and manipulate the class's data members. To achieve this C++ provides a keyword called *friend*. It permits a function or all the functions of another class to read and write the original class's *private* data members.

Suppose we want a function to operate on objects of two different classes. If the two classes are inherited from the same base class, then we may be able to put the function in the base class. But what if the classes are unrelated? This is an ideal situation where a *friend* function can be used as a bridge between two classes. The following program will help you in understanding how this concept is put to work.

```cpp
#include <iostream.h>

class two ;

class one
{
    private :

        int data1 ;

    public :

        one( )
        {
            data1 = 100 ;
        }

        friend int accessboth ( one, two ) ;
};

class two
{
    private:
```

```
        int data2 ;

    public:

        two( )
        {
            data2 = 200 ;
        }
        friend int accessboth ( one, two ) ;
} ;

int accessboth ( one a, two b )
{
    return ( a.data1 + b.data2 ) ;
}

void main( )
{
    one a ;
    two b ;
    cout << accessboth ( a, b ) ;
}
```

Here, we have declared two classes *one* and *two*. The constructors in these classes initialize their *private* data items to a fixed value (*100* in *one* and *200* in *two*). We want the function *accessboth( )* to have access to both these *private* data members. Hence we have made it a *friend* function. It has been declared with the *friend* keyword in both the classes as,

friend int frifunc (alpha, beta) ;

This declaration can be placed either in the *private* section or the *public* section of the class.

An object of each class has been passed as an argument to the function *accessboth( )*. Being a *friend* function it can access the *private* data member of both classes through these arguments.

Though the function doesn't do much, I think the program serves to illustrate the concept.

A function like *accessboth( )* is often called a global friend function. It doesn't belong to either of the two classes (otherwise in its definition we would have been required to use *one::accessboth* or *two::accessboth*) but can access *private* data of both of them. Note that the *friend* declaration is necessary in both the classes. Try commenting it out from class *one*. Immediately the compiler would flash an error that it can't access *data1*, which belongs to class *one*. ·

Note that the function *accessboth( )* has not been declared as global. This is because when we mention *friend* in the class it declares the function and also gives it a *friend* status.

Observe the declaration at the beginning of the program:

class two ;

This declaration is necessary since a class can't be referred to until it has been declared. Class *two* is being referred to in the declaration of the function *accessboth( )* in class one. So *two* must be declared before one. This declaration tells the compiler that the class *two* is defined later.

9.2.2   Static Functions

Firstly, we would use the *static* keyword with data members and then see how it can be used with member functions.

If a data member of a class is declared as *static*, then only one such item is created for the entire class, irrespective of the number of objects created from that class. A *static* data member is useful when all objects of the same class must share a common item of information. A *static* data member is available only within the class, but it continues to live till the time program execution doesn't come to an end. In that sense a *static* data member is similar to the ordinary *static* variable. However, their utility is different. While a normal *static* variable is used to retain information between calls to a function, *static* data members of a class are used to share information among the objects of a class. The following program shows *static* data member at work.

```cpp
#include <iostream.h>

class sample
{
    private :

        static int index ;  // declaration of index
        int count ;

    public:

        sample( )
        {
            index++ ;
            count++ ;
        }

        void showdata( )
        {
            cout << endl << "index = " << index ;
            cout << endl << "count = " << count ;
        }
};
int sample::index = 0 ;  // definition of index

void main( )
{
    sample s1, s2, s3 ;

    s1.showdata( ) ;
    s2.showdata( ) ;
```

```
        s3.showdata( ) ;
}
```

The class *sample* has two data members, *index*, which is of the type *static int*, and *count*, which is a normal *int*. The constructor for this class causes each of them to be incremented. In *main( )* we have defined three objects of class *sample*. Each time an object is created the constructor gets called. Hence, *index* and *count* would get incremented thrice. Another member function, *showdata( )*, displays the current values of *index* and *count*. Here is the output of the program.

```
index = 3
count = -29312
index = 3
count = 645
index = 3
count = -2012
```

As we expected, the value of *index* is reported as *3* for each object, whereas, the value of *count* is reported as *–29312, 645* and *–2012*. This is so because *index* is being shared amongst the three objects, whereas, each object enjoys its own *count*. Since *count* has not been specifically initialised its value is being reported as garbage.

If you observe carefully you would find that *static* data members require an unusual format. Ordinary variables like *count* are declared (the compiler is told about their name and type) and defined (the compiler sets aside memory to hold the variable) in the same statement. *static* data members like *index*, on the other hand, requires two separate statements. The variable's declaration appears in the class declaration, but the variable is actually defined outside the class.

Why such an approach is used for *static* data members? If *static* data members were defined inside the class declaration it would violate the idea that a class declaration is only a blueprint and does not set aside any memory. Defining the *static* member data outside the class also emphasizes two facts:

(a) The memory space for such data is allocated only once, before the program starts executing.

(b) There is only one *static* member variable for the entire class; each object does not have its own version of the variable.

A word of caution! If you include the declaration of a *static* variable but forget its definition, the compiler would pass it, whereas, the linker would tell you that you're trying to reference an undeclared external variable. This happens even if you include the definition, but forget the class name (the *sample::* in the program above).

Lastly, the most important question: when would we be required to use *static* member data? Imagine a situation where an object is required to know how many other objects of its class are in existence. In this case a *static* variable *index* can be included as a member of the class. Being *static*, this variable would be shared by all the objects.

The way we can have *static* data members in a class we can have *static* member functions as well. The following program shows how they can be used.

```
#include <iostream.h>

class sample
{
    private :

        static int count ;
```

```
        public :

            sample( )
            {
                count++ ;
            }

            static void showcount( )
            {
                cout << endl << "count = " << count ;
            }
    } ;

    int sample::count = 0 ;

    void main( )
    {
        sample s1 ;
        sample::showcount( ) ;
        sample s2 ;
        sample::showcount( ) ;
        sample s3 ;
        sample::showcount( ) ;
    }
```

In this program there is a *static* data member, *count*, in the class
sample. It keeps track of how many objects of the class there are.
It is incremented every time an object is constructed. We have
created a function *showcount( )* to display the current value of
count. Problem is how to access this function? We can do so in
two ways:

sample s1 ;

s1.showcount( ) ;
sample::showcount( ) ;

The first way is a little clumsy. We shouldn't need to refer to a specific object when we're doing something that relates to the entire class. The second way is more elegant:

sample ::showcount( ) ;

It's more reasonable to use the name of the class itself with the scope resolution operator. However, for this form to work it is necessary to define *showcount( )* as a *static* member function.

9.2.3   Comparing Macros and Inline Functions

Inline functions are similar to *#define* macros. However, they provide better type checking and do not have the side effects so typically associated with macros. For example consider the following program:

```
#include <iostream.h>

#define SQUARE( x )  x * x

inline float square ( float y )
{
    return y * y ;
}

void main ( )
{
    float a = 0.5, b = 0.5, c, d ;
    c = SQUARE ( ++a ) ;
    d = square ( ++b ) ;
}
```

During preprocessing the macro SQUARE gets expanded into

c = ++x * ++x ;

You can notice the undesirable side effect in this macro expansion: the variable is getting incremented twice even though we have used the incrementation operator only once. Such side effects would not occur in the *inline* function.

Exercises

[A] State True or False:

(a) Virtual functions implement one form of polymorphism.

(b) Virtual functions permit calling of derived class functions using a base class pointer.

(c) Each object has its own VTABLE.

(d) There is only VTABLE per class.

(e) We can access the VTABLE using the *this* pointer.

(f) *this* pointer and *vptr* are same.

(g) There is one *vptr* per VTABLE.

(h) There is one *vptr* per object.

(i) The *vptr* always points to the VTABLE of the class.

(j) Virtual functions permit functions from different classes to be executed through the same function call.

(k) Pure virtual functions can never have a body.

(l) Pure virtual constructors can have a body.

(m) We can never build an object from a class containing a pure virtual function.

(n) A class containing a pure virtual function is called an abstract base class.

(o) Virtual function calls work faster than normal function calls.

(p) In a class hierarchy of several levels if we want a function at any level to be called through a base class pointer then the function must be declared as *virtual* in the base class.

(q) Virtual functions can be safely invoked using objects.

(r) The behaviour of virtual functions is same irrespective of whether we invoke them through pointers or references.

(s) A *static* data member is useful when all objects of the same class must share a common item of information.

(t) If a class has a *static* data member and three objects are created from this class, then each object would have its own *static* data member.

(u) A class can have *static* data members as well as *static* member functions.

(v) A function that is a *friend* of a class can access *private* data member of a class but cannot manipulate them.

[B] What will be the output of the following programs:

(a) #include <iostream.h>

```
class base
{
    public :
```

```cpp
        virtual void fun1( )
        {
                cout << endl << "In base::fun1" ;
        }
};

class derived1 : public base
{
    public :

        void fun1( )
        {
                cout << endl << "In derived::fun1" ;
        }

        virtual void fun2( )
        {
                cout << endl << "In derived1::fun2" ;
        }
};

class derived2 : public derived1
{
    public :

        void fun1( )
        {
                cout << endl << "In derived2::fun1" ;
        }

        void fun2( )
        {
                cout << endl << "In derived2::fun2" ;
        }
};
```

```
        void main( )
        {
            base *ptr1 ;
            derived1 *ptr2 ;
            base b ;
            derived2 d ;

            ptr1 = &b ,
            ptr2 = &d ;

            ptr1->fun1( ) ;
            ptr2->fun1( ) ;

            ( ( derived1 * ) ptr2 )->fun2( ) ;
        }
```

(b)   `#include <iostream.h>`

```
    class base
    {
        public :

            virtual void fun( )
            {
                cout << endl << "In base::fun( )" ;
            }
    };

    class derived1 : virtual public base
    {
        public :

            void fun( )
            {
                cout << endl << "In derived1::fun( )" ;
            }
    };
```

```cpp
class derived2 : virtual public base
{
    public :

        void fun( )
        {
            cout << endl << "In derived2::fun( )" ;
        }
} ;

class derived3 : public derived1, public derived2
{
    public :

        void fun( )
        {
            cout << endl << "In derived3::fun( )" ;
            derived1::fun( ) ;
        }
} ;

void main( )
{
    base *b ;

    derived1 d1 ;
    b = &d1 ;
    b->fun( ) ;

    derived2 d2 ;
    b = &d2 ;
    b->fun( ) ;

    derived3 d3 ;
    b = &d3 ;
    b->fun( ) ;
}
```

(c)
```
#include <iostream.h>

class base
{
    protected :

        int data ;
} ;

class derived1 : virtual public base
{
    protected :

        int data1 ;
} ;

class derived2 : virtual public base
{
    protected :

        int data2 ;
} ;

class derived3 : public derived1, public derived2
{
    private :

        int data3 ;
} ;

void main( )
{
    base b ;
    derived1 d1 ;
    derived2 d2 ;
    derived3 d3 ;

    cout << endl << sizeof ( b ) << endl << sizeof ( d1 )
```

```
            << endl << sizeof ( d2 ) << endl << sizeof ( d3 ) ;
}
```

[C] Answer the following:

(a) What is run-time polymorphism?

(b) In a virtual function scenario would the derived class function get called even when it is called through a non-upcasted pointer?

(c) What are virtual base classes? When should they be used?

(d) When we should declare a function as a *friend* of a class?

(e) How *static* data members are different than non-static data members?

(f) What is the performance penalty in case of late binding of functions?

[D] Attempt the following:

(a) Write a program that contains a class *derived*, derived from *base*. The *base* class should have a virtual function *fun( )* and it should be overridden in *derived*. Try to call *fun( )* from the constructor of the derived class and watch the results.

(b) A publication company has implemented a discount system for books. Company has three types of customers: library, shops and individuals. Libraries get 30 % discount, shops get 15 % discount and individuals get 10 % discount. The type of customer is known at runtime. According to the customer, appropriate discount should be given. To implement this system, design a class named *books* that has a member function *discount( )*. Inherit three classes *library*, *shop* and *individual* from *books* class. Override the *discount( )* function in these classes. The *discount( )* function should display a message specifying the percentage of discount. Define the *discount( )* function in such a way that if address of derived class's object is stored in pointer to the *books* class's object, derived class's *discount( )* function should get called.

10
Streams

10.1   Understanding Streams

We had an introduction to streams in Chapter 2. As discussed in Chapter 2, a stream is a general name given to the flow of data. Streams provide an interface independent to the device from which data is accessed. A stream can either be an input stream, an output stream or both. As the names suggest, data can be read from an input stream or written to an output stream. Likewise, data can be read from or written to an input-output stream. Input data comes to the input stream from any input device like keyboard. The output data from the output stream goes to the screen or any other output device. Using a stream we can access and manipulate input/output data. We have been frequently using *cin* and *cout* in our programs. *cin* represents an input stream since it is used to input data from keyboard. *cout*, on the other hand, represents output stream because it sends data to the output device. Strictly speaking, *cin* is an object of *istream_withassign* class, whereas, *cout* is an object of *ostream_withassign* class,

10.1.1   Stream Class Hierarchy

The C++ input/output stream library contains a hierarchy of classes. These classes are declared in 'iostream.h' file. Figure 10.1 shows some of the important classes of the I/O stream library.

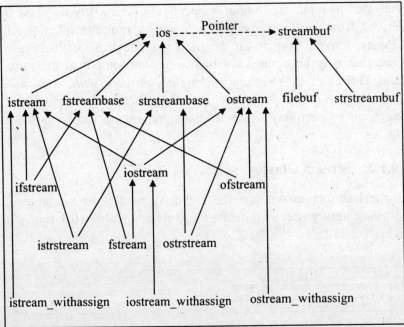

Figure 10.1. *Hierarchy of stream classes.*

As seen from Figure 10.1 the I/O specification class (*ios*) is at the root of the *iostream* class hierarchy. This class contains features that are common to all streams. There include flags for formatting the stream data, the error-status flags and the file operation mode. We would soon examine these in detail.

The *ios* class contains a pointer to the *streambuf* class, which contains the actual memory buffer into which data is read or written, and the routines to handle its data. Usually, you don't need to worry about the *streambuf* class, which is referenced automatically by other classes. However, if required you can access the buffer by calling the member functions of the *streambuf* class.

The *istream* and *ostream* classes are derived from *ios* and are dedicated to input and output, respectively. The *iostream* class is derived from both *istream* and *ostream* by multiple inheritance. Classes derived from it can be used with devices, such as disk files, that may be opened for both input and output at the same time. Three classes—*istream_withassign*, *ostream_withassign*, and *iostream_withassign*—are inherited from *istream*, *ostream*, and *iostream*, respectively. They add assignment operators to these classes.

10.1.2   Stream Classes

In the last section we saw the hierarchy of classes available in *iostream* library. Let us reiterate these classes. Table 10.1 shows it in brief.

Class	What It Does
streambuf	Provides methods for memory buffers
ios	Handles stream state variables and errors
istream	Handles formatted and unformatted character conversions *from* a *streambuf*
ostream	Handles formatted and unformatted character conversions *to* a *streambuf*
iostream	Combines *istream* and *ostream* to handle bi-directional operations on a single stream
istream_withassign	Provides copy constructor and assignment operators for the *cin* stream
ostream_withassign	Provides copy constructor and assignment operators for *cout*, *cerr* and *clog*

Table 10.1. *The stream classes.*

10.1.3 Header Files

The standard C++ I/O classes are distributed in several headers. They are shown in Table 10.2.

Header	Used for
<fstream>	File I/O
<iomanip>	Manipulators with arguments
<ios>	Basic I/O support
<iosfwd>	Forward declarations used by I/O system
<iostream>	General I/O
<istream>	Input stream
<ostream>	Output stream
<sstream>	String streams
<streambuf>	Low-level I/O support

Table 10.2. *The I/O header files.*

10.1.4 Ios flags

As said earlier, the *ios* class contains data members that help formatting of stream data, the error-status flags and the file operation mode. Some of the data used for formatting is stored in variables. For example, the floating-point precision, the output field width, and the character used to pad the output. The rest of the formatting is determined by flags, which are usually combined to save space. Table 10.3 gives a complete list of the formatting flags.

Flag	Meaning
skipws	Skip (ignore) whitespace (For input; this is the default)

showbase	Use base indicator on output (0 for octal, 0x for hex)
showpoint	Show decimal point and trailing zeros for floats in output
uppercase	Use uppercase A-F for hex values and E for scientific values
showpos	Display + before positive integers
unitbuf	Unit Buffering. Flush all streams after each insertion
stdio	Synchronize the stream with C standard I/O system
dec	Convert to decimal
oct	Convert to octal
hex	Convert to hexadecimal
left	Left justify output
right	Right justify output
internal	Use padding between sign or base indicator and number
scientific	Use exponential format on floating-point output
fixed	Use fixed format on floating-point output
boolalpha	Convert *bool* to "true" or "false" strings

Table 10.3. *ios formatting flags.*

There are two types of flags:

(a) On/Off flags
(b) Flags that work in a group

The on/off flags are simple. They can be turned on through the *setf( )* function and off through the *unsetf( )* function. For example, by default a string is displayed right justified. If we are to left-justify it we can say,

```
cout.setf ( ios::left ) ;
cout << "Open your eyes. Donate them!"
```

To remove the left justification for subsequent output we can say,

```
cout.unsetf ( ios::left ) ;
```

The flags that can be set/unset in this manner include *skipws*, *showbase*, *showpoint*, *uppercase*, *showpos*, *unitbuf* and *stdio*.

The second type of formatting flags work in a group. You can have only one of these flags on at a time. To set these flags you must use the second form of *setf( )* function. For example, there's a flag for each of the number bases: hexadecimal, decimal, and octal. Collectively, these flags are referred to as the *ios::basefield*. If the *ios::dec* flag is set and you call *setf (ios::hex)*, you'll set the *ios::hex* flag, but you won't clear the *ios::dec* bit, resulting in undefined behavior. The proper thing to do is call the another form of *setf( )* like this:

```
cout.setf ( ios::hex, ios::basefield ) ;
```

This call first clears all the bits in the *ios::basefield*, then sets *ios::hex*.

Similarly, the flags *scientific* and *fixed* are referred to as *ios::floatfield*. Also, the flags *left*, *right* and *internal* are collectively referred as *ios::adjustfield*. The following code snippet shows use of these group flags.

```
float a = 3.142800 ;
cout.setf ( ios::scientific, ios::floatfield ) ;
cout << a << endl ;
cout.setf ( ios::left, ios::adjustfield ) ;
cout << "Diamonds are for ever" ;
```

There are data members in the *ios* class that control the width of the output field, the fill character used when the data doesn't fill the output field, and the precision for printing floating-point numbers. The values of these variables can be read and written by member functions of the same name. A list of these functions is given in Table 10.4.

Function	Effect
int ios::width( )	Reads the current width. (Default is 0.)
int ios::width (int n)	Sets the width, returns the previous width.
int ios::fill( )	Reads the current fill character, (Default is space).
int ios::fill (int n)	Sects the fill character, returns the previous fill character.
int ios::precision( )	Read current floating-point precision (Default is 6)
int ios::precision (int n)	Sets floating-point precision, returns previous precision.

Table 10.4. *ios formatting functions.*

A small note about the field width values. When the specified width is less than the number of characters that represent the value the specified width is ignored. Thus, if you try to print 412 with a width of two, you'll still get 412. The field width specifies a minimum number of characters; there's no way to specify a maximum number.

Also, the width is reset to zero by each insertion and extraction. If we want to have a constant width, we need to call *width( )* after each insertion or extraction.

Let us now put together all that we have learnt about stream formatting in a program. Carefully go through the program and the output that follows it. I am sure it would clarify your understanding of the *iostream* formatting.

```
#include <iostream.h>
#include <conio.h>

void main( )
{
    int i = 52 ;
    float a = 425.0 ;
    float b = 123.500328 ;
    char str[ ] = "Dream. Then make it happen!" ;

    clrscr( ) ;
    cout.setf ( ios::unitbuf ) ;
    cout.setf ( ios::stdio ) ;

    cout.setf ( ios::showpos ) ;
    cout << i << endl ;

    cout.setf ( ios::showbase ) ;
    cout.setf ( ios::uppercase ) ;
    cout.setf ( ios::hex, ios::basefield ) ;
    cout << i << endl ;

    cout.setf ( ios::oct, ios::basefield ) ;
    cout << i << endl ;

    cout.fill ( '0' ) ;
    cout << "Fill character: " << cout.fill( ) << endl ;

    cout.setf ( ios::dec, ios::basefield ) ;
    cout.width ( 10 ) ;
    cout << i << endl ;

    cout.setf ( ios::left, ios::adjustfield ) ;
    cout.width ( 10 ) ;
    cout << i << endl ;

    cout.setf ( ios::internal, ios::adjustfield ) ;
    cout.width ( 10 ) ;
```

```
cout << i << endl ;
cout << i << endl ; // without width ( 10 )

cout.width ( 10 ) ;
cout << str << endl ;
cout.width ( 40 ) ;
cout << str << endl ;
cout.setf ( ios::left, ios::adjustfield ) ;
cout.width ( 40 ) ;
cout << str << endl ;

cout.precision ( 6 ) ;
cout << "Precision: " << cout.precision( ) ;
cout.setf ( ios::showpoint ) ;
cout.unsetf ( ios::showpos ) ;
cout << endl << a ;
cout.unsetf ( ios::showpoint ) ;
cout << endl << a ;

cout.setf ( ios::fixed, ios::floatfield ) ;
cout << endl << b ;
cout.setf ( ios::scientific, ios::floatfield ) ;
cout << endl << b ;

b = 5.375 ;
cout.precision ( 14 ) ;
cout.setf ( ios::fixed, ios::floatfield ) ;
cout << endl << b ;
cout.setf ( ios::scientific, ios::floatfield ) ;
cout << endl << b ;

cout.unsetf ( ios::showpoint ) ;
cout.unsetf ( ios::unitbuf ) ;
cout.unsetf ( ios::stdio ) ;
}
```

Here is the output of the program...

```
+52
0X34
064
Fill character: 0
0000000+52
+520000000
+000000052
+52
Dream. Then make it happen!
0000000000000Dream. Then make it happen!
Dream. Then make it happen!0000000000000
Precision: +6
425.000000
425
123.500328
1.235003E+02
5.375
5.375E+00
```

Most of the output is self-explanatory. The *unitbuf* and *stdio* flag deserve some explanation. The unit buffering should be turned on when we want to ensure that each character is output as soon as it is inserted into an output stream. You can also use unbuffered output, but unit buffering provides better performance.

The *ios::stdio* flag is used when you have a program that uses both iostreams and the C standard I/O library (not unlikely if you're using C libraries). If you discover your *iostream* output and *printf( )* output are occurring in the wrong order, try setting this flag.

The value of any format flag can be enquired using *ios::flags( )* member function. This function takes no arguments and returns a *long* (*typedef*ed to *fmtflags*) that contains the current format flags.

10.1.5   Stream Manipulators

We have seen what manipulators are in Chapter 2. We know that
manipulators are of two types—those that take an argument and
those that don't. We have used predefined manipulators belonging
to both these categories in Chapter 2. However, so far we have not
seen how to create our own manipulators. We would demonstrate
how to create both types of manipulators—those that do not take
arguments and those that do. Let us begin with the first one.

To understand how to develop a zero-argument manipulator we
need to understand the internal working of some existing
manipulator, say *endl. endl* is simply a function that take as its
argument an *ostream* reference. The declaration for *endl( )* in
'iostream.h' looks like this.

ostream& endl (ostream&) ;

Consider the statement

cout << endl ;

Since << is an overloaded operator, internally this statement
becomes,

cout.operator << (endl) ;

endl( ) being a function what is being passed to the overloaded
operator is a pointer to a function. The << operator has been
defined in 'iostream.h' as follows:

ostream & ostream::operator << (ostream & (*_f) (ostream &))
{
        return (*_f)(*this) ;
}

This indicates that when we pass the address of *endl( )* to this
function it collects it in a pointer to a function that receives an
ostream reference and returns an *ostream* reference. If you observe

carefully this matches the prototype of the *endl( )* function. Since this operator function is called through the *cout* object the *this* pointer contains the address of *cout*. Hence **this* yields the object. This object is then passed to the *endl( )* function through the statement.

(*_f)(*this) ;

On getting called all that the *endl( )* function does is emit a '\n' to the output stream.

Simple enough! Now we can proceed to develop our own manipulator called *tab*. Here it is.

```
#include <iostream.h>
ostream & tab ( ostream &o )
{
    return o << '\t' ;
}

void main( )
{
    cout << "Don't" ;
    cout << tab << tab ;
    cout << "panic" ;
}
```

This program works exactly on the similar lines as the previous one. The only difference is instead of calling the function *endl( )*, here the *tab( )* function gets called. Trace the flow of control in the program. This would help you understand its working better.

User-defined Manipulators with Arguments

As we saw in the previous section it is easy to create zero-argument manipulators. However, the way to create manipulators with arguments is pretty convoluted. Hence, let us try to understand it with an example. Here we would try to create a manipulator called *roman* which would receive an *unsigned long* as an argument and output its roman equivalent. To implement this *roman( )* manipulator we need to define a class called *roman*. This class consists of a constructor and an overloaded << operator function. This function has been implemented as a *friend* function.

Take a look at the listing of the program that defines and uses the *roman* class.

```cpp
#include <iostream.h>

class roman
{
    private :

        unsigned long num ;

    public :

        roman ( unsigned long n ) ;
        friend ostream & operator << ( ostream& o, roman& r ) ;
} ;

roman::roman ( unsigned long n )
{
    num = n ;
}

ostream & operator << ( ostream& o, roman& r )
{
    struct key
    {
        char ch ;
        int val ;
    } ;
    key z[ ] = {
```

```
                'm', 1000,
                'd', 500,
                'c', 100,
                'l', 50,
                'x', 10,
                'v', 5,
                'i', 1
            } ;
    int sz ;
    int k ;

    sz = sizeof ( z ) / sizeof ( z [ 0 ] ) ;

    for ( int i = 0 ; i < sz ; i++ )
    {
        k = r.num / z [ i ].val ;
        for ( int j = 1 ; j <= k ; j++ )
            o << z [ i ].ch ;

        r.num = r.num % z [ i ].val ;
    }
    return o ;
}

void main( )
{
    long yr = 1999 ;
    cout << roman ( yr ) ;
    cout << endl << roman ( 1752 ) << endl ;
}
```

Observe the following statement carefully

```
cout << roman ( yr ) ;
```

Here *roman (yr)* creates a temporary object of the type *roman*. Naturally, while creating this temporary object the constructor gets called and the value passed to it gets set in the *private* variable *num*. This temporary object and the *cout* object are then passed to the overloaded *operator <<( )* function. Note that in case of a *friend* the call to the operator function *doesn't* get converted into the form

cout.operator << (roman (yr)) ;

Within the operator function we have converted the value in *num* into its roman equivalent and outputted it using the reference of the *cout* object. At the end we have returned the reference. This returning of reference is necessary if we are to use the manipulator in a cascaded *cout* like

cout << endl << roman (1752) << endl ;

Thus we can implement any other manipulator with an argument— by developing a class for it. Does this mean that for every one-argument manipulator provided by the *iostream* library there is a separate class? Yes. However, instead of writing a separate class for each manipulator, the writers of the *iostream* library have put together a generic class hidden behind a complicated set of *#define*s in the file 'iomanip.h'. You can examine this file and try to understand this generic class.

10.2   Types of I/O Streams

In this section we would discuss various types of streams.

10.2.1   String Streams

A string stream allows the string to act as an internal text file. For string I/O we have an input stream, an output stream or a stream that does both simultaneously. The iostreams library provides different types of classes to perform string I/O. They are *istringstream*, *ostringstream*, and *stringstream*. These classes are declared in the header *<sstream>*. The string stream classes work with the standard C++ *string* class. For extracting characters from a string stream, we must create an *istringstream* object. For writing characters into a string stream, we must create an *ostringstream* object.

Following program shows how to use input string stream class *istringstream*.

```
#include <sstream>
#include <string.h>
#include <iostream.h>

using namespace std ;

void main( )
{
    istringstream is ( "260 125.00, C++Quiz" ) ;
    int pg ;
    double pr ;

    is >> pg >> pr ;

    string n ;
    is >> n ;
    cout << pg << endl << pr << endl << n.data( ) ;
}
```

You can understand that using string stream is a flexible and general approach to transform the value in string to the typed values. The string is delimited by a whitespace. So, the variables *pg* and *pr* would contain the first two values i.e *260* and *125.00*. *n* would contain the string 'C++Quiz'.

Here is the program that shows output string at work.

```
#include <iostream.h>
#include <sstream>
```

```
#include <string.h>

using namespace std ;

void main( )
{
    ostringstream os ;
    os << "Hello!\t" << 44 << '\t' << 3.14f ;
    string s = os.str( ) ;

    int i ;
    float j ;
    string t ;

    istringstream is ( s ) ;
    is >> t >> i >> j ;
    cout << t.data( ) << endl << i << endl << j << endl ;
}
```

Here, we have passed a string, an *int* and a *float* value to the output string. These values are then stored in a *string* object. We have then created an input string and associated the string with input string. Next, we have transformed the value to the typed variables and displayed them.

If we wish to perform both input and output using single object we can use the *stringstream* class.

10.2.2   Character Streams

We have already learnt how to input/output characters to the *istream* and *ostream* streams in Chapter 2. We have used the *get( )* and *put( )* functions for reading and writing a character respectively.

Reading/Writing characters with respect to file is discussed in section 10.2.4.

10.2.3 Object Streams

The term 'object stream' means writing an entire object to the output string and reading the object from the input stream. In other words if we have an object *c1* of class *complex*, then we can display it through the statement

cout << c1 ;

Or we can read it by saying,

cin >> c1 ;

This makes the user-defined types' handling similar to that of basic data types. To achieve this, we need to overload the << and >> operators. The following program shows how this overloading can be achieved.

```
#include <iostream.h>
class complex
{
    private :

        double real, imag ;

    public :

        complex( )
        {
        }

        complex ( double r, double i )
        {
            real = r ;
            imag = i ;
        }

        friend ostream& operator << ( ostream& s, complex& c ) ;
        friend istream& operator >> ( istream& s, complex& c ) ;
```

```
};

ostream& operator << ( ostream& s, complex& c )
{
    s << "(" << c.real << ", " << c.imag << ")" ;
    return s ;
}

istream& operator >> ( istream& s, complex& c )
{
    s >> c.real >> c.imag ;
    return s ;
}

void main( )
{
    complex c1 ( 1.5, 2.5 ), c2 ( 3.5, 4.5 ), c3 ;
    cout << endl << "c1 = " << c1 << endl << "c2 = " << c2 ;
    cout << endl << "Enter a complex number: " ;
    cin >> c3 ;
    cout << "c3 = " << c3 ;
}
```

You may note that the statements

```
cout << endl << "c1 = " << c1 << endl << "c2 = " << c2 ;
cout << endl << "Enter a complex number: " ;
cin >> c3 ;
cout << "c3 = " << c3 ;
```

are much more expressive and are similar to the way we would perform I/O with standard data types.

Here we have defined two *friend* functions *operator << ( )* and *operator >> ( )*. Since the *friend* declaration of these functions occurs only in the *complex* class and not in *istream* or *ostream* classes these functions can access only the *public* data of the *complex* class.

The operator functions are not members of the class *complex*. Hence the statement *cin >> c3 doesn't* get converted into the form

cin.operator >> (c3)

The object on either side of >> gets passed to the operator function. Both are collected as references. This prevents creation of copies of these objects. The *complex* object accesses the *private* data of the *complex* class. The function returns the *istream* object by reference to permit cascading, as in

cin >> c4 >> c5 ;

Exactly same argument applies to the *operator << ( )* function.

10.2.4   File Streams

Almost all programs need to carry out disk file I/O. To carry out reading/writing from/to files we need to use another set of classes. These are given in Table 10.5.

Class	Derived From	Purpose
ifstream	istream, fstreambase	Input from file
ofstream	ostream, fstreambase	Output to file
fstream	iostream, fstreambase	Both input and output

Table 10.5. *File stream classes.*

The *ifstream*, *ofstream* and *fstream* classes are declared in the file 'fstream.h'.

Let us now look at a simple program that writes standard data types to a disk file and then reads them back and displays them on the screen.

```cpp
#include <fstream.h>

void main( )
{
    // create file for output
    ofstream outfile ( "SAMPLE.TXT" ) ;

    char ch = 'Z' ;
    int i = 25 ;
    float a = 473.14 ;
    char str[ ] = "Hyperbole!" ;

    // send data to file
    outfile << ch << endl << i << endl << a << endl << str ;

    outfile.close( ) ;

    ifstream infile ( "SAMPLE.TXT" ) ;

    //  read data from file
    infile >> ch >> i >> a >> str ;

    //  send data to screen
    cout << ch << endl << i << endl << a << endl << str ;
}
```

Opening File

To begin with, we have defined an object called *outfile* of type *ofstream* class through the statement

```cpp
ofstream outfile ( "SAMPLE.TXT" ) ;
```

This invokes the one argument constructor of the *ofstream* class. This constructor allocates resources and opens the file SAMPLE.TXT. But we didn't mention whether the file is to be opened for reading or writing. This is not necessary since the constructor uses the defaults. The prototype of the constructor looks like this.

```
ofstream ( const char*, int = ios::out, int = filebuf::openprot ) ;
```

When we do not pass the second parameter to this constructor it uses the *ios::out* as the default file opening mode. Hence the file gets opened for writing.

The third parameter corresponds to the access permission under DOS, and it is used unless *ios::nocreate* is specified in the file opening mode. The default value is set to read and write permission.

Sometimes, we may not know the name of the file when the *ofstream* object is created. In such a case we may first create the object and then call *ofstream::open( )* function to open the file. This procedure is shown below.

```
ofstream outfile ;
outfile.open ( "SAMPLE.TXT" ) ;
```

Once again we have not mentioned the file opening mode. The reason is same–*ios::out* has been binarily included (ORed) into the mode (second parameter).

Later when the file is opened for reading once again a one-argument constructor of *ifstream* class is invoked. This constructor uses the *ios::in* by default to open the file for input.

Writing Data

The insertion operator << has been appropriately overloaded in the *ostream* class (from which *ofstream* is derived) to write different data types to the relevant stream. We can use the same operator functions to output data to the file. This we have done through the statement

```
outfile << ch << endl << i << endl << a << endl << str ;
```

Note that while writing this data we have separated each data item from the other using a newline. This is necessary because when we attempt to write numbers like 25 and 473.14 they are written as numeric strings. That is, 473.14 is written as '4', '7', '3', '.', '1', '4'. This results into two disadvantages:

(a) 473.14, which occupied only four bytes in memory ends up occupying 6 bytes in the file. This means more the number of digits in the number more space would it demand in the file.

(b) Every data item needs to be separated from the other using a delimiter (usually '\n'). This is necessary otherwise while reading the file it would not be possible for the extraction operator to figure out where one number is ending and the other beginning. Also, using this method if we write a multiword string, during extraction only the first word of the string would be read back.

Reading Data

For reading the data back we have built an object of the *istream* class. Constructor of this object opens the 'SAMPLE.TXT' file for reading. Once opened we have used the overloaded extraction operator of the class *istream* to read the data from the file. The '\n' written at the end of every data item helps the overloaded operator to distinguish the various items. When the numeric strings are read back from the file they are converted back to their binary representation for storage in program variables.

Closing File

We have specifically closed the file once writing is over by calling the function *ostream::close( )*. This is necessary since we wanted to open the same file for reading. Ideally, we should have opened the file for reading as well as writing. This file opening mode we would see later.

Note that we didn't close the file once reading from the file was over. This is because on termination of the program the *infile* object goes out of scope. As a result, the destructor gets called which closes the file.

The *ifstream*, *ofstream*, and *fstream* classes are declared in the header file 'fstream.h'. This file also includes the 'iostream.h' header file, so there is no need to include it explicitly.

A Better way

Not being able to read multi-word strings is a serious limitation. We can overcome it by using the *getline( )* function in place of the extraction operator as shown below.

```
#include <fstream.h>

void main( )
{
    // create file for output
    ofstream outfile ( "SAMPLE.TXT" );

    // send text to file
    outfile << "You should be enthusiastic about your future\n" ;
    outfile << "That is where you are going to spend the rest of your life\n" ;

    outfile.close( ) ;

    const int MAX = 100 ;
```

```
char str [ MAX ] ;

// create file for input
ifstream infile ( "SAMPLE.TXT" ) ;

// so long as end of file is not encountered
while ( !infile.eof( ) )
{
    // read a line of text
    infile.getline ( str, MAX ) ;

    // display the text read from the file
    cout << endl << str ;
}
}
```

Here we have read the text from the file one line at a time using the *getline( )* function. This function is a member of *istream* (from which *ifstream* is derived). It reads characters until it encounters the end of line character, '\n', and places the resulting string in the buffer *str* supplied as an argument. The maximum size of the buffer is given as the second argument. The contents of the buffer are displayed after each line is read. This goes on till all the lines have been read.

Detecting End Of File

Within the *while* loop we keep checking whether we are through with reading the entire contents of the file. For this we have called the function *ifstream::eof( )*. This function returns a value zero if the end of file is reached, non-zero otherwise.

At times the same effect can be obtained through a statement like .

while (infile)

It seems truly magical that in this case a zero or non-zero value is correctly returned. Let us try to understand what is happening behind the screen. When the statement *while (infile)* gets executed the following function gets called

```
ios::operator void * ( )
{
    return fail( ) ? 0 : this ;
}
```

This is a conversion function that tries to convert an *ifstream* object into a *void* pointer. Within it, it calls a *ios::fail( )* function which looks like this:

```
int fail( )
{
    return state & ( failbit | badbit | hardfail ) ;
}
```

Here *state* is an *ios* class variable and what is being tested is the status of various error flags (these are discussed towards the end of this chapter). If this function returns a non-zero value (meaning end of file is not reached) then the conversion function simply returns the address of the object (*this*), otherwise it returns a zero. It is this address or zero that is checked in the *while* loop. If zero is returned the control jumps out of the *while* loop.

Note that the address returned has no significance except to be tested for a zero or non-zero value.

A Filecopy Program

Let us now try to write a program that copies the contents of one file into another. To perform file copying we would read the source file character by character and keep writing every character read to the target file. The process would continue till the end of file is not reached. Here is the program.

```
#include <fstream.h>
void main( )
{
    char source [ 67 ], target [ 67 ] ;  // max allowable path length usually 66
    char ch ;

    cout << endl << "Enter source filename" ;
    cin >> source ;

    cout << endl << "Enter target filename" ;
    cin >> target ;

    // create file for input
    ifstream infile ( source ) ;

    // create file for output
    ofstream outfile ( target ) ;

    // continue reading file until EOF is reached
    while ( infile )
    {
        infile.get ( ch ) ;
        outfile.put ( ch ) ;
    }
}
```

Here the characters are read using the *istream::get( )* function and they are written to the target file using *ostream::put( )*.

File Opening Modes

So far we have opened a stream object either for reading or for writing. There are several other modes in which a stream object can be opened. Each mode is defined by a bit in the *ios* class. We can combine these bits using the logical OR operator. Each combination of mode bits specifies various aspects of how a stream object will be opened. Table 10.6 shows the various possibilities.

Mode Bit	Result
in	Open for reading (default for *ifstream*)
out	Open for writing (default for *ofstream*)
ate	Start reading or writing at end of file (AT End)
app	Start writing at end of file (APPend)
trunc	Truncate file to zero length if it exists (TRUNCate)
norcreate	Error when opening if file does not already exist
noreplace	Error when opening for output if file already exists, unless *ate* or *app* is set
binary	Open file in binary (not text) mode

Table 10.6. *File opening modes.*

If we want to preserve whatever was in the file we should use *ios::app*. In this case whatever we write to the file will be added at the end of the existing contents.

If we want to perform both input and output on the file in binary mode we can use the following open command.

```
fstream file ;
file.open ( filename, ios::in | ios::out | ios::binary ) ;
```

The vertical bars between the flags cause the bits representing these flags to be logically combined into a single integer, so that several flags can be applied simultaneously.

Quick now! Can you suggest the bit flag combination for opening a file for reading as well as writing? If the file does not exist a new one should get created, whereas if it already exists then it should not get overwritten. The answer is

```
fstream file ;
file.open ( filename, ios::in | ios::out | ios::noreplace ) ;
```

Binary I/O

Imagine that we wish to read/write records from/to file. Assume that each record contains employee information like name, age, basic salary and gross salary. If we use the overloaded operator << to write such records we would end up consuming more space for a record on the disk as compared to the space occupied by the same record in memory. This is because normally each number (integer or float) is written as a character string rather than as binary bits of the number. If the records were huge in number this would lead to a lot of wastage of precious disk space. If we are to avoid this we need to open the file in binary mode and then carry out the record input/output. The following program shows how this can be achieved.

```
#include <fstream.h>

void main( )
{
    struct employee
    {
        char name [ 20 ] ;
        int age ;
        float basic ;
        float gross ;
    } ;
    employee e ;
```

```
char ch = 'Y' ;

// create file for output
ofstream outfile ;
outfile.open ( "EMPLOYEE.DAT", ios::out | ios::binary ) ;

while ( ch == 'Y' )
{
    cout << endl << "Enter a record" ;
    cin >> e.name >> e.age >> e.basic >> e.gross ;
    outfile.write ( ( char * ) &e, sizeof ( e ) ) ;
    cout << endl << "Add another Y/N" ;
    cin >> ch ;
}

outfile.close( ) ;

// create file for input
ifstream infile ;
infile.open ( "EMPLOYEE.DAT", ios::in | ios::binary ) ;

while ( infile.read ( ( char * ) &e, sizeof ( e ) ) )
{
    cout << endl << e.name << '\t' << e.age << '\t'
        << e.basic << '\t' << e.gross ;
}
}
```

On execution the program asks the user to enter employee records. Each record entered is written to disk using the *ofstream::write( )* function. Once all the records are written the file is closed. The same file is then opened for reading in binary mode and it is read record by record. Every record read is displayed on the screen.

We have used two new functions here: *write( )*, a member of *ofstream*; and *read( )*, a member of *ifstream*. These functions think about data in terms of bytes. They don't care how the data is formatted, they simply transfer a buffer full of bytes from and to a disk file. Consider the call to *write( )*.

```
outfile.write ( ( char * ) &e, sizeof ( e ) ) ;
```

Here we are trying to tell *write( )* to write everything from the address given by *&e* upto the next *sizeof (e)* bytes. Note that it is necessary to cast the address passed to *write( )* into a *char **, since *write( )* doesn't know about an *employee **.

The parameters passed to *read( )* are identical to the ones passed to *write( )*—the address of the data buffer and its length in bytes.

Exercises

[A] State True or False:

(a) In the *iostream* library the *ios* class is at the root.

(b) Some of the *ios* flags can be set either through the *setf( )* function or through the manipulators.

(c) Only for those manipulators which need an argument we need to include the file 'iomanip.h'.

(d) When we are using a manipulator we are in fact calling a member function.

(e) It is possible to create your own manipulators.

(f) The *istream_withassign* class has been derived from the *istream* class and overloaded assignment operator has been added to it.

(g) *cout* and *cin* are predefined stream objects.

(h) Objects can read and write themselves.

(i) *strstreams* serve the same purpose as *sprintf( )* and *sscanf( )*.

(j) The *istream::getline( )* function cannot tackle multi-words strings.

[B] Answer the following:

(a) Draw a chart showing hierarchy of various classes in the *iostream* library.

(b) What are the three parts of an *iostream* system?

(c) Why is *ios::* necessary in the following statement:

cout << setiosflags (ios::showbase) ;

(d) How can the following statement work for testing the end of file, if *infile* is an *ifstream* object:

while (infile) ;

(e) What do the *nocreate* and *noreplace* flag ensure when they are used for opening a file?

(f) What problem do you think would we face if the following code is executed twice:

```
file.seekg ( 0L, ios::beg ) ;
while ( file.read ( char * ) &p, sizeof ( p ) )
    cout << t.name << endl << p.age ;
```

How would you solve the problem?

(g) How would you obtain the value of a *state* variable?

[C] What would be the output of the following programs:

(a)
```
#include <iostream.h>
void main( )
{
    char str[ ] = "The boring stuff" ;
```

```
        char *p = "That's interesting" ;
        cout << endl << str :
        cout << endl << p :


        cout << endl << ( void * ) str ;
        cout << endl << ( void * ) p :
    }
```

(b) ```
     #include <iostream.h>
     void main( )
     {
         int i = 650 ;
         float a = 425.123 ;
         cout << setiosflags (ios::showbase | ios::uppercase) ;
         cout << hex << i << endl ;
         cout.precision (4) ;
         cout << setiosflags (ios::showpoint) << a ;
     }
     ```

(c)  ```
     #include <iostream.h>
     void main( )
     {
         char str[ ] = "Just listing" ;
         cout.width ( 40 ) ;
         cout << str << endl ;
         cout.setf ( ios::left, ios::adjustfield ) ;
         cout.width ( 40 ) ;
         cout << str ;
     }
     ```

[D] Attempt the Following:

(a) Write a program that will create a manipulator with arguments. If row number and column number are passed as arguments to this manipulator it should position the cursor at that row and column.

(b) There are 100 records present in a file with each record containing a 6-character item code, a 20-character item name and an integer quantity. Write a program to read these records, arrange them in the ascending order and write them in the same file overwriting the earlier records.

11
Exception Handling

11.1   Exception Handling Mechanism

Exceptions are errors that occur at run time. The reasons why exceptions occur are numerous. Some of the more common ones are:

(a)   Falling short of memory
(b)   Inability to open a file
(c)   Exceeding the bounds of an array
(d)   Attempting to initialize an object to an impossible value

When such exceptions occur, the programmer has to decide a strategy according to which he would handle the exceptions. The strategies could be, displaying the error messages on the screen, or displaying a dialog box in case of a GUI environment, or requesting the user to supply better data or simply terminating the program execution.

Usually C programmers deal with exceptions in two ways:

(a)   Following the function calls with error checks on return values to find whether the function did its job properly or not.

(b)   Using the *setjmp* and *longjmp* mechanism. This approach is intended to intercept and handle conditions that do not require immediate program termination. For example, if a recursive descent parser detects an error, it should report it and continue with further processing.

C++ provides a systematic, object-oriented approach to handling run-time errors generated by C++ classes. The exception mechanism of C++ uses three new keywords: *throw*, *catch*, and *try*. Also, we need to create a new kind of entity called an *exception class*.

Suppose we have an application that works with objects of a certain class. If during the course of execution of a member function of this class an error occurs, then this member function informs the application that an error has occurred. This process of informing is called *throwing* an exception. In the application we have to create a separate section of code to tackle the error. This section of code is called an *exception handler* or a *catch block*. Any code in the application that uses objects of the class is enclosed in a *try block*. Errors generated in the *try* block are caught in the *catch* block. Code that doesn't interact with the class need not be in a *try* block. The following code shows the organisation of these blocks. It is not a working program, but it clearly shows how and where the various elements of the exception mechanism are placed.

```
class sample
{
    public :

        // exception class
        class errorclass
        {
        };

        void fun( )
        {
            if ( some error occurs )
                throw errorclass( ) ;  // throws exception
        }
};

// application
void main( )
{
    // try block
    try
    {
        sample s ;
        s.fun( ) ;
```

```
      }
      catch ( sampel :: errorclass )      // exception handler or catch block
      {
            // do something about the error
      }
}
```

Here *sample* is any class in which errors might occur. An exception class called *errorclass*, is specified in the *public* part of *sample*. In *main( )* we have enclosed part of the program that uses *sample* in a *try* block. If an error occurs in *sample::fun( )* we throw an exception, using the keyword *throw* followed by the constructor for the *errorclass*:

```
throw errorclass( ) ;
```

When an exception is thrown control goes to the *catch* block that immediately follows the *try* block.

11.1.1   Try Block

The keyword *try* is used to declare the *try* block followed by a pair of braces. It contains code that may raise an exception. The code in the *try* block executes until a statement that raises an exception is encountered. The syntax of the *try* block is given below:

```
try
{
      // statements that may throw exception
}.
```

If an exception is thrown control jumps to the *catch* block. It never returns back to the *try* block.

The *try* block may also contain a call to the function that can throw an exception. A *try* block is always associated with a *catch* block.

11.1.2 Catch Handler

When an exception is encountered, the program flow shifts to the *catch* block. The *catch* block handles the exception by executing the code written in it. The syntax of the *catch* block is given below.

```
catch ( type arg )
{
    // statements that handle exception
}
```

Note that an exception is actually an object that contains information about the error. If the type of object matches the type given in *catch* the statements in the *catch* block get executed. If the exception is not thrown the control directly goes to the statement after *catch* block. Following program illustrates the usage of try-catch blocks.

```
#include <iostream.h>
class excep
{
};

class math
{
    public :

        int fun ( int n, int d )
        {
            if ( d == 0 )
            {
                throw new excep( ) ;
            }

            return n / d ;
```

```
        }
};

void main( )
{
    int  num = 120,  div = 0 ;
    math  e ;

    try
    {
        int res = e.fun ( num. div ) ;
    }
    catch ( excep  *m )
    {
        cout << "Divide by zero error" ;
    }

    cout << endl << "reached here " ;
}
```

In this program we have done exception handling for a divide by
zero error. The *try* block contains a call to the *fun( )* member
function. In the *fun( )* function if the denominator is zero an
exception of type *excep* is thrown. The exception is caught in the
catch block and the message "Divide by zero error" is displayed.
After the execution of *catch* block control falls to the next
statement and the message "reached here" gets displayed. Had we
not have written the *try-catch* block the program would have been
terminated abnormally.

If a set of statements are likely to throw exception of different
types we can write them in a single *try* block and handle the
exceptions in separate *catch* blocks. Thus, a *try* block can have
multiple *catch* blocks. This is shown in the following example.

```
try
{
    // statement that causes divide by zero exception
    // statement that causes array bounds out of range exception
}

catch ( dividebyzero *e )
{
    cout << "Divide by zero error" ;
}
catch ( arraybounds  *e )
{
    cout << "Index out of bounds" ;
}
```

Here, the two *catch* blocks are written to handle the 'divide by zero' and 'index out of range' exceptions. The *dividebyzero* and *arraybounds* classes represent these exceptions respectively.

When an exception is thrown the exception blocks are searched serially for the matching block. If the matching block is found, it gets executed and control goes to the statement next to the *catch* blocks.

11.1.3   Throw Statement

The *throw* keyword is used to throw an exception. The syntax of the *throw* statement is given below.

```
throw exception ;
throw ;
```

The second *throw* statement is used for re-throwing an exception. Re-throwing an exception is discussed in section 11.2.3. The exception thrown by the *throw* statement is handled by the *catch* block.

If an exception is thrown the control jumps to the *catch* block and never returns to the statement next to the *throw* statement. For example, if a function throws an exception, control never returns back to that function after execution of the *catch* block.

11.2   Exception Handling Options

In section 11.1 we saw basic mechanism and usage of exception handling. In this section we would see few more things associated with *try, catch* and *throw*.

11.2.1   Catching All Exceptions

Sometimes, we may not anticipate how many types of exceptions a code is likely to throw. Therefore, we may not write *catch* blocks for these exceptions. At such times we can make a single *catch* block to handle all the exceptions by writing ellipses (…) instead of a type inside the definition of *catch*. This is shown below.

```
catch ( ... )
{
}
```

Here is the sample program that illustrates catching all exceptions.

```
#include <iostream.h>
class excep
{
} ;

void fun ( int n )
{
    if ( n > 10 )
        throw new excep( ) ;

    if ( n < 0 )
```

```
        throw -1 ;
}
void main( )
{
    try
    {
        fun ( 11 ) ;
    }
    catch ( ... )
    {
        cout << "Caught" << endl ;
    }

    try
    {
        fun ( -2 ) ;
    }
    catch ( ... )
    {
        cout << "Caught" << endl ;
    }

}
```

We can also write one *catch* handler by specifying a type and another using ellipses. In such a case if an exception of the specified type is thrown the first catch handler would get executed. If an exception of any other type were thrown, second *catch* handler would be executed. However, it is necessary to write *catch* block with ellipses at the end of all the *catch* blocks. Otherwise, it would handle all the exceptions.

11.2.2   Restricting Exceptions

We can restrict a function to throw only a specified type of exception. This is done by adding a *throw* list while defining the function. The syntax of adding the *throw* list is given below.

type function_name (<argument list>) throw (type list)

The types specified in *type-list* are separated by comma. Following code snippet shows how to declare a *throw* list.

```
void fun ( int  n ) throw ( int, excep* )
{
    if ( n > 10 )
        throw new excep( ) ;
}
```

If the function throws any exception other that the specified ones' the program terminates.

To prevent a function from throwing an exception we should keep the *throw* list empty as shown below:

void fun (int n) throw ( )

11.2.3   Rethrowing an Exception

Suppose an exception is thrown and a *catch* handler is invoked. If this *catch* handler does not want to handle the exception it can rethrow the same to another *catch* handler. This is done by writing a *throw* statement without any type inside the *catch* handler. In the following program the *catch* in *fun( )* rethrows the exception. This exception is then handled by the *catch* in *main( )*.

```
void fun ( int  n )
{
    try
    {
        if ( n < 0 )
```

```
            throw -1 ;
    }
    catch ( int i )
    {
        cout << "Negative value" << endl ;
        throw ;
    }
}

void main( )
{
    try
    {
        fun ( -1 ) ;
    }
    catch ( int i )
    {
        cout << "Caught" << endl ;
    }
}
```

Exercises

[A] State True or False:

(a) The exception handling mechanism is supposed to handle compile time errors.

(b) It is necessary to declare the exception class within the class in which an exception is going to be thrown.

(c) Every thrown exception must be caught.

(d) For one *try* block there can be multiple *catch* blocks.

(e) The *catch* block and the exception handler are one and the same thing.

(f) When an exception is thrown an exception class's constructor gets called.

(g) *try* blocks cannot be nested.

(h) A single *catch* block can handle multiple exceptions.

(i) *throw* is used to either throw an exception or to rethrow an exception.

(j) We can decide which type of exception a function can throw.

[B] Answer the following:

(a) What is the difference between run-time errors and compile time errors?

(b) When should we write multiple *catch* blocks for a *try* block?

(c) State advantages of exception handling.

[C] Attempt the following:

(a) Implement an exception handling mechanism, which reports stack full and stack empty mechanism for a class called *stack*.

(b) Implement a class called *student* containing appropriate data members to store roll number, name, and age. Make arrangements that if the age and roll number is entered as a negative value then an exception is thrown.

(c) Call a function that calls another function and which in turn calls the third function. This function throws an exception. Apply appropriate exception handling mechanism.

12
Class Libraries

12.1   Types of Class Libraries

Reuse of existing code is one of the primary goals that C++ addresses. Existing classes can be made available for reuse by packaging them in a library. Several such class libraries are available. We would discuss three such class libraries in this chapter. They are Standard C++ Library, Standard Template Library and Microsoft Foundation Class Library.

12.1.1   Standard C++ Library

A C++ program can call on a large number of functions from the Standard C++ Library that provide efficient implementations of frequently used operations such as input and output. Each and every entity in the library is declared in one or more header files. To use the classes declared in these header files we need to *#include* them in out program. We have been using header files like 'iostream.h' and 'iomanip.h' in our programs. We have used standard objects like *cin* and *cout* declared in 'iostream.h' and manipulators declared in 'iomanip.h' file. The Standard C++ Library consists of 50 headers files. These headers together host implementation of the C++ library. Table 12.1 shows some of the header files belonging to the standard C++ library.

Header Name	Description
<algorithm>	Contains functions performing algorithms
<bitset>	Contains the class bitset and functions for representing and manipulating fixed-size sequences of bits
<exception>	Contains types and functions for handling exceptions
<functional>	Contains functions that help construct function objects
<iosfwd>	Contains forward references to several template classes used in iostreams
<iterator>	Contains the predefined iterators, stream iterators and several supporting templates

<new>	Contains functions that control the allocation and de-allocation of memory
<memory>	Contains entities that help allocate and free objects
<numeric>	Contains containers that perform algorithms provided for numerical processing
<sstream>	Contains several classes that support iostreams operations on an array object
<string>	Contains the container template class *basic_string* and various supporting templates
<stdexcept>	Contains several standard classes used for reporting exceptions
<valarray>	Contains the template class *valarray* and supporting template classes and functions
<strstream>	Contains classes that support iostreams operations on array of *char* object.

Table 12.1. *List of standard C++ header files.*

12.1.2   Standard Template Library

The C++ Standard Template Library referred to, as STL is a C++ programming library that has been developed by Alexander Stepanov and Meng Lee at the Hewlett Packard laboratories in Palo Alto, California. The Standard Template Library (STL) is a general-purpose C++ library of algorithms and data structures. It is a built-in container class library, used to store and process data. It is a part of the standard ANSI/ISO C++ library.

The STL is implemented by means of the C++ template mechanism, hence the name Standard Template Library. The STL can be applied in a very straightforward way, facilitating reuse of the sophisticated data structures and algorithms it contains. It provides many of the basic algorithms and data structures of computer science. The STL consists of various types of entities most important of which are containers, algorithm, and iterators. We would discuss various container classes later in this chapter.

Algorithms in STL are certain procedures that are applied to containers to process the data. STL provides algorithms for operations like search, sort, merge, copy, etc. The algorithms are provided by means of a template function. These template functions are not written as part of the container class, but are provided as standalone template functions. Moreover, these functions can also be used on ordinary C++ data members like arrays, or user-defined container classes. Table 12.2 lists the functions provided by STL.

Function	Description
find( )	Returns an iterator referring to the first element in the container that matches the element to be searched
count( )	Counts the occurrences of a given element
equal( )	Compares the contents of two containers and returns true if the corresponding elements are similar
search( )	Searches for the given pattern of elements in the container
copy( )	Copies a sequence of elements from one container to another
swap( )	Interchanges the element at one location with the element at the same location in the other container

Table 12.2. *List of STL functions.*

Iterators are special STL objects that are used to represent positions of elements in various STL containers. More clearly, iterators play a role similar to that of a subscript in a C++ array. Iterators are like references that allow the programmer to access a particular element, and to traverse through the container. There are many different kinds of iterators depending on the type of container with which they are associated. At any given time, an iterator object is associated with only one container object. There are 3 basic types of iterators as given in Table 12.3.

Type of Iterator	Description
Forward	Specifies the position of a single element in a container. It can move in one direction from element to element in a container
Bi-directional	Same as forward iterator, but can move in two directions i.e. forward and reverse from element to element
Random Access	Same as bi-directional iterator, but can move in bigger steps by skipping multiple elements

Table 12.3. *Types of iterators.*

In addition to the above given types, the iterators can be *const* (e.g., "const_iterator") or non-*const*. Constant iterators can be used to examine container elements, but cannot be used to modify the elements in the container. Non-constant iterators cannot be used with constant container objects.

Container Class

A *container* is a template class that is used to store objects of other types such as *int*, *float*, *double*, *char*, etc. It actually manages the objects of different data types. By saying managing the objects, we mean that the container as a template class provides constructor, destructor, necessary operator functions and additional member functions. Container classes form one of the most crucial components of STL.

The container classes are divided into three categories, depending on the way the elements are arranged. The categories are:

- Sequence Containers
- Associative Containers
- Derived Containers — *implemented in terms of prev 2*

The sequence containers are implemented using vector, deque and list. The associative containers are implemented by set, multiset, map and multimap. The derived containers are stack, queue and priority_queue. We would learn more about containers in Chapter 13.

Stack Class

A *stack* object is a sequential container that allows insertion and deletion of elements only at one end. It follows Last In First Out system for adding and retrieving the stack elements. Here is the program for maintains a stack of integers.

```cpp
#include <iostream.h>
#include <stack>

using namespace std ;

void main( )
{
    stack <int> stk ;

    // add elements to the stack
    stk.push ( 16 ) ;
    stk.push ( 10 ) ;
    stk.push ( 19 ) ;
    stk.push ( -3 ) ;
    stk.push ( 22 ) ;
    stk.push ( 18 ) ;

    int sz = stk.size( ) ;
    cout << "The stack contains " << sz << " elements" << endl ;
```

```
// remove elements from the stack
while ( !stk.empty( ) )
{
     int i = stk.top( ) ;
     cout << i << " " ;
     stk.pop( ) ;
}
}
```

A stack can be implemented using vector, list or deque. We can specify the type of the underlying container as the second parameter in the constructor of *stack* as shown below:

stack <int, vector<int> > stk ;

The default value is the class *deque*.

In the program we have created a stack to maintain integers. The object *stk* is a stack implemented as a *deque*. Then using *push( )* function we have added elements to the stack. The *size( )* function returns the total number of elements present in the stack. The *top( )* function returns an element present at the top of the stack. Hence we have called this function through a *while* loop that runs till the stack does not become empty. This we have checked using *empty( )* function. After displaying the element at the top we have called *pop( )* to remove an element at the top of the stack.

Important member functions of the *stack* class are given in Table 12.4.

Member Function	Description
empty( )	Tests if the stack is empty
pop( )	Removes the element from the top of the stack
push( )	Adds an element to the top of the stack
size( )	Returns the number of elements in the stack

| stack( ) | Constructs a stack that is empty or that is a copy of a base container object |
| top( ) | Returns a reference to an element at the top of the stack |

Table 12.4. *Member functions of stack class.*

Queue Class

Like stack we can implement a queue in our program. For example, if we wish to implement a queue of integers as a linked list then the statement to declare such a queue would be as given below:

queue < int, list <int> > q ;

where *q* is a container of type *queue* employed as a linked list of integers. The functions like *size( )* , *front( )*, *empty( )*, etc. work in the same manner. Hence writing a program to maintain a queue is left to you.

Consider some jobs, which are to be processed by the CPU. The job, which has to be processed first, depends on its priority. CPU should get these jobs in the ascending order of their priority number, i.e. lower the priority number higher is the priority. There should be some function, which would arrange these jobs as per their priorities. Let us see how this can be done with the help of *priority_queue* container.

```
#include <iostream>
#include <queue>
#include <string>
#include <vector>

using namespace std ;

namespace std
```

```
{
    class tasks
    {
        private :

            int prno ;
            string pname ;

        public :

            tasks ( string pnm, int pr ) ;
            friend class prioritizetasks ;
            friend ostream& operator << ( ostream &s, tasks &task ) ;
    } ;

    tasks :: tasks ( string pnm, int pr )
    {
        pname = pnm ;
        prno = pr ;
    }

    ostream& operator << ( ostream &s, tasks &task )
    {
        s << "Process: " << task.pname << " Priority: " << task.prno
            << endl ;
        return ( s ) ;
    }

    class prioritizetasks
    {
        public :

        int operator( ) ( const tasks &t1, const tasks &t2 )
        {
            return t1.prno > t2.prno ;
        }
    } ;
}
```

```
void main( )
{
    priority_queue<tasks, vector<tasks>, prioritizetasks> pq ;

    tasks t[ ] = { tasks ( "SWAP", 4 ), tasks ( "PRNT", 17 ),
                tasks ( "WORD", 18 ), tasks ( "COPY", 3 ),
                tasks ( "RENM", 6 ), tasks ( "DELT", 5 ),
                tasks ( "CRET", 1 ), tasks ( "DUMP", 9 ) } ;

    for ( int i = 0 ; i < sizeof ( t ) / sizeof ( t [ 0 ] ) ; i++ )
        pq.push( t [ i ] ) ;

    while ( !pq.empty( ) )
    {
        tasks tk = pq.top( ) ;
        cout << tk ;
        pq.pop( ) ;
    }

    cout << endl;
}
```

In this program a priority queue holds objects of a class *tasks* in the form of a vector. Note the statement that builds a priority queue.

priority_queue<tasks, vector<tasks>, prioritizetasks> pq ;

The above statement builds a priority queue *pq* to hold objects of class *tasks* as a vector. Furthermore, the class *prioritizetasks* provides a function to decide the order in which the tasks should get placed.

Here, first we have created an array *t* of *tasks* and initialized it at the same place. Then through a *for* loop we have added the objects to the priority queue *pq*, by calling function *push( )*. While adding objects to *pq* an overloaded function for the operator *( )* (which is a member function of *prioritizetasks*) gets called. This function compares the priorities of the two objects *t1* and *t2* and returns 0 or 1. Finally, we have displayed the contents of *pq* through a loop.

Vector Class

The *vector* container resembles a C++ array in that it holds objects of the same type, and that each of these objects can be accessed individually. The *vector* container is defined as a template class, and hence it can be used to hold objects of any type. For example,

vector <int> vec_int ;

Here, *vector* *<int>* is a container data type, where *vector* is a template and holds objects of type *int*. Vectors are smarter than C++ arrays, as they manage the storage allocation for the elements, if we add or remove elements from it. Vector always occupies contiguous memory locations. If the size of a vector grows too large, then it is moved to a new location where it can get enough space. The iterator provided for the vector is a random access iterator. The header file required to be *#include*d in a program for vectors is:

#include <vector>

Various operations can be performed on vector. These operations are listed in Table 12.5.

Function	Description
push_back( )	Adds an element at the end of the vector
pop_back( )	Removes an element from the end of the vector
front( )	Returns an element present at the beginning of the vector
back( )	Returns an element present at the end of the vector

at( )	Returns an element present at the specified position in the vector
insert( )	Inserts an element in the vector at the position specified by the iterator
erase( )	Removes elements from a vector
clear( )	Erases all elements from a vector

Table 12.5. *Member Functions of Vector class.*

Let us now see a program that performs various operations on a vector.

```cpp
#include <iostream.h>
#include <vector>

using namespace std ;

void main( )
{
    vector<int> vec ;

    // add elements to the vector
    vec.push_back ( 18 ) ;
    vec.push_back ( 29 ) ;
    vec.push_back ( -4 ) ;
    vec.push_back ( 12 ) ;
    vec.push_back ( 44 ) ;

    vector<int>::iterator vitr ;

    // display elements of the vector
    cout << "The elements in the vector: " << endl ;
    for ( vitr = vec.begin( ) ; vitr != vec.end( ) ; vitr++ )
        cout << *vitr << " " ;
    cout << endl ;
```

```
cout << "An element at front: " << vec.front( ) << endl ;
cout << "An element at 2nd position: " << vec.at ( 2 ) << endl ;
cout << "An element at end: " << vec.back( ) << endl ;

// replace the elements
vitr = vec.begin( ) ;
*vitr = 35 ;
vec [ 2 ] = 20 ;
vitr += 4 ;
*vitr = 99 ;

cout << "The elements in the vector after replacements: " << endl ;
for ( vitr = vec.begin( ) ; vitr != vec.end( ) ; vitr++ )
    cout << *vitr << " " ;
cout << endl ;

// insert an element
vitr = vec.begin( ) ;
vec.insert ( vitr, 25 ) ;

cout << "The elements in the vector after insertion: " << endl ;
for ( vitr = vec.begin( ) ; vitr != vec.end( ) ; vitr++ )
    cout << *vitr << " " ;
cout << endl ;

// erase an element
vitr = vec.begin( ) ;
vitr += 2 ;
vec.erase ( vitr ) ;
cout << "The elements in the vector after
        erasing element at 2nd position: " << endl ;
for ( vitr = vec.begin( ) ; vitr != vec.end( ) ; vitr++ )
    cout << *vitr << " " ;
cout << endl ;

// remove elements from the vector
vec.pop_back( ) ;
vec.pop_back( ) ;
```

```
// display elements of the vector
cout << "The elements in the vector after
        removing top 2 elements: " << endl ;
for ( int i = 0 ; i < vec.size( ) ; i++ )
    cout << vec [ i ] << " " ;
cout << endl ;

cout << "Clearing elements of vector vec ..." << endl ;
vec.clear( ) ;
if ( vec.empty( ) )
    cout << "The vector vec is empty now" << endl ;
else
    cout << "The vector vec is not empty" << endl ;
}
```

List Class

The list is a container, which implements a classic list data structure. Unlike C++ array or STL vector, list does not allow to randomly accessing the elements. Lists are implemented as doubly linked list structures in order to support bi-directional iterators. Each element in the list contains a pointer to the preceding and the next element in the list. Lists are better used when we want to add or remove elements to or from the middle of the list. The header file required to be *#included* in a program for lists would be

#include <list>

The various functions provided by the list container are given in Table 12.6.

Function	Description
push_front( )	Adds an element at the beginning of the list
push_back( )	Adds an element at the end of the list
pop_front( )	Removes an element from the beginning of the list
pop_back( )	Removes an element from the end of the list
front( )	Returns an element present at the beginning of the list
back( )	Returns an element present at the end of the list
insert( )	Inserts an element in the list at the position specified by the iterator
erase( )	Removes elements from a list
clear( )	Erases all elements from the list
sort( )	Sorts the elements in the list

Table 12.6. *Member functions of List class.*

Let us now see a program that has used these functions to work on a list.

```
#include <iostream.h>
#include <list>
#include <algorithm>

using namespace std ;
void main( )
{
    list <int> ls ;

    // add elements to the list
    ls.push_back ( 12 ) ;
    ls.push_front ( 34 ) ;
```

```
ls.push_back ( 19 ) ;
ls.push_front ( 44 ) ;
ls.push_back ( 31 ) ;
ls.push_front ( 2 ) ;
ls.push_back ( 29 ) ;
ls.push_front ( -8 ) ;

list<int>::iterator litr ;

// display elements in the list
cout << "The elements in list ls: " << endl;
for ( litr = ls.begin( ); litr != ls.end( ) ; litr++ )
    cout << *litr << " " ;
cout << endl ;

cout << "An element at the front: " << ls.front( ) << endl ;
cout << "An element at the end: " << ls.back( ) << endl ;

// remove elements from the list
ls.pop_back( ) ;
ls.pop_back( ) ;

// display elements of the list
cout << "The elements in the list after removing top 2 elements: "
        << endl ;
for ( litr = ls.begin( ) ; litr != ls.end( ) ; litr++ )
    cout << *litr << " " ;
cout << endl ;

ls.pop_front( ) ;
ls.pop_front( ) ;

// display elements of the list
cout << "The elements in the list after removing first 2 elements: "
        << endl ;
for ( litr = ls.begin( ) ; litr != ls.end( ) ; litr++ )
    cout << *litr << " " ;
cout << endl ;
```

```
// insert an element
litr = ls.end( ) ;
litr-- ;
ls.insert ( litr, -20 ) ;
litr-- ;
litr-- ;
ls.insert ( litr, 67 ) ;
litr++ ;
ls.insert ( litr, 33 ) ;

cout << "The elements in the list after insertion: " << endl ;
for ( litr = ls.begin( ) ; litr != ls.end( ) ; litr++ )
     cout << *litr << " " ;
cout << endl ;

// erase an element
litr = ls.begin( ) ;
ls.erase ( litr ) ;
cout << "The elements in the list after erasing element at 1st position: "
     << endl ;
for ( litr = ls.begin( ) ; litr != ls.end( ) ; litr++ )
     cout << *litr << " " ;
cout << endl ;

ls.clear( ) ;

int arr[ ]  = { 5, 11, -4, 8, 12, 3, 20, 10 } ;
for ( int i = 0; i < sizeof ( arr ) / 4 ; i++ )
     ls.push_back ( arr [ i ] ) ;

cout << "The new values in the list ls: " << endl ;
for ( litr = ls.begin( ) ; litr != ls.end( ) ; litr++ )
     cout << *litr << " " ;
cout << endl ;

// sort the elements in the list
ls.sort( ) ;
cout << "The elements in the list after sorting: " << endl ;
```

```
for ( litr = ls.begin( ) ; litr != ls.end( ) ; litr++ )
    cout << *litr << " " ;
cout << endl ;

// reverse the order of elements in the list
ls.reverse( ) ;
cout << "The list ls after reversing its elements: " << endl ;
for ( litr = ls.begin( ) ; litr != ls.end( ) ; litr++ )
    cout << *litr << " " ;
cout << endl ;
}
```

In this program of maintaining a list, we wish to create list *ls* of integers. We have called two functions such as *push_back( )* and *push_front( )* to add elements at the end or at the beginning of the list respectively. While adding elements at the beginning of the list the existing elements would get shifted one place to the right. The functions *front( )* and *back( )* displays element at the first and last position of the list respectively.

The functions *pop_back( )* and *pop_front( )* called next, remove element at the end and at the beginning of the list respectively. In case of *pop_front( )* function, after removing the element at the beginning of the list, the remaining elements are shifted one place to the left of their existing positions.

The iterator provided for the list is a bi-directional iterator, which can move, sequentially in a forward or backward direction. As a result, random access to the elements in a list is not possible. This is the reason why list does not support subscript operator *[]*. Thus to insert an element at the 6th position (in a list of 7 elements), we have used the statement *litr = ls.end( )* ; which returns an iterator referring to the element at the 7th position. Next, we have decremented the value of iterator by 1, to refer *litr* to the element at the 6th position. The *insert( )* function then adds element -20 at

this position. Similar steps are carried out to insert element at the
3rd and 5th position.

The *erase( )* function called next erases an element to which the
iterator *litr* is referring to. The *clear( )* function on the other hand
removes all the elements from the list. The *sort* algorithm does not
work on a list hence a *sort( )* member function is provided for the
list container. The *sort( )* function called in the program sorts the
elements in the list *ls* in ascending order. The function *reverse( )*
too belongs to the list container and reverses the order of elements
in the list *ls*.

12.1.3 Microsoft Foundation Classes (MFC)

Microsoft Foundation Class (MFC) library contains hundreds of
C++ classes. These classes are used for programming Windows
Operating System. The MFC classes encapsulate the Windows
API functions. Before introduction of MFC, programmers used to
do Windows programming through C using the API functions.
Remembering thousands of API functions, each taking numerous
parameters was a big hurdle for programmers.

MFC has completely changed the scenario. It abstracts the API
and encapsulates the basic behavior of windows API in reusable
classes. This has made Windows programming much simpler.

MFC contains a class for virtually everything that you would want
to do under Windows. This includes creating and displaying a
window, painting the window, printing, file I/O and even for
maintaining popular data structures. The classes available for
maintaining data structures are known as 'collection classes'.
Table 12.7 (a) - (d) would give you a glimpse of MFC library.

Window supporting classes

Class	Description
CWnd	Base class for all window classes
CFrameWnd	Creates frame window
CSplitterWnd	Creates splitter window

Table 12.7 (a). *MFC window classes.*

View classes

Class	Description
CView	Base class for all views
CScrollView	Provides scrolling facility for views.
CFormView	Provides view that contains controls
CCtrlView	Base class of *CTreeView*, *CListView*, *CEditView*, and *CRichEditView*. These views encapsulate respective common controls

Table 12.7 (b). *MFC view classes.*

Collection classes

Class	Description
CByteArray	Array of 8-bit bytes (BYTEs)
CWordArray	Array of 16-bit words (WORDs)
CUIntArray	Array of Unsigned integers (UINTs)
CStringArray	Array of *CStrings*
CPtrArray	Array of void pointers

CObArray	Array of *CObject* pointers
CObList	Linked list of CObject pointers
CPtrList	Linked list of void pointers
CStringList	Linked list of CStrings
CMapWordToPtr	Stores void pointers keyed by WORDs
CMapPtrToWord	Stores WORDs keyed by void pointers
CMapPtrToPtr	Stores void pointers keyed by other void pointers
CMapWordToOb	Stores CObject pointers keyed by WORDs
CMapStringToOb	Stores CObject pointers keyed by strings
CMapStringToPtr	Stores void pointer keyed by strings
CMapStringToStrin	Stores strings keyed by other strings
CMapWordToPtr	Stores void pointers keyed by WORDs

Table 12.7 (c). *MFC collection classes.*

Control classes

MFC Class	Representing Control Type
CButton	Buttons
CListBox	List boxes
CEdit	Edit controls
CComboBox	Combo boxes
CScrollBar	Scroll bars
CStatic	Static controls
CAnimateCtrl	Animation
CImageList	Image list
CIPAddressCtrl	IP address
CListCtrl	List view

Table 12.7 (d). *MFC control classes.*

Though there are other class libraries available for programming Windows (Object Window Library, for example), a majority of Windows' programmers have settled for MFC.

12.2   Developing Programs for Class Library

In the last section we saw various libraries and studied various classes contained in these libraries. You can appreciate how using class libraries can make programmer's life simple.

Have you ever wondered how these re-distributable libraries have been created? In this section we would see how to create and use our own class library.

12.2.1 Creating Class Library File

Creating a class library involves creating the classes we want to distribute, creating header file and lastly compiling the source code to create a library. We would discuss the process of creation of library with Turbo C++ and Microsoft Visual C++ compilers.

12.2.2 Writing the source File

Using Microsoft Visual C++ Compiler

Given below are the steps that should be carried out for creating a source file in Visual C++.

(a) Create a Console Application called 'mymath' by selecting 'File | New' and then selecting the 'Win32 Console Application' project type. Select an empty project in the next step of the AppWizard.

(b) Create a header file named 'mymath.h' by selecting 'File | New' and then selecting 'C/C++ Header File'. We would declare a class called *mymath* having a member function *square( )*. The *square( )* function would return the square of an integer passed to it.

Write the following class declaration in the file.

```
class mymath
{
    public :

        int square ( int ) ;
};
```

(c) Define the *mymath* class in the 'mymath.cpp' file. Create this file by selecting 'File | New' menu item and then selecting 'C++ Source File'.

```
#include "mymath.h"
```

```
int mymath::square ( int i )
{
    return i * i ;
}
```

(d) Now compile the 'mymath.cpp' file by pressing Ctrl + F7.
The library file 'mymath.obj' gets created in the Debug folder
of the project.

Using Turbo C++ Compiler

Create the 'mymath.cpp' and 'mymath.h' files containing the same
code as above. Compile the 'mymath.cpp' file by pressing Alt +
F9. The library file 'mymath.obj' would get created in the output
directory.

12.2.3   Setting the Directories

Now our library file stands created. We can ship this file along
with the header file to the clients. Copy these files in a separate
folder, say, 'Library'. In order to use the classes in the library, the
clients have to link the library file and *#include* the header file in
their project. Here are the steps to be followed that discuss how to
use the library.

Using Microsoft Visual C++ Compiler

Create the client application named 'client'. Write the code as
given below in the 'client.cpp' file

```
#include <iostream.h>
#include <mymath.h>

void main( )
{
    mymath m ;
    int i = m.square ( 3 ) ;
```

```
    cout << i ;
}
```

Link the 'mymath.obj' file by selecting 'Project | Settings' menu option. Select the 'Link' tab. Write 'mymath.obj' in 'Object/library modules:' edit box.

Note that all compilers search for the *#included* files and library files linked to the project in the predefined paths. In order to use our header file and library file, client has to set the path of the 'Library' folder so that compiler would search the header file and library file in this folder. To set the path, select 'Tools | Options' menu item. Select 'Directories' tab. Select 'Include Files' from the 'Show Directories for:' combo box. Add the path by double clicking the blue bar appearing in the 'Directories' list box. Also add the same path for 'Library Files'.

Now run the program. It would give *9* as output.

Using Turbo C++ Compiler

To use the *mymath* library we would create a project by selecting 'Project | Open Project' menu item. Enter the project name as 'client'. Create the 'client.cpp' file by selecting 'Project | Add Item' option. Write the same code in it as we wrote in Visual C++ client. Add the 'mymath.obj' file to the project by selecting 'Project | Add Item' option.

Now set the directory path by selecting 'Options | Directories' menu item and run the program.

Exercises

[A] State True or False:

(a) The classes of Standard C++ Library are provided in the form of several header files.

(b) We don't need to mention extension '.h' while #*includ*ing the header files of Standard C++ Library.

(c) The algorithms in STL are provided by means of a template functions.

(d) Iterators are the objects that are used to represent positions of elements in STL containers.

(e) A vector contains elements of the same type.

(f) The size of a vector remains same even if its elements are removed.

(g) A map can have two or more elements with the same key value.

[B] Fill in the blanks:

(a) A _____ is a template class that stores objects of other types.

(b) The STL _____ container stores a finite set of objects in a linear arrangement, provided that the elements are of _____ type.

(c) The STL _____ containers are the ones that provide fast retrieval of data

(d) _____ , _____ and _____ are the STL sequence containers.

(e) An iterator provided for the vector is a _____ iterator.

[C] Pick up the correct alternative for each of the following questions:

(a) Iterators are
   (1) Used to represent positions of elements
   (2) Allow access to a particular element
   (3) Allow to traverse through the container
   (4) All of the above

(b) An algorithm is
   (1) A member function of its corresponding container class
   (2) A friend function of its corresponding container class
   (3) Type of iterator
   (4) A stand-alone function that works on containers

(c) The STL container deque supports
   (1) Bi-directional iterator
   (2) Random-access iterator
   (3) Forward iterator
   (4) None of the above

(d) The **find( )** algorithm
   (1) Returns an element found in the container
   (2) Returns an iterator refering to the element found in the container
   (3) Compares data in two given containers
   (4) None of the above

[D] Answer the following:

(a) What are different types of iterators? Explain each in brief.

(b) Write short notes on the following:
   – Container.class
   – stack class

- queue & deque class
- vector class
- sets and multisets
- maps & multimaps

[E] Attempt the following:

(a) Write a program that stores an array of double values entered by the user to a vector container and displays the elements in sorted order.

(b) Write a program that stores an array of words to a vector container and arranges them in alphabetical order.

(c) Write a program that stores even numbers to a vector container and odd numbers to a set container, and merges both to a new vector container.

13
Advanced Classes

13.1   Templates

Templates are a mechanism that makes it possible to use one function or class to handle many different data types. By using templates, we can design a single class/function that operates on data of many types, instead of having to create a separate class/function for each type. When used with functions they are known as *function templates*, whereas when used with classes they are called *class templates*. We would first look at function templates and then move on to class templates.

13.1.1   Template Function

Suppose we want to write a function that returns the minimum of two numbers. Ordinarily this function would be written for a particular data type. For example,

```
int min ( int a, int b )
{
    return ( a < b ) ? a : b ;
}
```

Here the function is defined to take arguments of type *int* and return a value of the same type. What if we want to find the minimum of two *long ints*—we would be required to write a completely new function. Similarly, to find minimum of two *floats* or two *doubles* or two *chars* we would be required to write separate versions of the same function. You would agree this is a suitable case for overloaded functions. These are given below:

```
// min for ints
int min ( int a, int b )
{
    return ( a < b ) ? a : b ;
```

```
}

// min for longs
long min ( long a, long b )
{
    return ( a < b ) ? a : b ;
}

// min for chars
char min ( char a, char b )
{
    return ( a < b ) ? a : b ;
}

// etc...
```

Have we gained anything by writing these overloaded functions? Not much, because we still have to write a separate definition for each type. This results into three disadvantages:

(a) Rewriting the same function body over and over for different types is time consuming.
(b) The program consumes more disk space.
(c) If we locate any error in one such function, we need to remember to correct it in each function body.

Won't it be nice if we could write such a function just once, and make it work for many different data types. This is exactly what function templates do for us.

The following program shows how to write the *min( )* function as a template, so that it will work with any standard type. We have invoked this function from *main( )* for different data types.

```
#include <iostream.h>

template <class T>
```

```
T min ( T a, T b )
{
    return ( a < b ) ? a : b ;
}

void main( )
{
    int i = 10, j = 20 ;
    cout << endl << min ( i, j ) ;

    float a = 3.14, b = -6.28 ;
    cout << endl << min ( a, b ) ;

    char ch = 'A', dh = 'Z' ;
    cout << endl << min ( ch, dh ) ;

    double d = 1.1, e = 1.11 ;
    cout << endl << min ( d, e ) ;
}
```

Here's the output of the program:

```
10
-6.28
A
1.1
```

As you can see, the *min( )* function now works with different data types that we use as arguments. It will even work on user-defined data types, provided the less-than operator (<) is appropriately overloaded in the class for the user-defined type.

Isn't this code reuse? Yes, but of a different type. Inheritance and containership provide a way to reuse *object* code. Templates provide a way to reuse the *source* code. Templates can significantly reduce source code size and increase code flexibility without reducing type safety.

Let us now understand what grants the templated function the flexibility to work with different data types. Here is the definition of the *min( )* function:

```
template <class T>
T min ( T a, T b )
{
    return ( a < b ) ? a : b ;
}
```

This entire syntax is called a function template. In a function template a data type can be represented by a name (*T* in our case) that can stand for any type. There's nothing special about the name *T*. We can use any other name like *type*, *mytype*, etc. *T* is known as a template argument. Throughout the definition of the function, wherever a specific data type like *int* would ordinarily be written, we substitute the template argument, *T*.

What Happens at Compile Time

Just seeing the function template doesn't swing the compiler into any real action, except for memorizing it for future use. The compiler cannot generate any code as yet because it doesn't know as yet what data type the function will be working with. The code generation takes place when the function is actually called from within the program through statements like:

```
cout << endl << min ( i, j ) ;
```

When the compiler sees such a function call, it knows that the type to use is *int*, because that's the type of the arguments *i* and *j*. Now it generates a specific version of the *min( )* for type *int*, replacing every *T* with an *int*. This process is often known as *instantiating* the function template. The compiler also generates a call to the newly instantiated function, and inserts it into the code where *min (i, j)* is.

Similarly, the expression *min (a, b)* causes the compiler to generate a version of *min( )* that operates on type *float* and a call to this function; while the *min (d, e)* call generates a function that works on type *double*. Note that the compiler generates only one version of *min( )* for each data type irrespective of the number of calls that have been made for that type.

Do templates help us save memory? Not really—because, even when we use templates the four functions (for *int, float char* and *double*) do get generated. The advantage is we are not required to type them out. The compiler creates them from the generic version that we pass on to it. This makes the listing shorter and easier to understand. Another advantage is, if we are to modify the function we need to make the changes at only one place in the listing instead of four places.

Here is another function template to help you fix your ideas. This one swaps the contents of two variables.

```
#include <iostream.h>

template <class T>
void swap ( T &a, T &b )
{
    T c ;

    c = a ;
    a = b ;
    b = c ;
}

void main( )
```

```
{
    int i = 10, j = 20 ;
    swap ( i, j ) ;
    cout << endl << i << "\t" << j ;

    char ch = 'A', dh = 'Z' ;
    swap ( ch, dh ) ;
    cout << endl << ch << "\t" << dh ;
}
```

This code defines a function template called *swap( )*. From this template the compiler generates functions that will swap *int*s and *char*s.

Note that standard type conversions are not applied to function templates. When a call is encountered the compiler first looks into the existing instantiations for an "exact match" for the parameters supplied. If this fails, it tries to create a new instantiation to create an 'exact match'. If this fails, the compiler generates an error.

13.1.2   Template Class

The concept of templates can be extended even to classes. Class templates are usually used for data storage (container) classes. We can create container classes for different data structures like stack and queue. However, if we create these classes they can store data of only a single basic type, say an integer. If we wish to store data of type *float* in a stack we would be required to define a completely new class. It follows that for every new data type that we wish to store, a new stack class would have to be created. Won't it be nice if we are able to write a single class specification that would work for variables of all types, instead of a single basic type. That's when we can use *class templates*. Here is a program with class template in action.

```cpp
#include <iostream.h>

const int MAX = 10 ;
template <class T>
class stack
{
    private :

        T stk [ MAX ] ;
        int top ;

    public :

        stack( )
        {
            top = -1 ;
        }
        void push ( T data )
        {
            if ( top == MAX - 1 )
                cout << endl << "stack is full" ;
            else
            {
                top++ ;
                stk [ top ] = data ;
            }
        }

        T pop( )
        {
            if ( top == -1 )
            {
                cout << endl << "stack is empty" ;
                return NULL ;
            }
            else
            {
                T data = stk [ top ] ;
```

```
                    top-- ;
                    return data ;
            }
        }
} ;

class complex
{
    · private :

        double real, imag ;

    public :

        complex ( double r = 0.0, double i = 0.0 )
        {
            real = r ;
            imag = i ;
        }

        friend ostream& operator << ( ostream &o, complex &c ) ;
} ;

ostream& operator << ( ostream &o, complex &c )
{
    o << c.real << "\t" << c.imag ;
    return o ;
}

void main( )
{
    stack < int > s1 ;
    s1.push ( 10 ) ;
    s1.push ( 20 ) ;
    s1.push ( 30 ) ;

    cout << endl << s1.pop( ) ;
    cout << endl << s1.pop( ) ;
```

```
        cout << endl << s1.pop( ) ;

        stack <float> s2 ;
        s2.push ( 3.14f ) ;
        s2.push ( 6.28f ) ;
        s2.push ( 8.98f ) ;

        cout << endl << s2.pop( ) ;
        cout << endl << s2.pop( ) ;
        cout << endl << s2.pop( ) ;

        complex c1 ( 1.5, 2.5 ), c2 ( 3.5, 4.5 ), c3 ( -1.5, -0.6 ) ;
        stack <complex> s3 ;

        s3.push ( c1 ) ;
        s3.push ( c2 ) ;
        s3.push ( c3 ) ;

        cout << endl << s3.pop( ) ;
        cout << endl << s3.pop( ) ;
        cout << endl << s3.pop( ) ;
}
```

We have created three stacks here: *s1*, *s2* and *s3* and pushed three values on each one. Then we have popped the values from the three stacks and displayed them on the screen. Here's the output of the program...

```
30
20
10
8.98
6.28
3.14
-1.5 -0.6
3.5  4.5
1.5  2.5
```

You can observe that the order in which the elements are popped from the stack is exactly reverse of the order in which they were pushed on the stack.

The way to build a class template is similar to the one used for building a function template. The *template* keyword and *<class T>* signal that the entire class will be a template.

```
template <class T>
class stack
{
      // data and member functions using template argument T
};
```

The template argument *T* is then used at every place in the class specification where there is a reference to the type of the array *stk*. There are three such places: the definition of *stk*, the argument type of the *push( )* function, and the return type of the *pop( )* function.

We have also declared a class called *complex* and then pushed/ popped *complex* objects to/from stack. This proves that we can create stacks of user-defined objects too from the class template. To be able to display the *complex* objects through *cout* we have overloaded the << operator. The working of such an overloaded operator has already been discussed in Chapter 10.

We saw that in function templates the instantiation takes place when a function call is encountered. As against this, classes are instantiated by defining an object using the template arguments. For example,

```
stack <int> s1 ;
```

creates an object, *s1*, a stack that can store numbers of type *int*. The compiler reserves space in memory for this object's data, using type *int* wherever the template argument *T* appears in the class specification. It also reserves space for the member functions (if these have not already been placed in memory by another object of type *stack <int>*). These member functions also operate exclusively on type *int*.

When we create a *stack* object that stores objects of a different type, say *float*, space is now created for data, as well as a new set of member functions that operate on type *float*.

As with normal classes can we not define the member functions of a class template outside the class? We can, but it needs a different syntax as shown below:

```
template <class T>
void stack<T>:: push ( T data )
{
    if ( top == MAX - 1 )
        cout << endl << "stack is full" ;
    else
    {
        top++ ;
        stk [ top ] = data ;
    }
}
```

Note that the expression *template <class T>* must precede not only the class definition, but each externally defined member function as well. The name *stack<T>* is used to identify the class of which *push( )* is a member.

Tips about Templates

It takes time to understand templates. Here are a few tips that you would find useful:

(a) The name of the template class (say *stack*) is expressed differently in different contexts. While declaring the class its simply the name, as in

```
class stack {    } ;
```

For externally defined member functions, it's the class name plus the template argument name as in

```
void stack<T>::push ( T data ) {    }
```

Lastly, when you define actual objects for storing a specific data type, it's the class name plus this specific type as in

```
stack <float> s1 ; // object of type stack <float>
```

You must exercise considerable care to use the correct name in the correct context. It's easy to forget to add the *<T>* or *<float>* to the *stack*. The compiler hates it when you get it wrong.

(b) Be careful about the syntax when a member function returns a value of its own class. Suppose we define a class template called *sample*. If a member function *fun( )* of this class returns a type *sample*, and we have to define this function outside the template class we need to use *sample<T>* for the return type as well as preceding the scope resolution operator. This is shown below:

```
sample<T> sample<T>::fun ( sample s )
{
}
```

The class name used as a type of a function argument, on the other hand, doesn't need to include the *<T>* designation.

(c) Template arguments can take default values. The values of these arguments then become compile-time constants for that particular instantiation of the template. For example:

```
template <class T, int max = 50 >
class sample
{
    private :
        T arr [ max ] ;
} ;
```

(d) We can inherit a new template from an existing one. For example:

```
template <class T>
class newsample : public sample <T>
{
} ;
```

(e) Every time we instantiate a template the code in the template is generated anew. If some of the functionality of a template does not depend on type, it can be put in a common base class to prevent unnecessary reproduction of that code.

(f) Templates should be used while creating a type-safe collection class that can operate on data of any type. For example a collection class to represent stack or queue.

(g) Many professional libraries heavily make use of templates. For example, the Standard Template Library (STL) and Microsoft Active Template·Library (ATL).

13.1.3   Template Function Specialization

Let us now see few miscellaneous issues regarding function templates.

Function Template Override

What if we want the function to behave in one way for all data types except one? In such a case we can override the function template for that specific type. For this we simply need to provide a non-templated function for that type. For example:

```
void swap ( double a, double b ).
{
    // some code here
}
```

This definition enables you to define a different function for *double* variables. Like other non-templated functions, standard type conversions (such as promoting a variable of type *float* to *double*) are now applicable.

Multiple Argument Types

We can as well write a function template that takes different types of arguments during one call. The following code shows such a function template.

```
#include <iostream.h>

template <class T, class S, class Z> void fun ( T a, S b, Z c )
{
    cout << a << endl << b << endl << c ;
}

void main( )
{
    int i = 10 ;
    float j = 3.14 ;
    char ch = 'A' ;

    fun ( i, j, ch ) ;
```

}

You must have noticed a small syntax variation in the function template of this program. We have put the template keyword and the function declarator on the same line:

```
template <class T, class S, class Z> void fun ( T a, S b, Z c )
```

This has got nothing to do with the multiple types of arguments that are being passed to the function template. We could as well have adopted the multi-line approach of earlier programs:

```
template <class T, class S, class Z>
void fun ( T a, S b, Z c )
```

Overloaded Template Functions

A template function may be overloaded either by template functions or ordinary functions of its name. In such cases the overloading resolution is accomplished as follows:

(a) Call an ordinary function that has an exact match.

(b) Call a template function that could be created with an exact match.

(c) Try normal overloading resolution to ordinary functions and call the one that matches.

An error is generated if no match is found. Note that no automatic conversions are applied to arguments on the template functions. Let us now see a program that shows how a template function is overloaded with an explicit function.

```
#include <iostream.h>

template <class T> void fun ( T x )
```

```
{
    cout << x << endl ;
}

void fun ( int f, char *s )
{
    cout << f << s << endl ;
}

void main( )
{
    fun ( 12.34 ) ;
    fun ( 100, " Non template" ) ;
    fun ( 10 ) ;
}
```

The output of this program would be:

```
12.34
100, Non template
10
```

Non-Type Template Arguments

We have seen that a template can have multiple arguments. It is also possible to use non-type arguments. That is in addition to the type argument **T**, we can also use other arguments such as strings, function names, constant expressions and built-in types. Consider the following example:

```
#include <iostream.h>

template <class T, int s>
class stack
{
```

```
    private:
        T arr [ s ] ;
    public :
        showlength( )
        {
            cout << sizeof ( arr ) / sizeof ( T) ;
        }
} ;

void main( )
{
    stack <int, 5> s1 ;
    stack <float, 3> s2 ;

    s1.showlength( ) ;
    s2.showlength( ) ;
}
```

This template supplies the size of the array as an argument. This implies that the size of the array is known to the compiler at the compile time itself. The arguments must be specified whenever a template class is created. We have specified the argument in main in the statements

```
stack <int, 5> s1 ;
stack <float, 3> s2 ;
```

The calls to the *showlength( )* function displays 5 and 3 respectively.

13.2   Containers

A *container* is a template class that is used to store objects of other types such as *int*, *float*, *double*, *çhar*, etc. It actually manages the objects of different data types. By saying managing the objects, we mean that the container as a template class provides constructor, destructor, necessary operator functions and additional member functions. Container classes form one of the most crucial components of STL.

The container classes are divided into three categories, depending on the way the elements are arranged. The categories are:

–   Sequence Containers
–   Associative Containers
–   Derived Containers

13.2.1   Sequence Containers

A *sequence* container is a kind of container that organizes a finite set of objects in a linear arrangement, provided that the elements are of the same type. Each element is related to the other elements by its position. STL provides three basic kinds of sequence containers—*vector*, *list* and *deque*.

13.2.2   Derived Containers

STL provides three derived containers. They are— *stack*, *queue* and *priority_queue*. They are also known as container adapters. Creation of these containers is based on sequence containers. The derived containers do not support iterators and therefore they cannot be used for data manipulation.

13.2.3   Associative Containers

Associative Containers are the one that provide fast retrieval of data from the collection, which is based on keys. Associative container is not sequential and hence uses keys to access data directly. The size of the collection can vary at runtime. The collection is maintained in order. There are four types of associative containers—set, multiset, map and multimap.

Set stores number of items and access them using a value as a key. These keys must be unique. Entries in set are kept in order. Set can be used to store the objects of user-defined classes or to hold simple data objects like *int*, *char*, *float*, *string*, etc. Set supports bi-directional iterators.

A *multiset* also stores a key value, but as against a set, multiset can store duplicate values. Rest of the working of multiset is similar to set. The various operations that can be performed on set or multiset are listed in Table 13.1.

Functions	Description
includes( )	Checks if the two given sets contain same elements
set_union( )	Returns a unique set of similar and dissimilar elements of the two given sets
set_intersection( )	Returns a unique set of elements common to the given two sets
set_difference( )	Returns a unique set of elements of first given set, which are not in second set.
set_symmetric_difference( )	Returns a unique set of elements which are present either in the first or the second given set

Table 13.1. *List of set/multiset functions.*

Lets us now see how a set and a multiset can be used in a program.

```
#include <iostream>
#include <algorithm>
#include <set>

using namespace std ;

void main( )
{
```

```
int arr1[ ] = { 11, 32, -3, 14, 5, 56, 27, 18, 19, 10 } ;
set<int, less<int> > set1 ( arr1, arr1 + 10 ) ;

int arr2[ ] = { -3, 2, 4, 19, 11, 30, 19, 10, 5, 56 } ;
set<int, less<int> > set2 ( arr2, arr2 + 10 ) ;

set<int, less<int> > set3 ;
set<int, less<int> >::iterator sitr ;

// display elements in both the sets set1 and set2
set1.insert ( 23 ) ;
cout << "The elements in the set set1: " << endl ;
for ( sitr = set1.begin( ) ; sitr != set1.end( ) ; sitr++ )
    cout << *sitr << " " ;
cout << endl ;
cout << "The elements in the set set2: " << endl ;
for ( sitr = set2.begin( ) ; sitr != set2.end( ) ; sitr++ )
    cout << *sitr << " " ;
cout << endl ;

// search for an element
int f ;
cout << "Input a number to be search : " ;
cin >> f ;
sitr = find ( set1.begin( ), set1.end( ), f ) ;
if ( sitr != set1.end( ) )
    cout << "The number " << *sitr << " found in the set set1" << endl ;
else
    cout << "The number " << f << " not found in the set set1"
        << endl ;

// check if sets set1 and set2 contains same data
bool b = includes ( set1.begin( ), set1.end( ), set2.begin( ), set2.end( ) ) ;
if ( b )
    cout << "set1 and set2 are identical" << endl ;
else
    cout << "set1 and set2 are not identical" << endl ;
```

```
// get the union of two sets
set_union ( set1.begin( ), set1.end( ),
          set2.begin( ), set2.end( ), inserter ( set3, set3.begin( ) ) ) ;
cout << "The union of two sets set1 and set2: " << endl ;
for ( sitr = set3.begin( ) ; sitr != set3.end( ) ; sitr++ )
     cout << *sitr << " " ;
cout << endl ;


// get the common elements of two sets
set3.clear( ) ;
set_intersection ( set1.begin( ), set1.end( ),
               set2.bégin( ), set2.end( ), inserter ( set3, set3.begin( ) ) ) ;
cout << "The intersection of two sets set1 and set2: " << endl ;
for ( sitr = set3.begin( ) ; sitr != set3.end( ) ; sitr++ )
     cout << *sitr << " " ;
cout << endl ;


// get the elements of set1 not present in set2
set3.clear( ) ;
set_difference ( set1.begin( ), set1.end( ),
               set2.begin( ), set2.end( ),
               inserter ( set3, set3.begin( ) ) ) ;
cout << "The difference between two sets set1 and set2: " << endl ;
for ( sitr = set3.begin( ) ; sitr != set3.end( ) ; sitr++ )
         cout << *sitr << " " ;
cout << endl ;


// get the elements of set1 as well as set2 not present in either
set3.clear( ) ;
set_symmetric_difference ( set1.begin( ), set1.end( ),
                       set2.begin( ), set2.end( ),
                       inserter ( set3, set3.begin( ) ) ) ;
cout << "The symmetric difference between two sets set1 and set2: "
     << endl ;
for ( sitr = set3.begin( ) ; sitr != set3.end( ) ; sitr++ )
         cout << *sitr << " " ;
cout << endl << endl ;
```

```
int arr3[ ] = { 2, 3, 11, -6, 5, 3, 7, 10, 11, 2 } ;
multiset <int, greater<int> > mset1 ( arr3, arr3 + 10 ) ;
multiset <int, greater<int> >::iterator msitr ;

// display elements of the multiset
cout << "The elements in the multiset mset1: " << endl ;
for ( msitr = mset1.begin( ) ; msitr != mset1.end( ) ; msitr++ )
        cout << *msitr << " " ;
cout << endl ;

int arr4[ ] = { 8, 10, 9, 3, 11, 6, 3, 12, 2, 13 } ;
multiset <int, greater<int> > mset2 ( arr4, arr4 + 10 ) ;
multiset <int, greater<int> > mset3 ;
// display elements of the multiset
cout << "The elements in the multiset mset1: " << endl ;
for ( msitr = mset2.begin( ) ; msitr != mset2.end( ) ; msitr++ )
        cout << *msitr << " " ;
cout << endl ;

// get the union of two multisets
set_union ( mset1.begin( ), mset1.end( ),
                mset2.begin( ), mset2.end( ),
                inserter ( mset3, mset3.begin( ) ) ) ;
cout << "The union of two sets mset1 and mset2: " << endl ;
for ( msitr = mset3.begin( ) ; msitr != mset3.end( ) ; msitr++ )
        cout << *msitr << " " ;
cout << endl ;
}
```

In this program we have used a set to hold integers. To create and store elements in a set we have given the following statement,

Set < int, less <int> > set1 (arr1, arr1 + 10) ;

It indicates that the set would store integers values, which would get arranged in an ascending order. The function *less<int>* given in the statement is a predefined algorithm operation, which compares two elements (integers in our case) and arranges them in ascending order.

The values to be stored and compared are read from the array *arr1*. To arrange elements in descending order we can use *greater<type>* algorithm operation, or even name of any user-defined function can be given. Thus two sets *set1* and *set2* stores the values of *arr1* and *arr2* respectively in ascending order. The set *set3* has been kept empty since we want it to store results of various functions carried on sets *set1* and *set2*. Then in order to be able to traverse through the set we have declared an iterator *sitr*. The functions like *insert( )*, *empty( )*, *find( )*, etc. work in same manner on sets also.

Next, in this program the algorithm specific to sets have been used. The *includes( )* function compares elements to check if the sequence of elements in the set *set1* and *set2* are same. In our case, this function would evaluate to *false* as the elements in two sets are not identical.

The *set_union( )* function extracts those elements which are common as well as uncommon to both the sets. These elements would then get copied to the third set *set3*. The template function *inserter( )* copies these values to the set *set3*. The elements in the set *set3* too, would get arranged in an ascending order as the function *less<>* is mentioned in the syntax while declaring *set3*.

The function *set_intersection( )* extracts elements which are common to both the sets *set1* and *set2*. These elements are copied to *set3*. As *set3* is being used to store the results of various functions, we have called *clear( )* function each time before using it in a function.

The function *set_diiference( )* extracts such elements of *set1* which are not present in the *set2*. These elements too would then get copied to the *set3*. The *set_symmetric_difference( )* function on the other hand extarcts all those elements which are either present in the *set1* or *set2* but not in both. Note that the elements that would get copied to the *set3* (as a result of algorithm operations) would be unique.

In the same program we have also used a multiset of integers, which can hold duplicate or multiple key values. The statement,

```
multiset <int, greater<int> > mset1 ( arr3, arr3 + 10 ) ;
```

creates a multiset *mset1* which to hold integer values. Furthermore, the elements are arranged in descending order, as the algorithm operation given is *greater*<>. We have copied the elements of an array *arr3* to *mset1*. The functions *find( )*, *empty( )*, etc. works in the same manner on a multiset.

An important point to note here is that an iterator declared to traverse a set can be used on multisets or vice versa. Similarly, if an iterator is associated with a set of *int*s arranged in ascending order, then it can be used with the set of *int*s arranged in descending order or any other order specified by some user-defined function.

A *map* stores a pair of values, where the pair consists of a key object and the value object. The key object can be a data such as *string, int, float* or any other object of user-defined class. The key object contains a key for which the map can be searched for. The value object stores additional data. The value object usually stores numbers or strings but it can even store the objects of other classes. For example, if the key object in a map holds a word, then the value object could be the length of the word, or the number of times the word has been repeated, or even the meaning of the word.

The data in a map always gets stored in a sorted order of the key object. The order of arranging data is decided by the function given in the syntax while creating the map. A map always stores a unique pair of key and value. A multi-map on the other hand stores multiple pairs of key and value in a sorted order. The various operations, which can be performed, on a map or multi-map are listed in Table 13.2.

Functions	Description
size( )	Returns the number of elements
max_size( )	Returns the maximum possible number of elements
empty( )	Checks if map / multimap is empty
insert( )	Inserts a new element
swap( )	Swaps two elements

Table 13.2. *List of map/multimap functions*

Let us see a how to create a map and multimap.

```cpp
#include <iostream>
#include <map>
#include <string>
#include <algorithm>

using namespace std ;

void main( )
{
    string name1[ ] = { "Rahul", "Aditi", "Salil", "Vibha", "Beena" } ;

    int marks[ ] = { 600, 545, 382, 470, 120 } ;

    map <string, int, less<string> > map1 ;
    map <string, int, less<string> >::iterator mitr ;

    string nm ;
    int m ;
```

```
// add data to the map
for ( int i = 0 ; i < sizeof ( marks1 ) / 4 ; i++ )
{
    nm = name1 [ i ] ;
    m = marks1 [ i ] ;
    map1 [ nm ] = m ;
}

// display the data
cout << "Total elements in map map1: " << map1.size( ) << endl ;
cout << "Elements in map map1: " << endl ;
for ( mitr = map1.begin( ) ; mitr != map1.end( ) ; mitr++ )
    cout << "Name: " << ( *mitr ).first << " & Marks Obtained: "
        << ( *mitr ).second << endl ;

// search map for the given student
char *s ;
cout << endl ;
cout << "Enter name of the student whose data has to be searched: " ;
cin >> s ;
nm = s ;

mitr = map1.find ( nm ) ;
if ( mitr == map1.end( ) )
    cout << endl << "No such student exists!" << endl << endl ;
else
    cout << endl << ( *mitr ).first << " has scored "
        << ( *mitr ).second << " marks" << endl << endl ;

multimap <string, int, less<string> > map2 ;
multimap <string, int, less<string> >::iterator mmitr ;

string name2[ ] = { "Rahul", "Aditi", "Salil", "Aditi", "Beena" } ;

int marks2[ ] = { 800, 475, 650, 300, 420 } ;

pair<string, int> p ;
for ( i = 0 ; i < sizeof ( marks2 ) / 4 ; i++ )
```

```
        {
            p.first = name2 [ i ] ;
            p.second = marks2 [ i ] ;
            map2.insert ( p ) ;
        }

        // display the data
        cout << "Elements in a multimap map2: " << endl ;
        for ( mmitr = map2.begin( ) ; mmitr != map2.end( ) ; mmitr++ )
            cout << "Name " << ( *mmitr ).first << " & Marks Obtained "
                << ( *mmitr ).second << endl ;
}
```

In this program we have created a map to store students name and the total marks obtained by the student. Here the key is the name of a student and a total mark scored by the student is the value for the key. The elements in the map are stored in an alphabetical order. To create the map we have given the statement,

```
map < string, int, less<string> > map1 ;
```

which indicates that the map *map1* would store a pair of *string* and an *int* in an order sorted on the key object *string*. We have copied the elements to the map *map1* from the string array *name1* and an *int* array *marks1* through a loop. Using the subscript operator *[]* the elements are copied to the map.

Similarly, we have displayed elements stored in *map1* through a loop. The statement given in the loop to display data is slightly different. Till now we simply used an iterator to display the data. But, since a map stores a pair of key and a value, *(*mitr).first* is used to display the first that is the key value and *(*mitr).second* is used to display the value associated with the key.

The algorithm function *find( )* called next searches for the specified name in the map. If the specified name is found then we are displaying the marks obtained by the student, otherwise an appropriate message is displayed.

In the same program we have created a multimap *map2*. The statement,

multimap <string, int, less<string> > map2 ;

indicates that the multimap would contain a *string* as a key object and an *int* as a value, and the elements would get arranged in ascending order of the key object *string*. A multimap does not support the subscript *operator []*. Hence, to add elements to the multimap we have created an object *p* of the template class *pair*, which stores a pair of objects first and second.

The *insert( )* function adds pair *p* to the multimap *map2*. Then through a loop we have displayed the elements stored in *map2*.

13.3   Nested Classes

If two classes are related there can be two types of relationships between them—a *kind of* relationship or a *has a* relationship. The *kind of* relationship is supported by inheritance, whereas, the *has a* relationship is supported by *composition* or *containership*. This containership is also known as nesting.

In a *has a* relationship you simply create objects of your existing class inside the new class. For example, if there is a class called *carburetor* we can create an object of this class in the new class *car* as shown below.

```
class carburetor
{
};
class car
{
    carburetor c ;
```

```
};
```

The object creation of a *car* class is different than creation of other objects. While creating the object of *car* firstly the constructor of the *carburetor* class would get called then the constructor of the *car* class would get called.

Actually, we have been using composition in almost every class designed so far. We were composing classes using built-in types. Using composition with user-defined types is equally straightforward, as you would realize in the following program.

```cpp
#include <iostream.h>
#include <string.h>

class carburetor
{
    private :

        char type ;
        float cost ;
        char mfr [ 30 ] ;

    public :

        void setdata ( char t, float c, char *m )
        {
            type = t ;
            cost = c ;
            strcpy ( mfr, m ) ;
        }

        void displaydata( )
        {
            cout << endl << type << endl << cost << endl << mfr ;
        }
```

```
} ;

class car
{
    private :

        char model [ 25 ] ;
        char drivetype [ 20 ] ;

    public :

        void setdata ( char *m, char *d )
        {
            strcpy ( model, m ) ;
            strcpy ( drivetype, d ) ;
        }

        void displaydata( )
        {
            cout << endl << model << endl << drivetype ;
        }

        carburetor c ;  // embedded object
} ;

void main( )
{
    car mycar ;
    mycar.c.setdata ( 'A', 8500.00, "Mico" ) ;
    mycar.setdata ( "sports", "4-wheel" ) ;

    mycar.c.displaydata( ) ;
    mycar.displaydata( ) ;
}
```

Since the data members of the *carburetor* class are *private* it is completely safe to embed an object of type *carburetor* as a *public* object in the new class *car*. To access the member functions of the *carburetor* class we simply have to use the '.' operator twice.

In composition it is more common to make the embedded objects *private*. This permits us to make a change in the implementation of the embedded object, if required. For example, in the following program the function *carburetor::displaydata( )* is retained as it is in the *car* class's interface, but the functions *setcarbudata( )* and *getcost( )* have been used within member functions of *car*, thereby changing the interface.

```
#include <iostream.h>
#include <string.h>

class carburetor
{
    private :

        char type ;
        float cost ;
        char mfr [ 30 ] ;

    public :

        void setcarbudata ( char t, float c, char *m )
        {
            type = t ;
            cost = c ;
            strcpy ( mfr, m ) ;
        }

        void displaydata( )
        {
            cout << endl << type << endl << cost << endl << mfr ;
        }

        float getcost( )
```

```
            {
                return cost ;
            }
    } ;

class car
{
    private :

            char model [ 25 ] ;
            char drivetype [ 20 ] ;
            carburetor cc ;  // embedded object

    public :

            void setdata ( char t, float c, char *mf, char *m, char *d )
            {
                strcpy ( model, m ) ;
                strcpy ( drivetype, d ) ;
                cc.setcarbudata( t, c, mf ) ;
            }

            void displaydata( )
            {
                cout << endl << model << endl << drivetype ;
            }

            float getcost( )
            {
                return 2 * cc.getcost( ) ;
            }
    } ;

void main( )
{
    car mycar ;
    mycar.setdata ( 'A', 8500.00, "Mico", "sports", "4-wheel" ) ;
```

```
    mycar.displaydata( ) ;
    cout << endl << mycar.getcost( ) ;
}
```

Exercises

[A] State True or False:

(a) We can inherit a new class from the class template.

(b) If there is a function template called *max( )* then a specific version of it would be created when *max( )* is called with a new type.

(c) The compiler generates only one version of function template for each data type irrespective of the number of calls that are made for that type.

(d) Using templates saves memory.

(e) We can override a function template for a particular type.

(f) A function template can have multiple argument types.

(g) Templates are type safe whereas macros are not.

(h) Class templates are usually used for container class.

(i) A class template member function can be defined outside the class template.

(j) Template arguments can take default values.

(k) The phenomenon of writing a class within a class is known as composition.

(l) Composition and containership is one and the same thing.

(m) Composition and Inheritance both promote reuse of code.

[B] Answer the following:

(a) State the difference between a macro and a template.

(b) Distinguish between the terms class templates and template class.

(c) Identify which of the following function template definitions are illegal.

```
(a) template <class A, B>
    void fun ( A, B )
    {
    }
(b) template <class A, class A>
    void fun ( A, A )
    {
    }

(c) template <class A>
    void fun ( A, A )
    {
    }

(d) template <class A, int r>
    void fun ( A, r )
    {
    }

(e) template <class A>
    A fun ( int *A )
    {
    }
```

(d) State in brief three types of containers.

(e) What is the difference between sequence container and associative container?

(f) Explain the types of associative containers.

[C] Attempt the following:

(a) Write a function template for finding the minimum value contained in an array.

(b) Write a program that will implement a binary tree as a class template.

(c) Write a program to implement a doubly linked list as a class template.

(d) Write a class template to represent a generic vector. Include member functions to perform the following tasks:
  - To create the vector
  - To modify the value of a given element
  - To multiply by a scalar value
  - To display the vector in the form (10, 20, 30, ...) ;

Appendix A
Testing and Debugging Simple Programs

Testing and debugging of programs is an important step in the application development cycle. Both Turbo C++ and Visual C++ provide good debugging tools that help in locating bugs, following flow of execution, enquiring values of variables/expressions, etc. This helps in overall program development. Let us first discuss how to use the debugging provisions available in Turbo C++ IDE (Integrated Development Environment).

Compiling and Running the Program

To compile the program in Turbo C++ we need to select the 'Compile' menu item from the 'Compile' menu or press *Alt + F9*. This compiles the program and reports the number of warnings and syntax errors, if any, in the program. On pressing a key a message window gets displayed with list of warnings and errors. When we use an up arrow or down arrow key it highlights the line of the program that caused an error/warning. This helps in quickly locating the errors and removing them. We may also select 'Compile | Build All' option to compile the program.

To run an error free program select 'Run | Run' menu option or press *Ctrl + F9*.

Tracing Into a Program/Function

Sometimes to rectify the logical errors it becomes essential to know the intermediate results of the variables and expressions used in the program. Turbo C++ IDE provides us a tool to trace the flow of execution of the program step by step.

For this Select 'Run | Trace into' option or press *F7*. This would first compile the program and if the compilation and linking is successful then it would begin the execution by highlighting the first line in *main( )*. Further pressing *F7* sequentially moves the control over the statements in the program. We can go to the output window to view the output while debugging is going on (by using *Alt F5*).

If there is any call to a function, then pressing *F7* transfers the control inside the function. Use *F8* if you don't want to trace the flow of execution inside the function. Using *F8* executes the function and moves the control to the next statement in the program. Thus, to step into a function, use *F7* and to step over it, use *F8*.

Suppose you don't want to debug a program right from the first statement but from a certain step onwards, then use 'Run | Go to cursor' option. This option runs the program from first line to the line on which the cursor is currently present. Once the control reaches this line the execution is stopped temporarily. From this line onwards now we can use *F7* or *F8* to trace the flow of execution of the rest of the program.

Examining the Values of Variables/Expressions

While debugging the program we can check for the values of variables or expressions. In debug mode, select 'Debug | Inspect...' option. A window gets displayed. Type the variable name (which can be an *int*, *float*, *char*, array, structure, etc.). The contents of that variable now get displayed in a 'Watch' window.

Evaluating a Variable/Expression

The Turbo C++ IDE allows us to evaluate the values of variables or valid C expressions. While in a debug mode select 'Debug | Evaluate/modify...' option or press *Ctrl + F4*. This displays a window. Type the expression to be evaluated in a box labeled as 'Expression' and click the 'Evaluate' button to see the result. We can provide simple variable as an expression and see its value in the 'Result' box. We can assign a new value to the variable by supplying the new value in the 'New Value' box. Now if you click the 'Evaluate' button, it would show the new value.

Using Watch Window

To see the intermediate results or how the values in a variable change while we step through a program, we can use 'Watch' window. 'Select Debug | Watches', a sub menu gets displayed. Select 'Add watch' or press *Ctrl + F7*. Type the name of the variable or expression, which has to be inspected in 'Add watch' window. A watch window gets displayed which gives the variable name and its current value. Any number of variables/expressions can be added to watch window.

We can edit an expression added to a watch window or can even delete it from the watch window. Selecting 'Debug | Watches | Remove all watches' clears the watch list.

Breakpoints

Breakpoints allow us to stop the program at any arbitrary location. Sometimes in a program that contains lots of loops and/or nested *if-else*s it becomes tedious to stepwise debug the program. At such times we can insert two break points—one before the loop and one after it. To insert break points open the program in an editor window, place the cursor on the line where a breakpoint has to be inserted and press *Ctrl + F8*. The line would get highlighted in red color. Any number of breakpoints can be inserted in a program. To remove a breakpoint press *Ctrl + F8* again on the same line. The option 'Debug | Breakpoints...' gives a list of breakpoints added for the current program.

Suppose a program contains about four different *for* loops and we want to debug 2nd and 4th *for* loop. So, insert one breakpoint on the line where 2nd *for* loop begins and insert second breakpoint on the line where 4th *for* loop begins. Run the program by pressing *Ctrl + F9*. The control will wait on the line where first breakpoint has been added. We can use the debug tolls to debug the program or after view result for the particular statement run the program by selecting 'Run | Run'. This would further part of the program that come before second breakpoint. The control would now wait on the line where second breakpoint has been added. Thus whenever you run this program, the control will stop at the breakpoints. Then we can examine the values of variable or step through the program code.

Let us now discuss the debugging support provided by VC++ IDE.

Compiling and Running the Program

The debugging environment of Visual C++ IDE provides a range of debugging tools. To compile a program select 'Build | Build <exename>' option. This compiles the program and lists the warnings or errors in an output window. A single file can be compiled by pressing *Ctrl + F7*.

Pressing F4 key highlights the warnings or errors displayed in an output window. It also highlights the line in the program code, which has caused an error. The error free program can then be executed by pressing *Ctrl + F5*.

Tracing Into a Program/Function

To debug a program step wise, select 'Build | Start Debug' menu item and then select the 'Step Into' option. This lets you debug a program one step at a time. Pressing *F11* also lets you step through a program. Repeatedly pressing *F11* moves the control to the next statement of the code. If there is any call to a function then this keystroke shifts the control inside the program.

If you want to trace the control flow from a certain statement then use *Ctrl + F10*. Place the cursor on the statement and press *Ctrl + F10*. Then you can use *F11* to sequentially execute the program or use *F10*, which does not transfer control inside the function, but executes the function as if one statement of the program has been executed. Thus *F11* is used to step into a function, whereas, *F10* is used to step over it. Pressing *F5* starts or continues the program execution.

Using Watch Window

While debugging a program, to examine the values of variables we can use Watch window. To open watch window, select 'View | Debug Windows | Watch' option. A window gets displayed. We can also press *Alt + 3* to get watch window. To add variables to the watch window, select 'Debug | Quick Watch...' option (or press *Shift + F9*). A window as shown in Figure A.1 would get displayed.

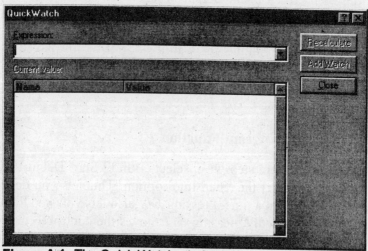

Figure A.1. *The Quick Watch window.*

Add the expression in the 'Expression' edit box and click on 'Add Watch' button. This would add the expression to watch window. If you don't want to add an expression to watch window, then you can view its contents in the Quick Watch window also. Any number of expressions/variables can be added to watch window. Now, we can examine the resulting values while stepping through the program.

Breakpoints

VC++ provides a very sophisticated way of debugging a program using Breakpoints. We can set breakpoints anywhere throughout the code, and run the program. When a control reaches a statement where breakpoint is given, it places the cursor on that statement. From this statement onwards we can use either *F11* to step through the program or use *F5* to continue program execution.

When we start debugging a program a menu called 'Debug' gets added to top-level menu. Following table lists the options available in this menu and their purpose.

Option	Shortcut Key
Go	F5
Restart	Ctrl + Shift + F5
Stop Debugging	Shift + F5
Step Into	F11
Step Over	F10
Step Out	Shift + F11
Run to Cursor	Ctrl + F10
Quick Watch	Shift + F9

Table A.1. *The debug options.*

Appendix B
DOEACC Solved Paper

NOTE:

1. There are two parts in this paper.

2. Part One is objective type and Part Two is descriptive type. Time allotted for Part One is one hour out of the maximum of three hours for the entire paper.

PART ONE

1   **Each question below gives a multiple choices of answers. Choose the most appropriate one.**

1.1 A *private* member function of a class can be called by

   (a)   Any normal function
   (b)   Invoking it directly in the *main*
   (c)   Object of the same class with '.' Operator
   (d)   Only *public* member function of the same class.

   Ans: (d)

1.2 A variable declared within a block { } has the following scope

   (a)   File scope
   (b)   Local scope
   (c)   Class scope

(d)   Global

Ans: (b)

1.3 The functions 'cin' and 'cout' resolve the necessary conversions at

(a)   Compile time
(b)   Execution time
(c)   Linking time
(d)   None of the above

Ans: (a)

1.4 C++ provides signed and unsigned character data type because

(a)   Characters can be used to hold small integer numbers
(b)   To allow the representation of lower and upper case characters
(c)   To allow the use of extended ASCII character set
(d)   To allow the variable names to be characters.

Ans: (a)

1.5 A value that is automatically passed to a function when no explicit argument is specified in the function call is called

(a)   Call-by value
(b)   Default argument
(c)   Constant argument
(d)   Virtual function

Ans: (b)

1.6 Reference to an object behaves like

(a) A Pointer and can be used in call-by reference in function call
(b) An alias
(c) A constant pointer
(d) A pointer to the object

Ans: (c)

1.7 A Generic Function can be created using the following

(a) Inheritance
(b) Data hiding
(c) Polymorphism
(d) Template

Ans: (d)

1.8 A constructor which can be used to open an output file

(a) *cout*
(b) *ofstream*
(c) *fstream*
(d) Constructor can not be used for this purpose

Ans: (b)

1.9 Identify the error in the following function

int emp_sal (basic, da, hra, cca = 1000, conveyane) {.............}

(a) One can not assign values in the functional arguments
(b) *cca* is a default argument hence it should be at the extreme right or conveyance also should have default value
(c) *cca* is a. default argument hence the rest of the arguments also should have default values

(d) *cca* is a default argument hence it should be at the extreme left or *basic, da, hra* also should have default values

Ans: (b)

2 Each statement below is either True or False. Identify and mark them accordingly in the answer book

2.1 The code of the inline function is expanded during compilation process rather than a functional call at the time of execution.

True

2.2 One can have pointers to reference variables -

False

2.3 A *protected* variable behaves like a *private* variable within that class but can be inherited as *protected* in *public* inheritance.

True

2.4 A *friend* function can not be used to overload the operator [ ] because 'this' pointer is not available.

True

2.5 Templates provide a method of parameterizing the data types and the data type can be passed as one of the arguments.

True

2.6 Constant arguments in a function cannot be modified by the function but can be used within the function for comparison or modifying other variables.

True

2.7 A pure virtual function is one, which is defined in the abstract base class.

True

2.8 One cannot define a virtual constructor but virtual destructor.

True

2.9 A constructor that accepts no arguments is known as the default constructor.

True

2.10 In multiple inheritance all the constructors are invoked in the reverse order of derivation and the destructors are invoked in the same order of derivation.

False

3 Match words and phrases in column X with the nearest in meaning in column Y.

	X		Y
3.1	Abstract class	A	When an object is assigned to another object using assignment statement.
3.2	Reference variables	B	A class with at least one member as the Pure virtual function
3.3	Virtual base class	C	this pointer
3.4	Shallow copy	D	Are used to set various format flags
3.5	Copy constructor	E	Are useful in a better way during call-by-reference
3.6	An implicit argument to all the members	F	Binding of data and the code that manipulate the data together
3.7	Enumeration	G	In the multiple inheritance, the duplication of members in a derived class can be avoided by

			making a
3.8	Manipulators in stream	H	Have the same name as the class with ~ prefix
3.9	Destructors	I	Is invoked automatically when an object is used to declare another object.
3.10	Encapsulation	J	Assigns an integral value to a list of variables.

Ans:

1	B
2	E
3	G
4	A
5	I
6	C
7	J
8	D
9	H
10	F

4 Fill in the blanks in 4.1 to 4.10 below, by choosing appropriate words and phrases given in the list below:

a) Call-by-value b) Public c) Inline d) Execution e) Private
f) virtual   g) compile h) pointers i) Shallow copy j) copy

4.1 Defining a member function within a class declaration makes the member function as _____.

Ans: (c)

4.2 In the _____ functional call, only a copy of the passed variables are copied into the arguments.

Ans: (a)

4.3 A *private* member function can be invoked only by another _____ member function of the same class.

Ans: (b)

4.4 When an object is used to initialize another object during declaration, the constructor invoked is known as _____. constructor.

Ans: (j)

4.5 The copy operation involved in passing of variables to arguments in a simple call by value functional call is known as _____.

Ans: (i)

4.6 The *protected* variable behaves like a _____ variable within the scope of that class.

Ans: (e)

4.7 The duplication of inherited members due to the multiple paths arising out of multiple inheritance can be avoided by declaring the common base class as _____ base.

Ans: (f)

4.8 An abstract class cannot have objects but can have _____ to objects.

Ans: (h)

4.9 In C++, *cin* and *cout* perform the necessary conversions at _____ time.

Ans: (g)

4.10 The corresponding code of the *virtual* function is linked during _____ time.

Ans: (d)

PART TWO

(Answer any four questions)

5   (a)   What is dynamic initialization of objects, what are the advantages of this and how is it achieved?

Ans:

When an object of a class is initialized using dynamic constructor, then it is called dynamic initialization or creation of an object. A dynamic constructor is used when the pointer members of an object of a class are to be initialized by allocating memory dynamically. It is very important that the pointer member of a class must get initialized before any member function of the class uses it.

The dynamic initialization of an object is done by using the *new* operator as shown in following code snippet.

```
class sample
{
    private :
        int *arr ;
        int size ;

    public :
        sample ( int sz )
        {
            size = sz ;
```

```
            arr = new int [ sz ] ;
    }
};
```

Suppose, instead of initializing pointer data member in the constructor, we initialize in some other member function of class, then there are chances of getting errors. This is because we may forget to call such function. However, it is sure that when an object is created the constructor is going to get called. This is the reason why object initialization is done in the constructor.

(b) What are the limitations on constructors and destructors?

A Constructor suffers from two constraints. These are as under:

1) A constructor cannot return a value. So, we cannot do error checking in constructor like this.

```
bool stack( )
{
    if ( i > 10 )
        return false ;
    else
        return true ;
}
```

2) We cannot invoke constructor for the same object twice. So, if we want to set up different values for an existing object we have to either call a member function using this object or create a new object with the new values and assign it to the existing object.

A destructor too can't return any value, so we cannot check for the successful execution of destructor.

Secondly, we cannot invoke a destructor explicitly to destroy an object.

(c) Can a 'friend' function be used for overloading the assignment operator? Justify your answer.

No. A *friend* function cannot be used for overloading assignment operator. If this were made possible, then a *friend* function would try to assign an object of one class containing totally different data members to an object of some other class, which too contains different members. This is not expected from an assignment operator. Hence, a friend function cannot be used to overload assignment operator.

(5, 5, 5)

6   (a) What is visibility in inheritance? Explain the role of *protected* members in inheritance.

Ans:

In case of inheritance, visibility decides whether the features, i.e. data members as well as member functions of a class are to be made available to the derived class. While deriving a class from a base class, we have to mention visibility mode like *public*, *private* and *protected*.

A *protected* member of a class can be accessed by member functions in its own class or in any class derived from its own class. It can't be accessed from functions outside these classes, such as *main( )*. This is what is required for data security while deriving a new class from an existing class. Hence the *protected* access specifier is used.

(b) Design a class 'Employee' of an organization with members *Employee_no*, *Name*, *Designation*, *Basic_pay*. Define a derived class 'Executive' such that the derived class inherit the common properties of base class *Employee* and also has 'Conveyance' as additional *private* member. Define also the necessary constructors.

```cpp
#include "iostream.h"
#include "string.h"

class Employee
{
    private:
        int Employee_no ;
        char Name [ 20 ] ;
        char Designation [ 20 ] ;
        float Basic_pay ;

    public:
        Employee ( int no, char *n, char * d, float pay )
        {
            Employee_no = no ;
            strcpy ( Name, n) ;
            strcpy ( Designation, d ) ;
            Basic_pay = pay ;
        }
} ;

class Executive : public Employee
{
    private:
        float Conveyance ;
    public:
        Executive ( int no, char * n, float pay, float con ) :
                        Employee ( no, n,"Executive", pay )
        {
            Conveyance = con ;
        }
} ;
```

```
void main( )
{
    Executive e ( 1, " Rakesh Sharma ", 10000, 4000 ) ;
}
```

(c)   Illustrate with example a Template class

Class templates are usually used for data storage
(container) classes. We can create container classes for
different data structures like stack and queue. However,
if we create these classes they can store data of only a
single basic type, say an integer. If we wish to store data
of type *float* in a stack we would be required to define
a completely new class. Thus, for every new data type
that we wish to store, a new stack class would have to
be created. However, using template class we are able
to write a single class specification that would work
for variables of all types, instead of a single basic type.
In short, a class template is a generic class. The general
format of class template is:

```
template <class T>
class classname
{
    // class members
};
```

Following is the class template declaration that
implements a stack.

```
template <class T>
class stack
{
    private :
        T stk [ MAX ] ;

    public :
```

```
            void push ( T data ) ;
            T pop( ) ;
};
```

The elements of any data type can be pushed in the stack using the following syntax.

```
stack < int > s1 ;
s1.push ( 10 ) ;

stack <float> s2 ;
s2.push ( 3.14f ) ;
```

(5, 5, 5)

7   (a)   Write a C++ program to define a stack as a class and define the necessary member functions to define the operations of stack.

```
#include < iostream.h >

const int max = 100 ;
const int error = -1 ;

class stack
{
    private :
        int arr [ max ] ;
        int top ;

    public :
        stack ( )
        {
            top = 0 ;
        }

        void push ( int n )
```

```
            {
                if ( top == max )
                    cout << " Stack Full " << endl ;
                else
                    arr [ top++ ] = n ;
            }

            int pop( )
            {
                if ( top == 0 )
                {
                    cout << " Stack Empty " << endl ;
                    return ( error ) ;
                }
                else
                {
                    int t = arr [ --top ] ;
                    return ( t ) ;
                }
            }

            void display( )
            {
                if ( top == 0 )
                    cout << " Stack Empty " << endl ;
                else
                {
                    cout << " Elements of stack are: " << endl ;
                    for ( int i = top - 1 ; i >= 0 ; i-- )
                        cout << arr [ i ] << endl ;
                }
            }
        } ;

    void main( )
    {
        stack s1 ;
```

```cpp
    s1.push ( 10 ) ;
    s1.push ( 20 ) ;
    s1.push ( 30 ) ;
    s1.push ( 40 ) ;

    s1.display( ) ;

    int r = s1.pop( ) ;
    if (r != error )
        cout << " Value Popped: " << r << endl ;
    r = s1.pop( ) ;
    if (r != error )
        cout << " Value Popped: " << r << endl ;
    r = s1.pop( ) ;
    if (r != error.)
        cout << " Value Popped: " << r << endl ;
    r = s1.pop( ) ;
    if (r != error )
        cout << " Value Popped: " << r << endl ;
    r = s1.pop( ) ;
    if (r != error )
        cout << " Value Popped: " << r << endl ;
}
```

(b) Write a program for evaluation of Post-fix expression using the above.

```cpp
#include <iostream.h>
#include <stdlib.h>
#include <math.h>
#include <ctype.h>

const int max = 100 ;
const int error = -1 ;

class stack
{
```

```
private :

    int arr [ max ] :
    int top ;

public :

    stack ( )
    {
        top = 0 ;
    }

    void push ( int n )
    {
        if ( top == max )
            cout << " Stack Full " << endl ;
        else
            arr [ top++ ] = n ;
    }

    int pop ( )
    {
        if ( top == 0 )
        {
            cout << " Stack Empty " << endl ;
            return ( error ) ;
        }
        else
        {
            int t = arr [ --top ] ;
            return ( t ) ;
        }
    }

    void display ( )
    {
        if ( top == 0 )
            cout << " Stack Empty " << endl ;
```

```cpp
            else
            {
                cout << " Elements of stack are: " << endl ;
                for ( int i = top - 1 ; i >= 0 ; i-- )
                    cout << arr [ i ] << endl ;
            }
        }
};

class postfix
{
    private :
        stack st ;
        int nn ;
        char *s ;

    public :
        postfix( )
        {

        }

        void setexpr ( char *str )
        {
            s = str ;
        }

        void push ( int item )
        {
            st.push(item);
        }
        int pop ( )
        {
            int data = st.pop();
            return(data);
        }

        void calculate( )
```

```
{
    int n1, n2, n3 ;
    while ( *s )
    {
        // skip whitespace, if any
        if ( *s == ' ' || *s == '\t' )
        {
            s++ ;
            continue ;
        }

        // if digit is encountered
        if ( isdigit ( *s ) )
        {
            nn = *s - '0' ;
            push ( nn ) ;
        }
        else
        {
            // if operator is encountered
            n1 = pop ( ) ;
            n2 = pop ( ) ;
            switch ( *s )
            {
                case '+' :
                    n3 = n2 + n1 ;
                    break ;

                case '-' :
                    n3 = n2 - n1 ;
                    break ;

                case '/' :
                    n3 = n2 / n1 ;
                    break ;

                case '*' :
                    n3 = n2 * n1 ;
```

```
                                break ;

                    case '%' :
                            n3 = n2 % n1 ;
                            break ;

                    case '$' :
                            n3 = pow ( n2 , n1 ) ;
                            break ;

                    default :
                            cout << "Unknown operator" ;
                            exit ( 1 ) ;
                }

                push ( n3 ) ;
            }
            s++ ;
        }
    }

    void show ( )
    {
        nn = pop ( ) ;
        cout << "Result is: " << nn ;
    }
} ;

void main( )
{
    char expr [ max ] ;

    cout << "\nEnter Postfix expression to be evaluated: " ;
    cin.getline ( expr, max ) ;

    postfix q ;

    q.setexpr ( expr ) ;
```

```
        q.calculate ( ) ;
        q.show ( ) ;
}
```

(5, 10)

8   (a)   Define a class 'complex_no', which has 2 real nos. as
          private variables one represents the real part and one for
          complex part. Define constructors to initialize the object.

```
class complex_no
{
    private :
        float real ;
        float imag ;

    public:

        complex_no( )
        {
            real = 0.0f ;
            imag = 0.0f ;
        }

        complex_no ( float r , float i )
        {
            real = r ;
            imag = i ;
        }
};
```

   (b)   Write a program, which takes two objects of the type
         Complex_no and returns an object of the same type
         which is the sum of two complex numbers. (Use answer
         of (a) above).

```cpp
#include < iostream.h >

class complex_no
{
    private :

        float real ;
        float imag ;
    public:

        complex_no ( )
        {
            real = 0.0f ;
            imag = 0.0f ;
        }

        complex_no ( float r , float c )
        {
            real = r ;
            imag = c ;
        }

        complex_no operator + ( complex_no c )
        {
            complex_no t ;
            t.real = real + c.real ;
            t.imag = imag + c.imag ;
            return t ;
        }

        void display ( )
        {
            cout << " Real Part: " << real << endl ;
            cout << " Complex Part: " << imag << endl ;
        }
} ;

void main ( )
```

```
{
    complex_no c1 ( 20 , 40 ), c2 ( 10 , 20 ) ;
    cout << " Displaying c1: " << endl ;
    c1.display ( ) ;
    cout << " Displaying c2: " << endl ;
    c2.display ( ) ;

    complex_no c3 ;
    c3 = c1 + c2 ;
    cout << " Displaying c3: " << endl ;
    c3.display ( ) ;
}
```

(c)   Distinguish clearly between 'Macros' and Inline functions.

a) Macros get expanded before compilation. Inline functions get added at the place of function calls during compilation.

b) Inline functions provide better type checking and do not have the side effects so typically associated with macros. For example consider the following program:

```
#include <iostream.h>

#define AREA( r )  3.14 * r * r
inline float area ( float r )
{
    return 3.14 * r * r ;
}

void main ( )
{
    float r = 1.5 ;

    float c = AREA ( ++r ) ;
```

```
        float d = area ( ++r ) ;
}
```

During preprocessing the macro AREA gets expanded into

```
c = ++r * ++r ;
```

This causes an undesirable side effect in the macro expansion. The variable is getting incremented twice even though we have used the incrementation operator only once. Such side effects would not occur in the inline function.

(5, 5, 5)

9   (a) Design a program to implement a linked list data structure to store integer data types, defining suitable member functions (delete a node which contains *int i* and add a node with data *j* after an element *k* in the) and a constructor.

```
#include < iostream.h >

class linkedlist
{
    private :

        struct node
        {
            int data ;
            node *link ;
        } *p ;

    public :
        linkedlist( )
        {
            p = NULL ;
        }
```

```
void addnode ( int n )
{
    node *q, *t ;
    if ( p == NULL )
    {
        p = new node ;
        p -> data = n ;
        p -> link = NULL ;
    }
    else
    {
        q = new node ;
        q -> data = n ;
        q -> link = NULL ;
        t = p ;
        while ( t -> link != NULL )
            t = t -> link ;
        t -> link = q ;
    }
}

void addafter ( int c , int n )
{
    node *q , *t ;int i ;
    for ( i = 0 , q = p ; i < c - 1 ; i++ )
    {
        q = q -> link ;
        if ( q == NULL )
        {
            cout << c << " is not present in list " ;
            return ;
        }
    }
    t = new node ;
    t -> data = n ;
    t -> link = q -> link ;
    q -> link = t ;
}
```

```
void delnode ( int n )
{
    node *q ,*t ;
    q = p ;
    if ( p -> data == n )
    {
        p = q -> link ;
        delete q ;
        return ;
    }
    t = q ;
    while ( q != NULL )
    {
        if ( q -> data == n )
        {
            t -> link = q -> link ;
            delete q ;
            return ;
        }
        t = q ;
        q = q -> link ;
    }
    cout << endl << " Element " << n << " is not present in
                    the list " ;
}

void display( )
{
    node *q ;
    q = p ;
    while ( q != NULL )
    {
        cout << q -> data << " " ;
        q = q -> link ;
    }
    cout << endl ;
}
```

```
~linkedlist( )
{
    node *q ;
    if ( p == NULL )
        return ;
    while ( p != NULL )
    {
        q = p -> link ;
        delete p ;
        p = q ;
    }
}
};
```

(b) Define class of square matrix n X n of integers. Define the necessary constructors/destructors and other members. Write a program to find the trace (sum of the diagonal elements) of a matrix.

```
#include < iostream.h >
const int MAX = 10 ;
class matrix
{
  private :

        int size ;
        int arr [ MAX ] [ MAX ] ;

  public :

        matrix ( int n )
        {
            size = n ;
            for (int i = 0 ; i < size ; i++ )
            {
                for ( int j = 0 ; j < size ; j ++ )
```

```
                    {
                        cout << " Enter " << i << " row " << j << "
                            column element: " ;
                        cin >> arr [ i ] [ j ] ;
                    }
                }
            }

            int trace ( )
            {
                int sum = 0 ;
                for ( int i = 0 ; i < size ; i++ )
                    sum += arr [ i ] [ i ] ;
                return ( sum ) ;
            }

            void display ( )
            {
                for ( int i = 0 ; i < size ; i ++ )
                {
                    for ( int j = 0 ; j < size ; j ++ )
                        cout << arr [ i ] [ j ] << " " ;
                    cout << endl ;
                }
            }
    } ;

void main ( )
{
    matrix m1 ( 2 ), m2 ( 3 ) ;

    m1.display( ) ;
    int t = m1.trace( ) ;
    cout << " Trace of m1 \n" << t << endl ;

    m2.display( ) ;
    t = m2.trace( ) ;
    cout << " Trace of m2 \n" << t << endl ;
```

}

(c)   Illustrate with example the use of default arguments in a function. What are the constraints on them?

C++ has an ability to define default values for arguments that are not passed when the function call is made. Consider the following example:

```
void rectangle ( int x1 = 0, int y1 = 0, int x2 = 50, int y2 = 50 )
{
    // code to draw rectangle
}
```

When we call the function *rectangle( )* with 4 arguments, it draws the rectangle using the arguments passed. However, when we call it with 3 arguments the default value mentioned in the prototype of *rectangle( )* is used for the last argument. Likewise, when we call it with two arguments default values are used for the last two arguments, and finally when we call it without any arguments, a rectangle gets drawn with all the four default values mentioned in the prototype. Thus, the default arguments are used if the calling function doesn't supply the arguments when the function is called.

Note that if one argument is missing when the function is called, it is assumed to be the last argument. Thus, the missing arguments must be the trailing arguments. You can leave out last three arguments, but you cannot leave out the last but one and then put in the last.

The default arguments are given only in the function prototype and should not be repeated in the function definition.

(5, 5, 5)

Appendix C
Practical Assignments

Assignment –1: Write program to take name, address as character array, *age* as *int*, *salary* as *float* & display it. (Note: use *cin* and *cout*).

Ans:

```
#include < iostream.h >

void main( )
{
    int age ;
    char name [ 15 ], addr [ 50 ] ;
    float salary ;

    cout << "Enter your name: " ;
    cin >> name ;
    cout << "Enter your address: " ;
    cin >> addr ;
    cout << "Enter your age: " ;
    cin >> age ;
    cout << "Enter your salary: " ;
    cin >> salary ;

    cout << endl << endl ;
    cout << " The name of the Employee is :    " << name << endl ;
    cout << " The address of the Employee is : " << addr << endl ;
    cout << " The age of the Employee is :    " << age << endl ;
    cout << " The salary of the Employee is :  " << salary << endl ;
```

}

Assignment – 2: Using concept of function overloading write function for calculating area of Triangle, Circle and Square.

```cpp
#include < iostream.h >

class shape
{
    public:
        //area of square
        float area ( float a )
        {
            return ( a * a ) ;
        }

        // area of triangle
        float area ( float b, float h )
        {
            return ( 0.5f * b * h ) ;
        }

        // area of circle
        double area ( double r )
        {
            return ( 3.14f * r * r ) ;
        }
} ;


void main( )
{
    shape s ;
    float a, b, h, r, sqr, tri ;
    double cir ;

    cout << " enter the side of square " << endl ;
```

```
        cin >> a ;
        sqr = s.area ( a ); // area of square

        cout << " enter the radius of circle " << endl ;
        cin >> r ;
        cir = s.area ( r ); // area of circle

        cout << " enter the base and height of triangle " << endl ;
        cin >> b >> h ;
        tri = s.area ( b, h );// area of triangle

        cout << endl << " the area of Square is : " << sqr ;
        cout << endl << " the area of Triangle is : " << tri ;
        cout << endl << " the area of Circle is : " << cir ;
}
```

Assignment – 3: Create a class student with *reg_no*, *name*, *age* and *address* as data members and contains inline functions to set the values and show the values of the data members.

```
#include < iostream.h >

class student
{
    private:
        char name [ 10 ], addr [ 20 ] ;
        int reg_no ;
    public:
        void getdata( )
        {
            cout << "enter registration number,
                    name and address of the student'" << endl ;
            cin >> reg_no >> name >> addr ;
        }

        void display( )
```

```
        {
                cout << " Registration number is : " << reg_no << endl ;
                cout << " Name of Student is : " << name << endl ;
                cout << " Address of Student is : " << addr << endl ;
        }
};

void main( )
{
    student s ;
    s.getdata( ) ;
    s.display( ) ;
}
```

Assignment – 4: Write a function *power( )* to raise a number *m* to a power *n*. The function takes a *double* value for *m* & *int* value for *n*. Use default value of and for *n* to make the function to calculate squares when this argument is omitted.

```
#include < iostream.h >

class calculation
{
    public:

        double power ( double m, int n = 2 )
        {
            double f = 1 ;

            for ( int i = 0 ; i < n ; i++ )
            {
                f = f * m ;
            }

            return f ;
        }
```

```
    } ;

    void main( )
    {
        calculation c ;
        double p ;

        p = c.power ( 100.0 ) ;
        cout << p << endl ;

        p = c.power ( 100.0, 3 ) ;
        cout << p ;
    }
```

Assignment – 5: Create a class called *stack*. Write member functions to push and pop data into/from stack.

```
    #include < iostream.h >

    class stack
    {
        private:
            int arr [ 20 ] ;
            int top ;

        public:
            stack( )
            {
                top = 0 ;
            }

            void push( int n )
            {
                if ( top > 19 )
                {
                    cout << " stack overflow " ;
                    top-- ;
```

```
            }
            else
            {
                arr [ top ] = n ;
                top++ ;
            }
        }

        int pop( )
        {
            if ( top < 0 )
            {
                cout << " Stack underflow " ;
                top++ ;
            }
            else
            {
                top-- ;
                int n = arr [ top ];
                cout << " Top is at " << top << endl ;
                return n ;
            }
        }

        void show( )
        {
            cout << "Elements of stack are:" ;
            for ( int i = 0 ; i < top ; i++ )
                cout << arr [ i ] << endl ;
        }
};

void main( )
{
    stack a ;

    a.push ( 10 ) ;
    a.push ( 20 ) ;
```

```
        a.push ( 30 ) ;
        a.push ( 50 ) ;

        a.show( ) ;

        int n = a.pop( ) ;
        cout << " The popped element is " << n << endl ;

        n = a.pop( ) ;
        cout << " The popped element is " << n << endl ;
}
```

Assignment – 6: Create a class time with members hours, minutes & seconds. Take input, add two time objects passing objects to function and display result.

```
#include < iostream.h >

class time
{
    private:
        int hr, min, sec ;

    public:
        time( )
        {
            hr = min = sec = 0 ;
        }
        time ( int hh, int mm, int ss )
        {
            hr = hh ;
            min = mm ;
            sec = ss ;
        }

        void display( )
```

```
        {
            cout << hr << " hours " << "\t" ;
            cout << min << " minutes " << "\t" ;
            cout << sec << " seconds " << endl ;
        }


        // friend function to add time objects
        friend time add ( time t1, time t2  ) ;
};

time add ( time t1, time t2 )
{
    time r ;

    r.hr = t1.hr + t2.hr ;
    r.min = t1.min + t2.min ;
    r.sec = t1.sec + t2.sec ;

    if ( r.sec > 60 )
    {
        r.min++ ;
        r.sec = r.sec - 60 ;
    }

    if ( r.min > 60 )
    {
        r.hr++ ;
        r.min = r.min - 60  ;
    }

    if ( r.hr > 23 )
    {
        r.hr = r.hr - 24 ;
    }

    return ( r ) ;
};
```

```
void main( )
{
    time a ( 10, 20, 55 ), b ( 2, 25, 35 ), c ;

    c = add ( a, b ) ;
    c.display( ) ;
}
```

Assignment – 7: Create a class book, which has data members as book name, author name, pages. Initialize all these values first with zero & then with some initial values. Use constructor overloading. Display all results.

```
#include < iostream.h >
#include < string.h >

class book
{
    private:
        char book_name [ 10 ], author_name [ 15 ] ;
        int pages ;
    public:
        book( ) //zero argument constructor with initial values
        {
            strcpy ( book_name, " None " ) ;
            strcpy ( author_name, " Anon " ) ;
            pages = 0 ;
        }

        book ( char *b , char *a , int p ) // overloaded constructor
        {
            strcpy ( book_name, b ) ;
            strcpy ( author_name, a ) ;
            pages = 0 ;
        }
```

```
                void display( )
                {
                    cout << " Name of the Book : " << book_name << endl ;
                    cout << " Author of the Book : " << author_name << endl ;
                    cout << " No : of pages in the Book : " << pages << endl ;
                }
        } ;

        void main( )
        {
            book b, c ( "Discovery", " Nehru ", 390 ) ;
            b.display( ) ;
            c.display( ) ;
        }
```

Assignment – 8: The array subscript operator is used to define the size of the array. Overload the *[ ]* operator so that the array does not exceed the limit.

```
        #include <iostream.h>
        #include <stdlib.h>

        class limit
        {
            private:
                int r [ 10 ] ;
                int count ;

            public:
                int& operator [ ] ( int n )
                {
                    if ( n > 9 )
                    {
                        cout << " Exceeding the array limit " << endl ;
                        exit ( 0 ) ;
                    }
                    else
```

```
                          return r [ n ] ;
              }

          void display( )
          {
               for ( int i = 0 ; i < 10 ; i++ )
                    cout << r [ i ] << endl ;
          }
};

void main( )
{
     limit arr ;

     arr [ 0 ] = 10 ;
     arr [ 13 ] = 20 ; // shows error

     arr.display( ) ;
}
```

Assignment – 9: A *friend* function can be used to overload the binary operator. To overload + operator as a *friend* function. Also use the same for commutatively using the operator+ (like Obj + int or int + Obj interchangeably).

```
#include < iostream.h >

class binary
{
     private :
          int a;

     public :

          binary( )
          {
```

```
            a = 0 ;
        }

        binary ( int b )
        {
            a = b ;
        }

        void Display ( )
        {
            cout << a << endl ;
        }

        void setdata ( int i )
        {
            a = i ;
        }

        friend binary operator + ( binary b, binary c ) ;
};

binary operator + ( binary b1, binary b2 )
{
    binary d ;
    d.a = b1.a + b2.a ;
    return d ;
}

void main( )
{
    binary bin, bin1, bin2 ;
    bin.setdata ( 1 ) ;
    bin1 = 2 + bin ;
    bin2 = bin + 2 ;

    bin.Display( ) ;
    bin1.Display( ) ;
    bin2.Display( ) ;
```

```
}
```

Assignment – 10: Design a class 'employee' of an organization with members employee number, name, designation, basic pay. Define a derived class "executive" such that the derived class inherits common properties of base class "employee" and also has conveyance as additional private member. Define also the necessary constructor.

```cpp
#include < iostream.h >
#include < string.h >

class employee
{
    protected:
        unsigned long int emp_no ;
        char emp_name [ 20 ] ;
        char emp_des [ 20 ] ;
        float emp_baspay ;

    public :
        employee ( unsigned long int empnum,
                        char *name, char *des, float bas )
        {
            cout << " Constructor of Base\n " ;
            emp_no = empnum ;
            strcpy ( emp_name, name ) ;
            strcpy ( emp_des, des ) ;
            emp_baspay = bas ;
        }
};

class executive : public employee
{
    private:
        float exec_con ;
```

```
public :
    executive ( unsigned long int empnum = 0,
                char *name = NULL, char *des = NULL,
                float bas = 0.0, float con = 0.0) :
                employee ( empnum, name, des, bas )
    {
        cout << "Constructor of Derived\n" ;
        exec_con = con ;
    }

    void Display( )
    {
        cout << " Employee Name : " << emp_name << endl
             << " Employee Number : " << emp_no << endl
             << " Employee Designation : " << emp_des << endl
             << " Employee Basic Salary : " << emp_baspay << endl
             << " Employee Conveyance : " << exec_con ;
    }
};

void main( )
{
    executive ex ( 10, " Subhash ", " Manager ", 2500.50, 50.25 ) ;
    ex.Display( ) ;
}
```

Assignment – 11: Create a base class called *shape*. Use this class to store two *double* type values. Derive two specific classes called *triangle* and *rectangle* from the base *shape*. Add to the base class, a member function *get_data( )* to initialize base class data members and another member function *display_are( )* to compute and display the area of figures. Make *display_are( )* a *virtual* function and redefine this function in the derived classes to suit their requirements. Using these three classes design a program that will accept driven of a triangle or rectangle interactively and display the area.

```
#include < iostream.h >

class shape
{
    protected:
        double side1, side2 ;

    public:
        void get_data( )
        {
            cout << "Enter value of side1: " ;
            cin >> side1 ;
            cout << "Enter value of side2: " ;
            cin >> side2 ;
        }

        virtual void display_are ( )
        {
        }
};

class rectangle : public shape
{
    public:
        void display_are ( )
        {
            cout << " Area of rectangle " << side1 * side2 << endl;
        }
};

class triangle : public shape
{
    public:
        void display_are( )
        {
            cout << " Area of triangle " << 0.5 * side1 * side2 << endl;
        }
};
```

```
void main( )
{
    triangle t ;
    rectangle r ;
    shape *s1, *s2 ;

    s1 = &t ; // Upcasting of base pointer
    s2 = &r ;

    s1 -> get_data( ) ;
    s1 -> display_are( ) ;
    s2 -> get_data( ) ;
    s2 -> display_are( ) ;
}
```

Assignment – 12: Create a class list with two pure virtual function *store( )* and *retrieve( )*. To store a value call *store( )* function and to retrieve call *retrieve( )* function. Derive two classes 'stack' and 'queue' from it and override *store( )* and *retrieve( )*.

```
#include < iostream.h >

#define MAX 10
#define MIN -1

class list
{
    protected:
        int arr [ 10 ];
        int index;

    public:
        list( )
        {
            index = 0 ;
```

```
        }

        virtual void store ( int i ) = 0 ;
        virtual int retrieve ( ) = 0 ;
} ;

class stack : public list
{
    public:

        void store ( int i )
        {
            if ( index < MAX )
            {
                arr [ index ] = i ;
                index++ ;
            }
        }

        int retrieve( )
        {
            if ( index > MIN )
                return arr [ --index ] ;
        }
} ;

class queue : public list
{
    private:
        int front ;

    public:
        queue( )
        {
            front = 0 ;
        }

        void store ( int i )
```

```
        {
            if ( index < MAX )
            {
                arr [ index ] = i ;
                index++ ;
            }
        }

        int retrieve( )
        {
            if ( front <= index )
                return arr [ front++ ] ;
        }
} ;

void main( )
{
    list * p1 , * p2 ;
    stack st ;
    queue q ;

    p1 = & st ;
    p2 = & q ;

    p1 -> store ( 10 ) ;
    p1 -> store ( 20 ) ;
    p1 -> store ( 30 ) ;

    st.store( 90 ) ; // Calling store ( ) from derived object
    st.store( 100 ) ;

    cout << p1 -> retrieve( ) << endl ;
    cout << p1 -> retrieve( ) << endl ;

    p2 -> store ( 60 ) ;
    p2 -> store ( 70 ) ;
    p2 -> store ( 80 ) ;
```

```
        q.store ( 90 ) ;
        q.store ( 100 ) ;

        cout << p2 -> retrieve( ) << endl ;
        cout << p2 -> retrieve( ) << endl ;
}
```

Assignment – 13: Write a C++ program to read an existing file and display words of this file on screen (one word for line) in the order they appear in the file. Assume that successive words are separated by one or more white space characters.

```
#include < fstream.h >

void main( )
{
        char ch ;
        ifstream infile ( "hello.txt" ) ;

        while ( infile.read ( &ch, 1 ) )
        {
                if ( ( ch == ' ' ) || ( ch == '\t' ) )
                        cout << endl ;
                else
                        cout << ch ;
        }
}
```

Assignment – 14: Create an Input manipulator skip to later that reads and discards all characters which are not letters. When the first letter is found the manipulator puts it back into input string and returns. Write a suitable main that illustrates the use of manipulators.

```
#include <iostream.h>
#include <string.h>
```

```
class skiptoletter
{
    private:
        char *m_str ;

    public:

        skiptoletter ( char *str )
        {
            m_str = str ;
        }

        friend istream& operator >> ( istream& istr, skiptoletter &s )
        {
            istr >> s.m_str ;

            char *p = s.m_str ;

            while ( *p )
            {
                if ( ( *p >= 65 && *p <= 90 ) )
                {
                    *p = '\0' ;
                    break ;
                }
                else
                {
                    if ( ( *p >= 97 ) && ( *p <= 122 ) )
                    {
                        *p = '\0' ;
                        break ;
                    }
                }
                p++ ;
            }

            return istr ;
```

```
        }
};

int main( )
{
    char str [ 100 ] ;

    cin >> skiptoletter ( str ) ;
    cout << str ;

    return 0 ;
}
```

Assignment – 15: Write a program to delete white spaces such as horizontal tab, vertical tab, space, linefeed, new line and carriage return from a text file and to store the contents of the file without spaces on another file.

```
#include < fstream.h >

void main( )
{
    char ch ;
    ifstream infile ( "sample.txt" ) ;
    ofstream outfile ( "copy.txt" ) ;
    while ( infile . read ( &ch, 1 ) )
    {
        if ( ch==' ' || ch == '\t' || ch== '\n' || ch == '\r' )
            continue ;

        outfile << ch ;
    }
}
```

Assignment – 16: Implement the stack class as template class in C++. Using this template class form following stacks:

- Stack of students names of a class;
- Stack of roll numbers of the above students;
- Stack of marks obtained by the students.

Print a list having roll number, names, marks obtained and ranks.

```
#include < iostream.h >
#include < string.h >

const int MAX = 10 ;

template < class T >

class stack
{
private :

    T stk [ MAX ] ;
    int top ;

public :

    stack ( )
    {
        top = -1 ;
    }

    void push ( T data )
    {
        if ( top == MAX - 1 )
            cout << endl << "stack is full" ;
        else
        {
            top++ ;
            stk [ top ] = data ;
        }
```

```
        }

        T pop( )
        {
            if ( top == -1 )
            {
                cout << endl << "stack is empty" ;
                return NULL ;
            }
            else
            {
                T data = stk [ top ] ;
                top-- ;
                return data ;
            }
        }
};

void main ( )
{
    stack < char* > stu_names ;
    stack < int > stu_rno ;
    stack < int > stu_marks ;

    int marks [ 3 ] ;
    int ranks [ 3 ] ;
    int rollno [ 3 ] ;
    char names [ 3 ][ 20 ] ;

    stu_names.push ( "Naresh" ) ;
    stu_names.push ( "Suresh" ) ;
    stu_names.push ( "Ganesh" ) ;

    stu_rno.push ( 1 ) ;
    stu_rno.push ( 2 ) ;
    stu_rno.push ( 3 ) ;

    stu_marks.push ( 277 ) ;
```

```
        stu_marks.push ( 279 ) ;
        stu_marks.push ( 245 ) ;


        for ( int i = 2 ; i >= 0 ; i-- )
        {
            marks [ i ] = stu_marks.pop( ) ;
            rollno [ i ] = stu_rno.pop( ) ;
            strcpy ( names [ i ], stu_names.pop( ) ) ;
            ranks [ i ] = i + 1 ;
        }
        for ( i = 0 ; i < 2 ; i++ )
        {
            for ( int j = i + 1 ; j <= 2 ; j++ )
            {
                if ( marks [ i ] >  marks [ j ] )
                {
                    int t = marks [ i ] ;
                    marks [ i ] =  marks [ j ] ;
                    marks [ j ] = t ;

                    t = rollno [ i ] ;
                    rollno [ i ] = rollno [ j ] ;
                    rollno [ j ] = t ;

                    char x [ 10 ] ;

                    strcpy ( x, names [ i ] ) ;

                    strcpy ( names [ i ], names [ j ] ) ;
                    strcpy ( names [ j ], x ) ;
                }
            }
        }

        cout << endl << "Rank\t" ;
        cout << "Name\t" ;
        cout << "\tRoll No.\t" ;
```

```
        cout << "Marks obtained\t" ;

        cout << endl << endl << ranks [ 0 ] ;
        cout << "\t" << names [ 2 ]  ;
        cout << "\t\t" << rollno [ 2 ] ;
        cout <<"\t\t"<< marks [ 2 ] ;

        cout << endl << ranks [ 1 ] ;
        cout << "\t" << names [ 1 ]  ;
        cout << "\t\t" << rollno [ 1 ] ;
        cout <<"\t\t"<< marks [ 1 ] ;

        cout << endl << ranks [ 2 ] ;
        cout << "\t" << names [ 0 ]  ;
        cout << "\t\t" << rollno [ 0 ] ;
        cout <<"\t\t"<< marks [ 0 ] ;

        cout << endl << endl ;
}
```

Assignment – 17: A hospital wants to create a database regarding its indoor patients. The information to store include

- Name of the patient
- Date of admission
- Disease
- Date of discharge

Create a structure to store the data (Year, month and date as its members).

Create a base class to store the above information. The member function should include functions to enter information and display a list of all the patients in the data base. Create a derived class to store the age of the patients. How will you list the information about all the pediatric patients (less than 12 years in age).

```
#include < conio.h >
#include < iostream.h >
#include < string.h >
#include < iomanip.h >

class Hospital
{
    protected :
        char name [ 30 ] ;
        struct date
        {
            int year, mon, day ;
        }
        dt_admit, dt_discharge ;

        char disease [ 30 ] ;

    public :
        void getinfo( )
        {
            cout << "Enter Patient name" << endl ;
            cin >> name ;

            cout << "Enter admission date ( dd mm yy )" << endl ;
            cin >> dt_admit.day >> dt_admit.mon >> dt_admit.year ;

            cout <<"Enter disease" << endl ;
            cin >> disease ;

            cout << "Enter discharge date ( dd mm yy )" << endl ;
            cin >> dt_discharge.day >> dt_discharge.mon
                >> dt_discharge.year ;
        }

        virtual void display( )
        {
            cout << endl << endl << endl << endl <<
                "Patient name  " << name ;
```

```
                        cout << endl << "admission date ( dd mm yy )  "
                            << dt_admit.day << dt_admit.mon << dt_admit.year ;
                        cout << endl << "disease  " << disease ;
                        cout << endl << "discharge date ( dd mm yy )  "
                                        << dt_discharge.day << dt_discharge.mon
                                        << dt_discharge.year ;

            }
};

class derive : public Hospital
{
    public :
        int age ;

        void setage( )
        {
            cout << "Enter the age of Patient" << endl ;
            cin >> age ;
        }

        bool is_pediatric_patient( )
        {
            if ( age < 12 )
                return 1 ;
            else
                return 0 ;
        }

        void display( )
        {
            cout << endl << endl << endl << endl <<
                    "Patient name  " << name ;
            cout << endl << "admission date ( dd mm yy )  " <<
                    dt_admit.day .<< " / " << dt_admit.mon << " / "
                    << dt_admit.year ;
            cout << endl << "disease  " << disease ;
            cout << endl << "discharge date ( dd mm yy )  "
                    << dt_discharge.day << " / " << dt_discharge.mon
```

```
                    << " / " << dt_discharge.year ;
                cout << endl << "Patient age  " << age ;
        }
};

void main ( )
{
\   derive d [ 100 ] ;

    for ( int i = 0 ; i <= 1 ; i++ )
    {
        d [ i ].getinfo( ) ;
        d [ i ].setage( ) ;
    }

    for ( i = 0 ; i <= 1 ; i++ )
    {
        if ( d [ i ].is_pediatric_patient( ) )
            d [ i ].display ( ) ;
    }
}
```

Assignment – 18: Write a program, which reads a text from the keyboard and display the following information on the screen in two columns:

- Number of lines
- Number of words
- Number of characters

Strings should be left justified and numbers should be right justified in a suitable field width.

```
#include < conio.h >
#include < iostream.h >
#include < string.h >
#include < iomanip.h >
```

```
class Counter
{
    private :
        char text [ 100 ] ;
        int chars, words, lines ;

    public :
        Counter( )
        {
            chars = words = lines = 0 ;
        }

        void gettext( )
        {
            int i = 0 ;
            char ch ;

            ch = getche( ) ;
            while ( ch != '#' )
            {
                if ( ch == 13 )
                {
                    putch ( '\r' ) ;
                    putch ( '\n' ) ;
                }
                text [ i++ ] = ch ;
                ch = getche ( ) ;
            }

            text [ i ] = '\0'  ;
        }

        void operation ( )
        {
            char *p ;
            p = text ;

            while ( *p != '\0' )
```

```
            {
                if ( *p == 13 )
                {
                    lines++ ;
                    words++ ;
                }
                else
                {
                    if ( *p == ' ' )
                        words++ ;
                    else
                        chars++ ;
                }
                p++ ;
            }
        }

        void display ( )
        {
            cout << endl << "Number of characters" <<  setw ( 20 )
                << "Number of words" << setw ( 20 )
                << "Number of lines" << endl ;
            cout << endl << setw ( 20 ) << chars <<  setw ( 20 )
                << words << setw ( 20 ) << lines << endl ;
        }
} ;

void main ( )
{
    Counter c ;

    c.gettext( ) ;
    c.operation( ) ;
    c.display( ) ;
}
```

Assignment – 19: Given a string String s ("123456789") Write a program that displays the following:

```
        1
       232
      34543
     4567654
    567898765
```

```cpp
#include < string.h >
#include < iostream.h >

class String
{
    private :
        char str [ 9 ] ;

    public :
        String( )
        {
            strcpy ( str, "123456789" ) ;
        }

        void display( )
        {
            char *p ;
            p = str ;

            for ( int i = 1 ; i <= 5 ; i++ )
            {
                for ( int k = 1 ; k <= 5 - i ; k++ )
                    cout << " " ;

                for ( int j = 1 ; j <= i ; j ++ )
                    cout << *p++ ;
                --p ;

                for ( j = 1 ; j < i ; j++ )
```

```
                              cout << *--p ;

                       cout << endl ;
                       p++ ;
               }
       }
};

void main( )
{
    String s ;
    s.display( ) ;
}
```

Assignment – 20: Initialization of date objects after validating that the integer representing a month is between 1 and 12 and checking that the day part of the date is within the correct range for a month.

  – Comparing two dates for equality.
  – Obtaining the next day from a given date.
  – Obtaining the previous day from a given date.

```
#include < iostream.h >

struct newdate
{
    int dd, mm, yy ;
};

class date
{
    public :
        newdate e ;

    public :
        date(int d = 1, int m = 1, int y = 0 )
        {
                int month [ 12 ] = { 31, 28, 31, 30, 31, 30, 31,
```

```
                        31, 30, 31, 30, 31 } ;

    if ( ( m > 12 ) || ( d > month [ m-1 ] ) )
            · cout << " The data entered is incorrect " << endl ;
    else
    {
        e.dd = d ; e.mm = m ; e.yy = y ;
        cout << " The entered date is " << d << "-" << m << "-"
            << y << endl ;
    }
}

friend bool Comparedate ( newdate d1, newdate d2 ) ;
void nextday ( newdate d )
{
    int day ;
    int month [ 12 ] = { 31, 28, 31, 30, 31, 30,
                                31, 31, 30, 31, 30, 31 } ;

    int daysinmon = 0 ;

    if ( d . yy % 4 == 0 )
            month [ 1 ] = 29 ;

    for ( int i = 0 ; i < d . mm ; i++ )
        daysinmon = daysinmon + month [ i ];

    day = d . yy * 365 - ( d . yy / 400 ) + ( d . yy / 4 )
                + daysinmon + d . dd ;

    cout << endl << endl ;

    cout << " The Next day to the entered date is " ;
    nameofday ( ( day % 7 ) + 1 ) ;

    cout << endl << endl ;
    cout << " The Previous day to the entered date is " ;
    nameofday( ( day % 7 ) - 1 ) ;
}
```

```cpp
void nameofday ( int n )
{
    cout << endl ;

    switch( (n) )
    {
        case 0:
                cout << " Sunday" ;
                break ;
        case 1:
                cout << " Monday" ;
                break ;
        case 2:
                cout << " Tuesday" ;
                break ;
        case 3:
                cout << " Wednesday" ;
                break ;
        case 4:
                cout << " Thursday" ;
                break ;
        case 5:
                cout << " Friday" ;
                break ;
        case 6:
                cout << " Saturday" ;
                break ;
    }
    cout << endl << endl ;
  }
};

bool Comparedate ( newdate d1, newdate d2 )
{
    if ( ( ( d1 . dd == d2 . dd ) && ( d1 . mm == d2 . mm )
                        && ( d1 . yy == d2 . yy ) )
            return true ;
    else
```

```
            return false ;
}

void main( )
{
    date d1 ( 2, 10, 2003 ), d2 ( 2, 10, 2003 ) ;

    if ( Comparedate( d1.e, d2.e ) )
        cout << " the two dates are same " ;
    else
        cout << " the two dates are not same " ;

    d1.nextday( d1.e ) ;
}
```

Index